KU-404-683

TONY CRAGG
托尼·克拉格
SCULPTURES AND DRAWINGS
雕塑与绘画

中央美术学院美术馆 编著

主办：
中央美术学院美术馆
成都当代美术馆
上海喜玛拉雅美术馆
英国大使馆文化教育处

Organizers:
CAFA Art Museum
Museum of Contemporary Art Chengdu
Himalayas Art Museum
Cultural and Education Section of the British Embassy

协办：
苏格兰国立现代美术馆
伦敦霍特曼艺术公司

Exhibition organized in collaboration with
Scottish National Gallery of Modern Art, Edinburgh
Holtermann Fine Art, London

CAFA Art Museum

Chengdu MOCA 成都当代美术馆

SCOTTISH NATIONAL GALLERY OF MODERN ART

Holtermann fine art

目录

Contents

前言 I

约翰·雷顿
苏格兰国立美术馆总馆长

西蒙·格鲁姆
苏格兰国立现代美术馆馆长

托尼·克拉格成名于20世纪70年代末，成为新一波英国年轻雕塑家的领军人物。从那时起，他的作品就在以非凡的方式演变着，恐怕没有其他在世的雕塑家像他一样用这样丰富和充满创造力的方式尝试了如此包罗万象的材料。创作初期，他曾运用塑料瓶盖和容器，扩大、延展和改变基本形式，创造出奇妙的雕塑作品，这些作品诉说了人类化腐朽为神奇的能力。

在过去的35年，克拉格已在欧洲各地和美国举行展览。本次展览起初于2011年夏天在爱丁堡的苏格兰国立现代美术馆首次展出。感谢英国使领馆文化教育处，使展览有机会以微调的形式来到北京中央美术学院美术馆、成都当代美术馆和上海喜玛拉雅美术馆。虽然克拉格的个别作品曾在中国展出，但这是使中国观众有机会第一次深入了解他的艺术，这对艺术家，尤其对苏格兰国立美术馆来说是十分令人振奋的机会。希望这将是我们美术馆与中国许多新兴的优秀美术馆之间合作的开始。我们要感谢北京中央美术学院美术馆馆长王璜生先生、上海喜玛拉雅美术馆执行馆长王纯杰先生、成都当代美术馆馆长吕澎先生。

英国方面，非常感谢伦敦霍特曼艺术公司的玛丽安·霍特曼，她对展览在爱丁堡和在中国的所有方面起到至关重要的支持作用。苏格兰国立美术馆方面，感谢组织展览的帕特里克·艾略特。感谢卡斯雕塑基金会的威尔弗雷德和珍妮特·卡斯出借了雕塑作品《赤纬》，这件作品是他们在英格兰南部古德伍德雕塑公园的亮点之一。德国伍珀塔尔托尼·克拉格工作室方面，感谢萨宾·阿贝斯、马里斯·迈耶、卡洛琳·佩舍、约翰·麦科马克、大卫·卡鲁扎及团队其他成员的紧密合作。最后，当然最重要的是，我们要感谢托尼·克拉格，他的积极、活力和一如既往的支持促成了展览。克拉格经常被邀请在世界各地举办展览，当被问到是否愿意将中国三个重要场馆加入到档期中，他毫不犹豫的答应了。我们相信，中国观众将对他的作品赞叹不已。

Foreword I

John Leighton
Director-General, National
Galleries of Scotland

Simon Groom
Director, Scottish National
Gallery of Modern Art

Tony Cragg rose to prominence in the late 1970s as the leading figure in a new wave of young British sculptors. Since then his work has evolved in extraordinary ways, and there is probably no other sculptor alive who has used and exploited such a vast range of materials in such a rich and imaginative way. Using ordinary objects such as plastic bottles and containers as his starting point, he has enlarged and stretched and altered these basic forms to create fantastic sculptures which speak of man's ability to transform the ordinary into the extraordinary.

Over the past thirty-five years Cragg has held exhibitions all over Europe and America. This exhibition was first staged in the summer of 2011 at the Scottish National Gallery of Modern Art in Edinburgh. Thanks to the British Council, the opportunity arose to transfer the exhibition in a slightly altered form to the CAFA Art Museum, Beijing; the Museum of Contemporary Art, Chengdu; and the Himalayas Art Museum, Shanghai. Although Cragg has exhibited individual works in China, this is the first opportunity for a Chinese audience to see his work in depth. It is a tremendously exciting opportunity for the artist, and indeed for the National Galleries of Scotland. We hope that this will be the first of many collaborations between our Galleries and the extraordinary museums which are emerging in China. We would like to thank Professor Wang Huangsheng, Director of the CAFA Museum in Beijing, Mr Wang Shun-kit, Executive Director of Himalayas Art Museum in Shanghai, and Mr Lu Peng, Director General of Chengdu Museum of Contemporary Art.

In Britain, we are immensely grateful to Marianne Holtermann of Holtermann Fine Art Ltd., London, for her crucial support and for advising on all aspects of the exhibition in Edinburgh and in China. At the National Galleries of Scotland our thanks go to Patrick Elliott for organising the exhibition. We are also grateful to Wilfred and Jeanette Cass of the Cass Sculpture Foundation, for lending Declination, one of the highlights of their sculpture park at Goodwood, in the South of England. At Tony Cragg's studio in Wuppertal, Germany, we are grateful to Sabine Abesser, Marlies Meier, Caroline Pescher, John McCormack, David Kaluza, and the rest of the team for their close collaboration. Lastly, but of course foremost, our thanks go to Tony Cragg, whose enthusiasm, energy and constant support have made the exhibition possible. Cragg is in constant demand to stage exhibitions around the world, but when asked if he could add three major venues in China into his full schedule he agreed without a moment's hesitation. We are confident that the public in China will be amazed by his work.

前言 II

王璜生
中央美术学院美术馆馆长

托尼·克拉格是当今英国最伟大的艺术家之一。他获得了很多的重要奖项，如特纳奖，皮蓬布鲁克雕塑奖，日本皇室世界文化奖，英国CBE 勋章等，在世界众多重要美术馆和展览会如英国伦敦泰特美术馆、法国巴黎蓬皮杜文化中心、西班牙马德里国立博物馆、德国慕尼黑现代美术馆、柏林新国立美术馆、瑞士伯尔尼美术馆、比利时布鲁塞尔美术馆、美国纽约现代美术馆、日本东京大都会美术馆以及威尼斯双年展、卡塞尔文献展等举办个展或联展，这些荣誉和成果使他成为了当代艺术界一位引人瞩目的人物。而今天，托尼·克拉格的个展来到了中国最重要的美术馆之一中央美院美术馆展出，这对我们深入且近距离地欣赏、学习和研究托尼·克拉格的艺术，无疑是一次难得的机会。

去年，托尼·克拉格应邀参加了我馆举办的“超有机：首届CAFAM 泛主题展”，不仅呈现了他三件精彩的雕塑作品，而且以艺术家及德国杜塞尔多夫艺术学院院长身份，与同样是中国最重要的艺术家之一的中央美术学院潘公凯院长作了一个“高峰对话”，对当代艺术及创作问题、艺术教育问题等作了富于思考和机智的演讲和讨论。

托尼·克拉格对艺术问题和社会问题的思考具有很强的理性精神，这可能与他出身于一个电气工程师的家庭及他早年在天然橡胶研究所实验室工作的经历有关，他对艺术创作的理解和实践敏感并重视于材料、介质、比例、生成、技术、计算机等。他的作品，往往应用现成品、废弃物、工业社会制品，利用那些在当代社会环境中常见的物品和材料，也包括塑料、陶瓷、石膏、木材、钢铁、玻璃、聚氨酯、石头、铜、橡胶、水泥及新出现的材质。当代社会文化及物质环境，其突出特点是产生和存在着丰富的材质，并可自由应用发挥，从而形成艺术创造的新面貌和新观念。从杜尚等对现成品的创造性应用，到层出不穷的工业制品、废弃物及新的材料、科技介质等等，构成了眼花缭乱的艺术创造的“材料”世界，而艺术家如何在自由的选择应用不同介质的“材料”的同时，一方面挑战和超越材料及技术所存在的形而下的条条框框，而创造出材料潜在和超潜在的美学价值；另一方面，又能够赋予这样的“材料”以新的与人、与社会、与现实相关的感觉、情感、观念、思想，也就是说，赋予“材料”以活脱脱的生命。托尼·克拉格的艺术，正是体现了他作为一位当代艺术家对时代的“材料”的超越性理解和表达。他早期作品利用废弃物、塑料等，构造着的是对这样的“材料”本身的颜色、形态、质感的美感的发现，及由这样的“材料”在特殊的空间存在中所体现的与人的生命状态之间的关系；而后期的作品使用的聚氨酯、合成木材、化学合成物、石膏、玻璃，以及钢铁、铜、石头等等，更体现了他对“材料”新的潜在的美学价值的挖掘，及当代社会学丰富内涵的表现。这样的独特性和创造性，使得托尼·克拉格被放到当代艺术史的格局中来论述和定位。

其实，托尼·克拉格的艺术并不仅仅停留在这样的艺术作品呈现上，而是具有很强的理性思考和表达的意义，从艺术的方法论、艺术观念、理论表述，到当代性实践等方面，托尼·克拉格做出了他难得的贡献，阅读他的理论文章包括访谈录等，以及对他的艺术思想的深入研究，也许可以为我们更全面地了解这位重要的艺术家有丰富的帮助，同时也对我们更多元地研究和推进当代艺术的发展具有重大的意义。

我们期待着托尼·克拉格这次展览所带来的难得的学习研究机会！同时，本次展览作为2012年在中国举办的最大的英国艺术和创意产业盛会“艺述英国”项目的一部分，我们相信，这将为中英文化交流谱写新的篇章！

衷心感谢托尼·克拉格先生！

衷心感谢所有支持和促进这次文化交流盛事的机构和个人！

王璜生

2012年2月12日于中国广州

Foreword II

Wang Huangsheng
Director of CAFA Art Museum

Tony Cragg is one of Britain's greatest artists today. He has received many important awards such as the Turner Prize, the Piepenbrock Award, Japan's Praemium Imperiale award, the British CBE, among others. His works have been showcased in solo and group exhibitions in major museums and galleries around the world, including the Tate Modern in London, the Centre Georges Pompidou in Paris, the Museo del Prado in Madrid, the Pinakothek der Moderne in Munich, the New National Gallery in Berlin, the Kunstmuseum Bern in Switzerland, the Musee royaux des Beaux-Arts de Begique in Belgium, the Museum of Modern Art in New York, the Tokyo Metropolitan Art Museum, the Venice Biennale and the Kassel Documenta. These honors have distinguished him as an exceptional talent in contemporary art. Today, Tony Cragg's works are presented in a solo show at one of China's most important art museums: the Central Academy of Fine Arts Museum. It is a valuable opportunity for us to admire, examine and to learn from Tony Cragg's art at a close range.

Last year, Tony Cragg participated in our "The 1st CAFAM Biennale: Super-Organism" where he presented three of his marvelous sculptures. Speaking as an artist and the Director of Kunstakademie Dusseldorf, Cragg engaged in a dialogue with one of China's leading art educators Pan Gongkai, Director of the Central Academy of Fine Arts. The occasion featured thought-provoking speeches and conversations on contemporary art, the challenges of creativity, fine art education and other topics.

Tony Cragg is a deeply rational thinker on issues of art and society, which may reflect his having come from a family of engineers and his work experience in a natural rubber laboratory in his early years. He has great sensitivity toward the understanding and execution of art, with a special focus on material, texture, proportion, organism, technique and calculation. Many of his works utilize existing materials, garbage, industrial products, objects and elements that are common to the social environment at the time. They also include plastic, porcelain, gypsum, wood, iron, glass, polyrethane, stone, bronze, rubber, concrete and other materials from the contemporary social and cultural landscapes. The materials stand out for their richness and flexibility, as they are molded to create new facets and concepts of art. Starting from the use of existing materials by artists like Duchamp, art has been revamped into a many-faceted "material world" thanks to the diversified use of industrial products, garbage and other new materials. In choosing from an expanding variety of "materials," the artists challenge and transcend the confines of materials and techniques, to unearth and re-create a hidden aesthetic. On the other hand, the artists instill new connections between the "materials" and people, society and reality, as the emerging emotions, values and mindsets bring new lives to the materials. As a contemporary artist, Tony Cragg starts from and transcends rational understanding of materials of his time, which is manifested in his art. His early works often make use of garbage and plastic to discover the intrinsic colors, shapes and textures of the "materials" while illuminating the relation between this unique art space and human lives. His later works utilize polyrethane, imitation-wood plastic, synthetics, gypsum, glass, iron, bronze, stones and others. It points to a deeper exploration into new aesthetics of "materials" with a sociological touch. Such distinctive creativity puts Cragg at the forefront of contemporary art and its debates.

Beyond his personal artistic expression, Tony Cragg's art embodies exceptional rational thinking and communication. His work is an outstanding contribution to contemporary theories, concepts, rational critique and execution of art. From his theoretical texts including artists' conversations, as well as research into his artistic concepts, we can get broader views on the art of this important artist. This will be of great significance to our various efforts in the research and promotion of contemporary art.

We look forward to this Tony Cragg exhibition and the wonderful opportunities for learning and research it opens up. In the meantime, the exhibition is a part of "UK NOW", the largest festival of British art and culture ever to come to China. We believe that it will be a new chapter in our Chinese-British cultural dialogue.

We would like to extend our deepest gratitude to Mr Tony Cragg, and to all the individuals and organizations who have supported this amazing cultural exchange.

Guangzhou, China
February 12 2012

前言 III

吕澎
成都当代美术馆馆长

从亨利·摩尔(Henry Moore)以来，英国雕塑开始融入世界雕塑艺术的主流，在Lynn Chadwick、Kenneth Armitage、Bernard Meadows、Reg Butler 以及Elisabeth Frink 等一大批新一代雕塑家的努力下，英国雕塑已经是世界当代雕塑发展史中的重要组成部分。在社会对雕塑的公共性、参与性以及与环境的协调性的不断需求下，英国雕塑家为欧洲乃至世界雕塑艺术提供了符合当代社会特征的创造性范例。

也正是在不断突破雕塑概念的过程中，英国也产生了这样的艺术家，他们对雕塑的边界——当然本质上是对艺术的边界——进行了扩展，在雕塑与非雕塑、雕塑与装置、以及综合材料上进行了富于成果的试验，从更加自由的角度上开拓了人们对雕塑艺术的理解。

出生于利物浦的托尼·克拉格(1949-)正是这样的实验性艺术家，他发展了波普艺术的现成品观念——利用废旧物品构成崭新的雕塑；他尝试着使用不同材料——铜、钢、塑料、橡胶、玻璃、木头、石膏等——进行雕塑创作；他注意到在工业社会与信息技术社会中对雕塑提出挑战的种种问题，因而更加富于活力地利用人类精神活动的特质，创造出对人们习惯的格式与规范有突破的雕塑作品。托尼·克拉格通过对艺术范畴的不断开拓赢得了艺术批评界和艺术史家们的关注，这样的结果是，尽管托尼·克拉格的雕塑具有相当的实验性，可是，大众通过对他的艺术的不断阅读，也因思想受到开启而对实验性艺术以及人类的可能性有了充分的理解和认识。

改革开放在中国已经有了三十多年的时间，中国观众对于富于创造性的新艺术具有浓厚的兴趣，所以，对当代最具有活力的艺术给予关注、展示、研究和收藏是成都当代美术馆的基本理念，基于此，我对于来自当代雕塑最为活跃的英国的雕塑作品能够在本馆进行展出，感到非常荣幸。事实上，托尼·克拉格的雕塑艺术不仅能够给成都的观众带来对新艺术的享受，也给成都的雕塑家带来了一次学习和交流的机会。在这里，我要感谢英国总领事馆文化教育处给本馆带来的这次展览，当然，我也希望借此机会通过英国使领馆文化教育处表达对卓越的雕塑艺术家托尼·克拉格的感谢和敬意。我希望托尼·克拉格的这次展览能够成为我们进一步了解英国当代艺术和文化的一次良好的开端，并能够有与英国艺术家和艺术机构长期交流的机会。

2012年2月14日星期二

Foreword III

Lu Peng
Director of Museum of
Contemporary Art Chengdu

Since Henry Moore, British sculpture has entered the world's mainstream sculptural art. With the efforts of Lynn Chadwick, Kenneth Armitage, Bernard Meadows, Reg Bulter, Elisabeth Frink and other sculptors, British sculpture has come to occupy a central place in the history of contemporary sculptural art. As society places changing demands on the public nature and participation of sculpture, British sculptors have been representatives of sculptural art grounded in contemporary society, in the European and even international art worlds.

In the ongoing evolution of sculptural concepts, the diverse group of British sculptors have sought to expand the limits of sculpture--and essentially, the frontiers of art. Their experiment has instilled new synergy into the questions about sculpture and non-sculpture, sculpture and installation, and mixed materials, as it broadens our understanding of sculptural art from a more liberal perspective.

Born in Liverpool, Tony Cragg (1949-) is one of these experimental artists. He initiated the concept of POP existing art objects, the use of discarded objects in creating innovative sculptures. He uses different materials--bronze, steel, plastic, rubber, glass, wood, plaster and more--in his sculptures. Cragg observes the challenges posed by the industrial society and technological advancements on sculpture. Illuminating the essence of human thought in their various activities, he creates sculptural works that go beyond common conception of the art form with great vibrancy. Cragg continually expands the frontiers of art, which garners much attention from art critics and art historians. As a result, Cragg's highly experimental work is constantly studied by the public, which leads to further understanding of experimental art and human possibility in art.

It has been over thirty years since the opening of China, and the Chinese audience has developed a keen interest in new and innovative art. As an advocate of contemporary art, the Chengdu Museum of Contemporary Art is dedicated to the promotion, showcase, research and collection of the most vibrant art today. As British sculpture is at the center stage of contemporary sculptural art, we feel deeply honored to exhibit some of these works in our museum. The art of Tony Cragg brings not only new artistic delight to the local audience, but also an opening for learning and exchange for the sculptors in Chengdu. I wish to thank the Cultural and Education Section of the British Embassy for making this exhibition happen, and to express my gratitude and admiration for Tony Cragg, a brilliant sculptor. I hope that this exhibition of Tony Cragg's art will be an excellent start for our further understanding of contemporary British art and culture, and our future exchanges with British artists and arts organizations.

February 14 2012

前言Ⅳ

王纯杰
喜玛拉雅美术馆馆长

托尼·克拉格（Tony Cragg）的作品难以用言语描述，只有通过对作品的观察和体验才被感知。今秋专程去看托尼的个展，来到爱丁堡苏格兰国立当代美术馆，门口一片绿色草地，被深色的树林围绕，草地上隆起小丘和低洼水塘，星云状般的罗旋线状交织一起，二只鹅在水塘中游动，美术馆古老的建筑物上霓虹灯管组成一行字"Everthing is going to be alright"，美术馆的周围场所和环境艺术，形成令人向往的纯净的心灵空间。托尼·克拉格的几件不同色彩户外作品置入在建筑物门口和草坪的周围，远远望去这几件雕塑有点似中国的假山石，走近看它们既不是任何形态的自然物体或生活中熟悉的造型，也不是几何机械型或生物有机体。托尼不可名状的新作品形态有一股深深的吸引力，吸引人们走到作品近处，围绕四周看，并想进入其中。他的每件作品给人不同感受。

最初认识托尼·克拉格是通过他创作于八、九十年代的作品。他收集塑料碎片和使用过的工业产品，排列成生活造型和堆积抽象的造型。他对材料的敏感和运用材料的观念，他的艺术与当代生活密切相关。他探索物质、自然、人类生存状态的互动和反应成为英国新雕塑群体的代表性艺术家。近二十年来，他运用各种不同物质材料，深入形体的研究，从每个维度挤拉、扭转、延展与凹陷，自身体量感在空间上的不同延伸，展现出起伏和节奏，创造了想象力和可能性的雕塑肌理。托尼·克拉格创作无限可能的物体造型，给予广阔想象空间。托尼·克拉格就是这样一位非常智慧的雕塑大师，注重雕塑造型语言和材料的探索研究。他的作品形式感和创作观念表达上都让我们看到了他对人类社会生活的敏锐观察，严密的理性思维和不断创新的活力。

喜玛拉雅美术馆将举办托尼·克拉格个展。包括托尼·克拉格大约50件雕塑作品和近百件水彩和绘画作品。从展览呈现角度而言，这并不仅仅是一个个展的概念，更确切地说是一个充满活力、不断演变进行的英国当代雕塑展。托尼·克拉格的艺术折射了英国80年代至今的当代雕塑史的历程，我们相信，通过交流托尼·克拉格的作品会给中国艺术家们新的启示，带给观众新的体验。

最后，感谢英国使领馆文化教育处真诚合作，他们的敬业精神令人感动，感谢中央美术学院美术馆和他们为托尼中国巡展做的周密的前期工作。感谢上海对外文化协会的赞助。感谢证大集团的鼎立支持！

Foreword IV

Wong Shun-kit
Director of Himalayas Art Museum

The works of Tony Cragg are beyond words; they are only recognized through observation and experience of his art. Last autumn I attended Cragg's solo exhibition at the Scottish National Gallery of Modern Art in Edinburgh. At the entrance, the grass field was surrounded by dark-colored trees; small valleys swirled around a shallow pond on which two swans were swimming. Neon lights spelled the sentence, "Everything is going to be alright", on the exterior of the museum, adding an energized touch to the old architecture. The museum and its surroundings presented an inner realm of purity. A handful of Cragg's outdoor installations in different colors stood around the museum's entrance and the grass field. From a distance, the installations bore a slight resemblance to Chinese fake stone mountains. At close range they looked nothing like any natural or everydayobjects, or any mechanical or organic forms. These new works of Cragg remain undefinable as they lure the viewers to examine them from near and far, entering the artist's imagination. Each instills different emotions in the viewers.

I was first exposed to Tony Cragg through his works from the 80's and 90's. He collected plastic fragments and used materials, transformed them into everyday objects and abstract forms. He had great sensitivity to materials and their usage, which created a strong connection between his art and contemporary life. With his exploration into materials, nature, human existence and the interaction in between, Cragg became the representative artist of the New British Sculpture. In the past twenty years, Cragg has expanded his use of different materials for further exploration into form. Starting with head sculptures, Cragg molded, twisted, stretched and pitted his materials. The texture of the sculptures extended in multi-dimensional spaces to show a fluid unfolding of concepts and the ever-pulsating creative process; they encapsulate an imaginative mindset that strives for changeability in material creation. Tony Cragg is an intellectual sculptor who stresses the exploration of sculptural language and materials. From the forms and creative expression of his works, we see his shrewd observations of human life and society, his rational thinking and energy of innovation.

The Himalayas Art Museum will present Tony Cragg's solo exhibition. Featured works will include about 50 sculptures and 100 watercolor paintings and drawings by the artist. The artistic voyage of Tony Cragg also reflects the dynamic evolution of contemporary sculpture in England from the 80's to the present. We believe that Tony Cragg's works will bring new insights to our Chinese artists and audience through such meaningful exchanges.

Lastly, I would like to extend my gratitude to the Cultural and Education Section of British Embassy for their collaboration and professionalism; the Scottish National Gallery of Modern Art for their professional support; the Central Academy of Fine Arts Museum for their thorough preparation for the national exhibition of Tony Cragg. I would also like to thank the Shanghai International Culture Association for their sponsorship, and the Zendai Group for their generous support.

前言V

白琼娜
英国大使馆文化教育处文化参赞
英国文化协会中国地区主任

我非常高兴“托尼·克拉格：雕塑和绘画展”在中国的三个城市举办。本展览基于苏格兰国立现代美术馆2011年夏季同名展，是托尼·克拉格作品在中国的首个回顾展。

托尼·克拉格是至今仍活跃的英国最伟大的艺术家之一。他不仅是一个雕塑家，更重要的是始终致力于探索不同介质在材料、哲学意义和技术方面的限制。他运用陶瓷、Jesmonite、石膏、木材、钢铁、玻璃钢、石头和铜等材料进行创作，以及本次将展出的许多纸本作品。克拉格于1988年荣获特纳奖，2002年被授予皮蓬布鲁克雕塑奖，2007年获日本皇室世界文化奖，并于2001年获英国CBE勋章。

该展览是“艺述英国”项目的一部分，该项目是在中国举办的最大的英国艺术和创意产业盛会，从2012年四月至十一月，将有超过100个活动在17个城市开展。正值2012伦敦奥运会和两国建立外交关系40周年之际，这一盛会的目的在于使英国和中国的艺术机构、艺术家和艺术爱好者更紧密地联系起来。

我想感谢苏格兰国立现代美术馆，特别是最初展览的策展人帕特里克·艾略特，以及允许我们将展览引进到中国的西蒙·格鲁姆馆长。非常感谢霍特曼艺术公司的玛丽安·霍特曼女士，她是英国方面的展览负责人。中国方面，我要感谢中央美术学院美术馆王璜生馆长及其同事王春辰博士和岳君瑶；证大集团董事长戴志康、上海喜玛拉雅美术馆执行馆长王纯杰及其同事黄玥霖；成都当代美术馆馆长吕澎先生及其同事何蕾、蓝庆伟、钟红豆，还必须感谢上海市对外文化交流协会提供的经济支持。

英国文化与教育处方面，我想感谢戴维礼(艺术总监，中国)、项目负责人张妤以及他们的同事鲁昱熙和曾臻。

最后我想感谢托尼·克拉格，感谢他的艺术精神和对展览的慷慨。

Foreword V

Joanna Burke
Counsellor (Cultural), British
Embassy Beijing
Director China, British Council

I am delighted that the exhibition, Tony Cragg: Sculptures and Drawings, is being shown in three cities across China. The exhibition, based on the Scottish National Gallery of Modern Art's summer 2011 show of the same name, is the first ever retrospective of Tony Cragg's work to be shown in China.

Tony Cragg is one of Britain's greatest living artists. He is a sculptor first and foremost, forever pushing the material, metaphysicial and technological limits of the medium. He works with ceramic, jesmonite, plaster, wood, steel, fibreglass, stone and bronze, and included in this exhibition are many of his drawings. Cragg won the Turner Prize in 1988, was awarded the Piepenbrock Award for sculpture in 2002 and the Praemium Imperiale in 2007, and received the CBE for services to art in 2001.

The exhibition is part of UK Now, the largest festival of British arts and creative industries ever to take place in China, with over 100 events in 17 cities from April to November 2012. Coinciding with the London Olympics and the 40th anniversary of the resumption of diplomatic relations between our two countries, the festival's aim is to bring British and Chinese arts institutions, artists and art lovers closer together.

I would like to thank the Scottish National Gallery of Modern Art, particularly Patrick Elliott who curated the original exhibition, and also Simon Groom, its Director, for allowing us to bring the exhibition to China. I would very much like to thank Marianne Holtermann of Holtermann Fine Art who managed the project from the UK end. In China I would like to thank Professor Wang Huangsheng, Director of the CAFA Museum in Beijing, together with his colleagues Wang Chunchen and Yue Junyao; Dai Zhikang, Chairman of Zendai Group, Wong Shun-kit, Executive Director of Himalayas Art Museum in Shanghai, together with their colleague Yoyo Huang; and Mr Lu Peng, Director General of Chengdu Museum of Contemporary Art, together with his colleagues He Lei, Lan Qingwei, Zhong Hongdou. Thanks must also go to the Shanghai International Culture Association for their financial support.

Within the British Council I would like to thank David Elliott (Director Arts, China), Lisa Zhang (Shanghai office) who managed the project from our end, and colleagues Yuxi Lu (Beijing office) and Jenny Zeng (Chongqing office).

And finally I would like to thank Tony Cragg for the spirit and generosity in which he has collaborated on the project.

雕塑 SCULPTURES

S1《马铃薯头像》 / *Potato Heads*

摄影 / Photographs
213×183×5cm
1970

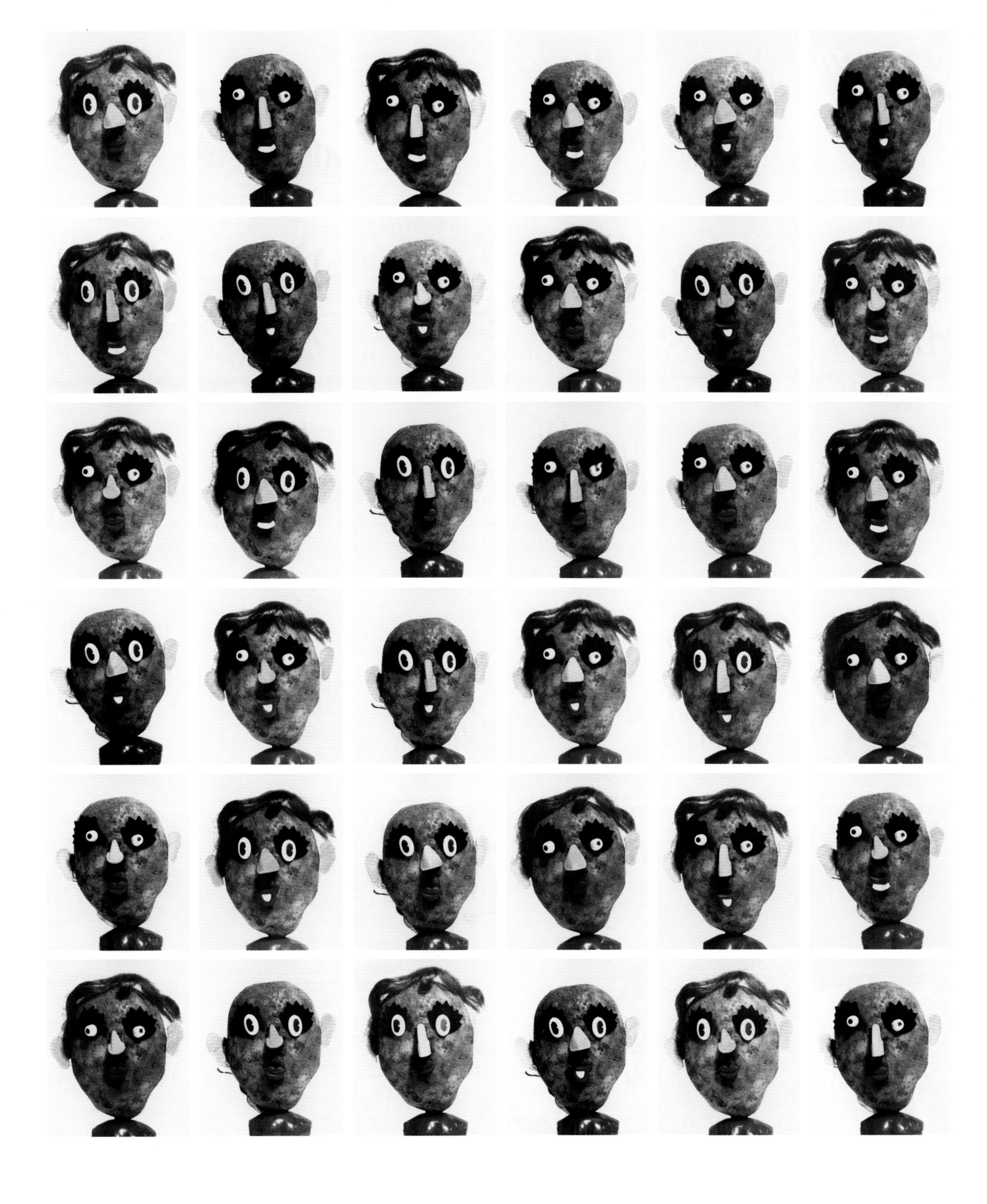

S2《元素平面》/ ***Element Plane***

木头、石 / Wood, stone
120×220×110cm
1983

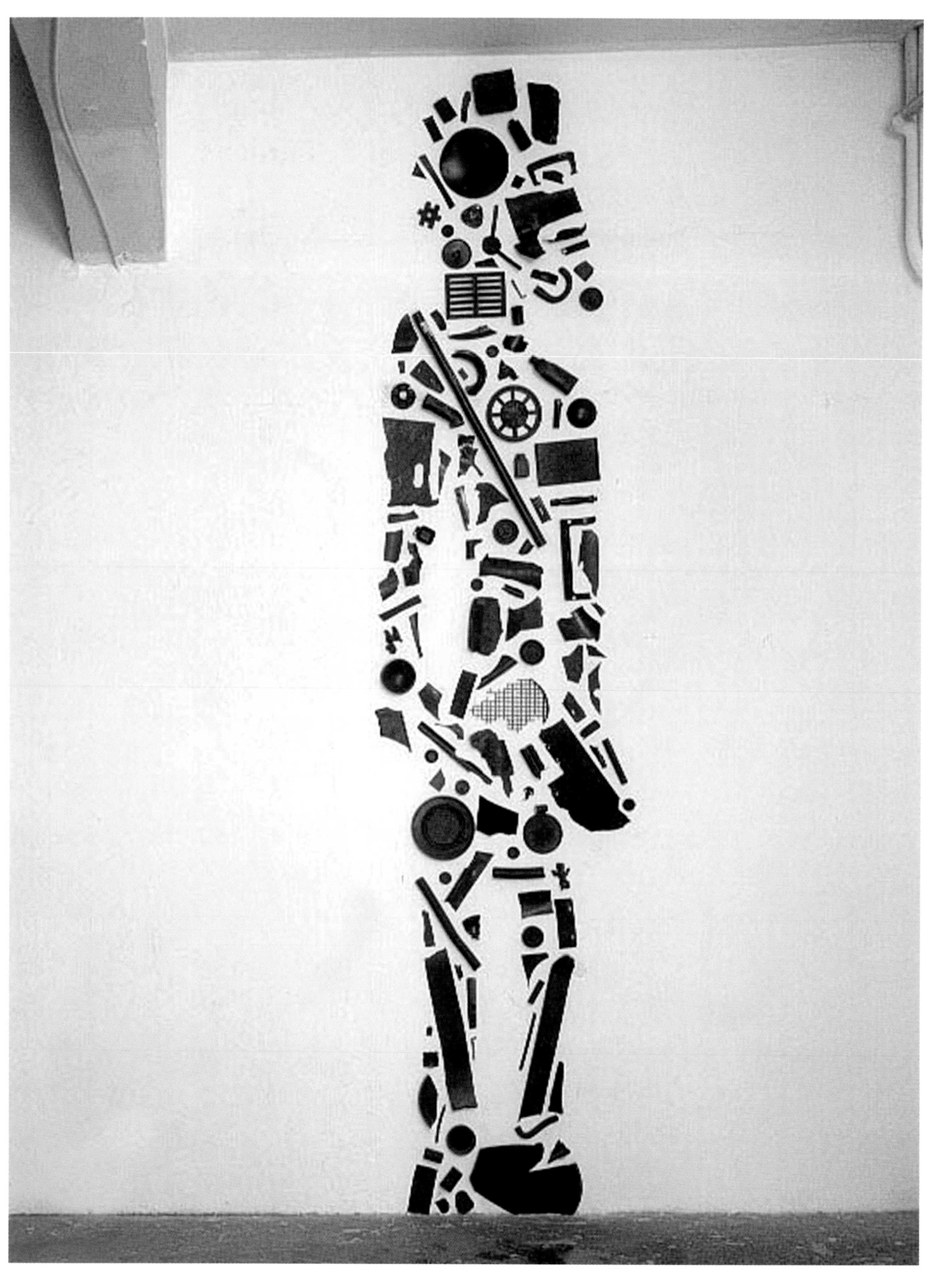

S3《非洲文化神话》/ *Element Plane*

塑料 / Plastic
323×63cm
1984

S4《大教堂》/ *Minster*

钢 / Steel
尺寸可变 / Size variable
1988
摄影 / Photo：David Kaluza

S5《测不准原理》/ *Unschärferelation*

木头 / Wood
160×115×85cm
1991
摄影 / Photo：Michael Richter

S6《完整的杂食动物》/ *Complete Omnivore*

石膏、木头、钢 / Plaster, wood, steel
160×200×200cm
1993

S7《早期形式》/ *Early Forms*

铜 / Bronze
60×65×60cm
1993
摄影 / Photo：David Kaluza

S8《早期形式》/ *Early Forms*

铜 / Bronze
45×57×75cm
1993
摄影 / Photo：Antje Zeis-Loh

S9《分泌物》/ *Secretions*

塑料 / Plastic
242×86×203cm, 33×225×167cm
1995
摄影 / Photo：Antje Zeis-Loh

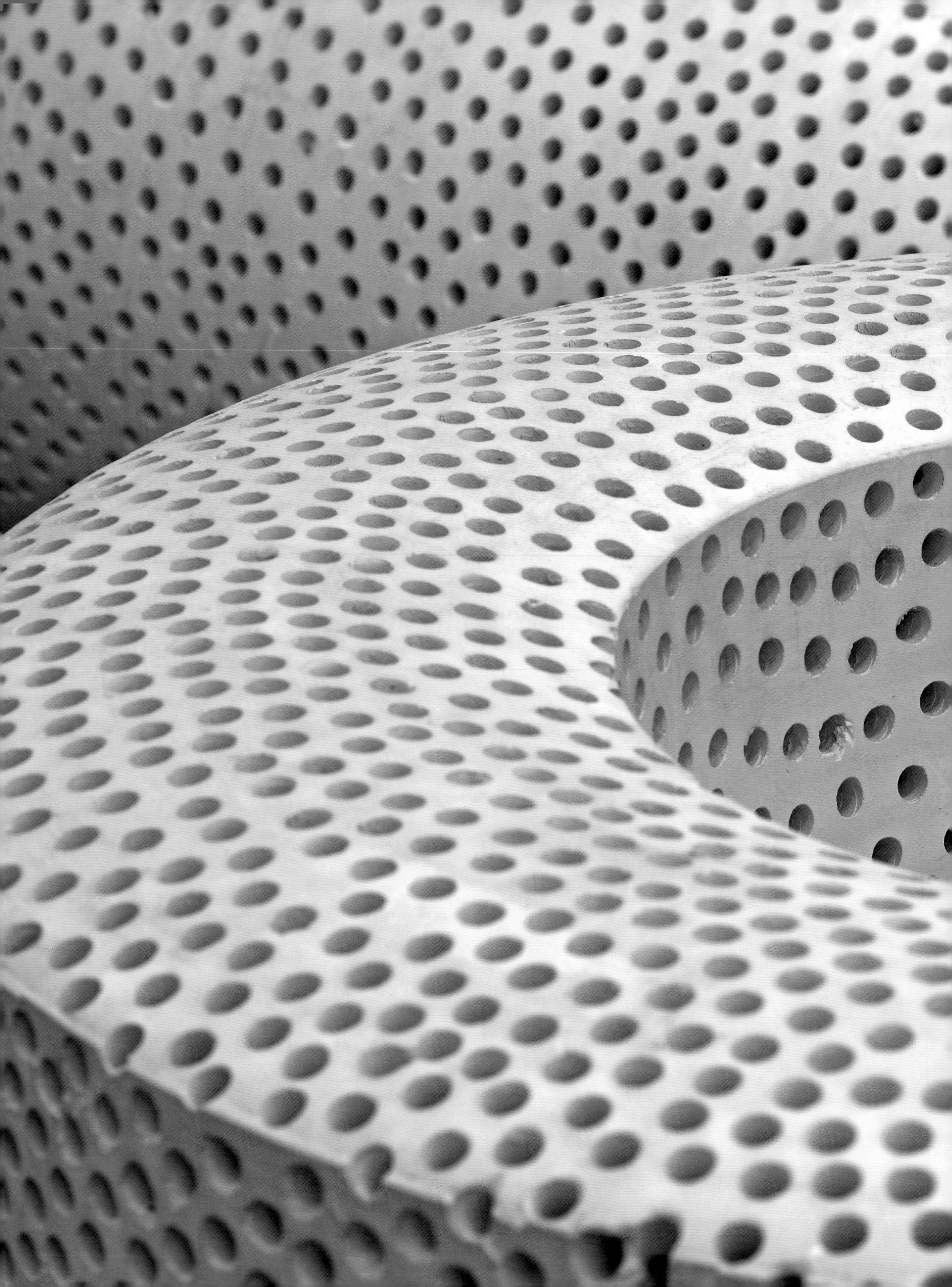

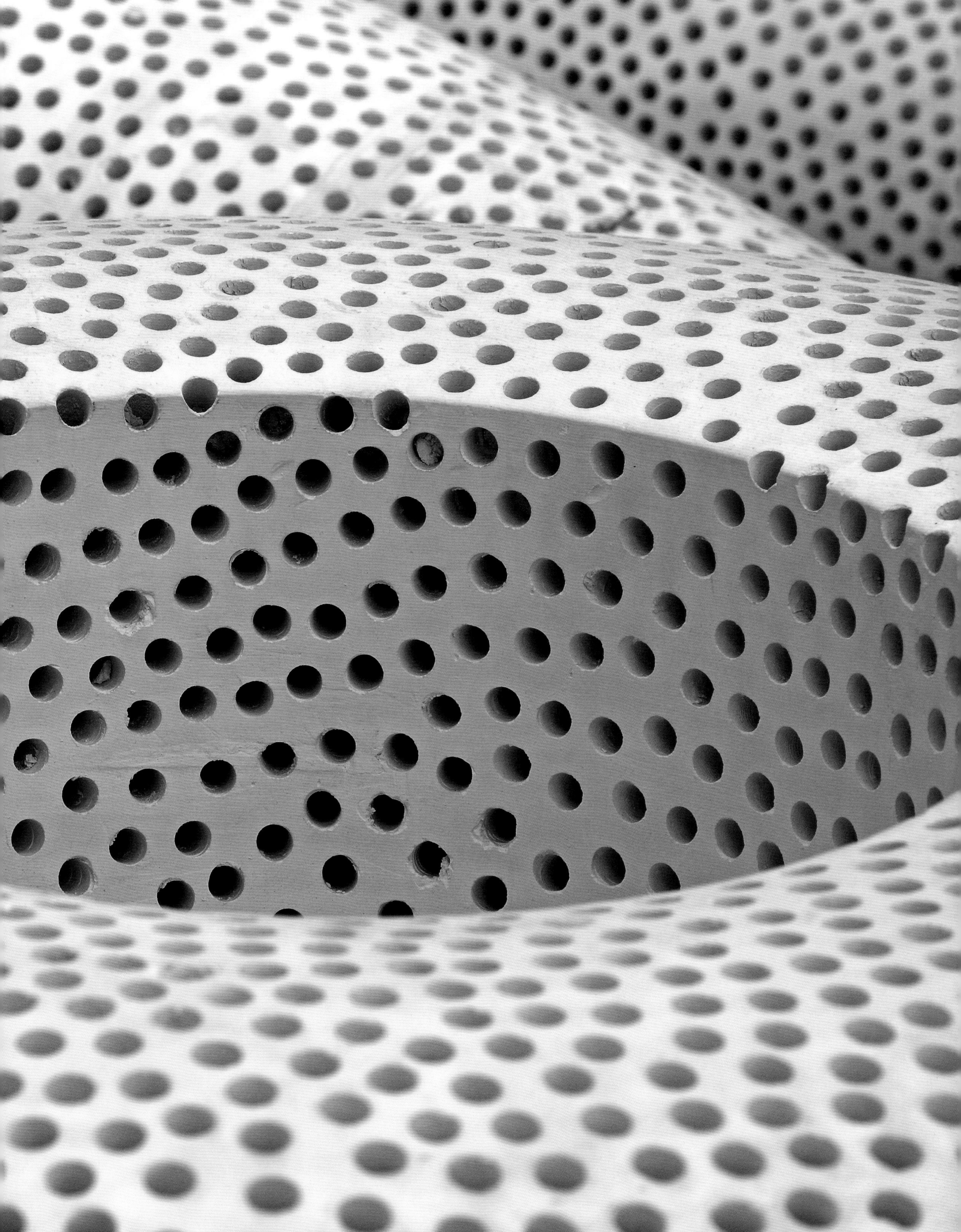

S10《有孔体》/ ***Forminifera***

石膏、钢 / Plaster, steel
250×300×300cm
1997
摄影 / Photo：Michael Richter

S11《早期形式圣加仑》/ *Early Forms St Gallen*

铜 / Bronze
85×105×265cm
1997
摄影 / Photo：Charles Duprat

S12《盒子》/ *Box*

铜 / Bronze
80×110×100cm
1999
摄影 / Photo：Jon Abbott

S13《康康舞》/ *Can-can*

铜 / Bronze
90×130×230cm
2000
摄影 / Photo：Charles Duprat

S14《构想（位置）》/ *Formulation (Stance)*

铜 / Bronze
218×109×107cm
2000
摄影 / Photo：Dave Morgan

S15《木制水晶》/ *Wooden Crystal*

木头 / Wood
407×108×108cm
2000
摄影 / Photo：Charles Duprat

S16《锥形瓶》/ *Conical Flask*

铜 / Bronze
58×62×37cm
2000
摄影 / Photo：Charles Duprat

S17《构想（右转，左转）》/ *Formulation (right turning, left turning)*

铜 / Bronze
114×127×119cm
2000
摄影 / Photo: John Abbot

S18《弯曲的思想》/ *Bent of Mind*

铜 / Bronze
120×80×70cm
2002
摄影 / Photo：Charles Duprat

S19《投以一瞥》/ *Cast Glances*

铜 / Bronze
240×190×160cm
2002
摄影 / Photo：Charles Duprat

S20《远房亲戚》/ *Distant Cousin*

玻璃钢 / Fiberglass
210×165×160cm
2003
摄影 / Photo：John Berens

S21《势如破竹》/ *On a Roll*

铜 / Bronze
82×95×95cm
2003
摄影 / Photo：Michael Richter

S22《赤纬》/ ***Declination***

铜 / Bronze
240×231×360cm
2004
摄影 / Photo：Charles Duprat

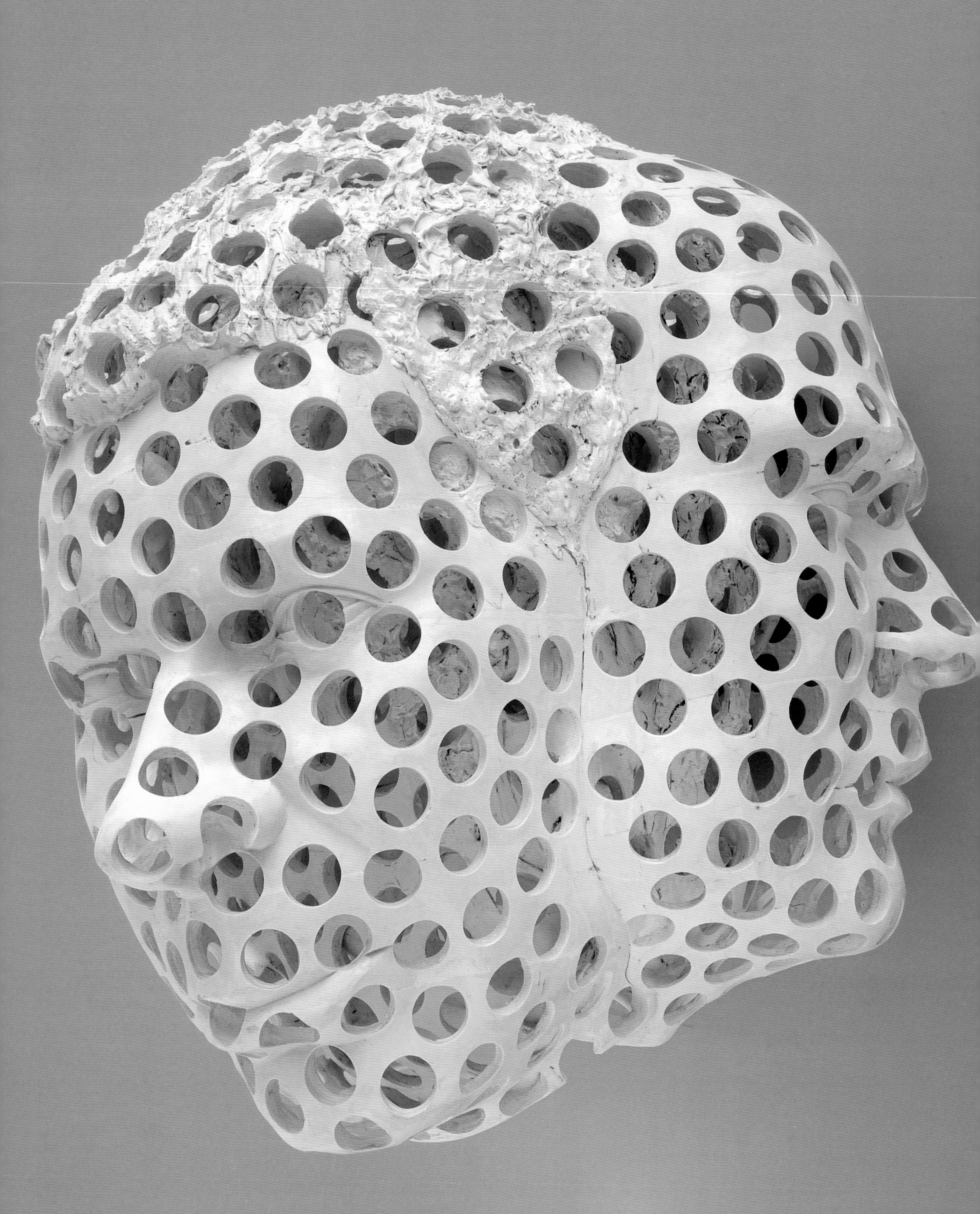

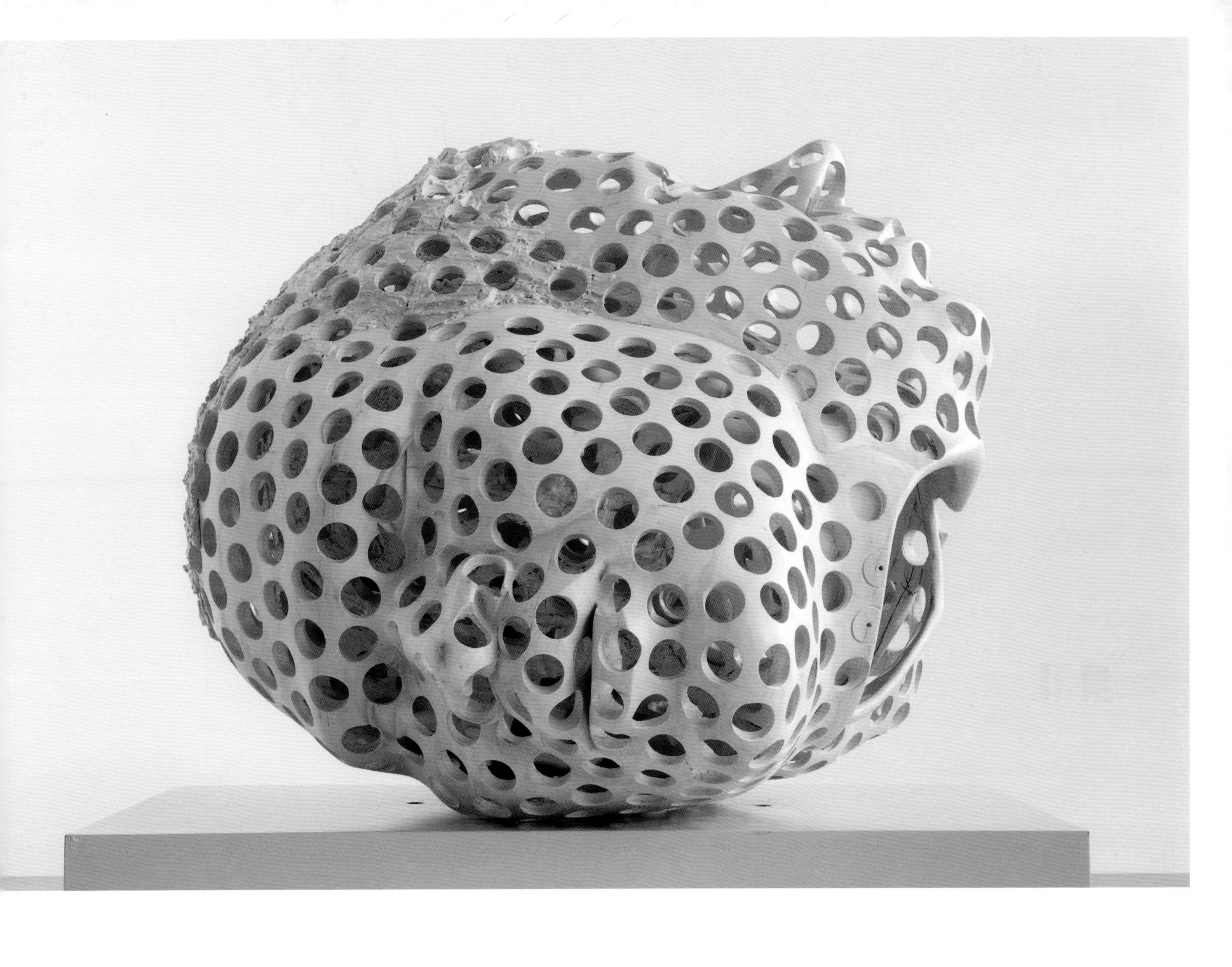

S23《共享》/ *Sharing*

Jesmonite 合成材料 / Jesmonite
100×110×120cm
2005
摄影 / Photo：Charles Duprat

S24《陷入沉思》/ *Lost in Thought*

铜 / Bronze
250×100×60cm
2005
摄影 / Photo：Michael Richter

S25《数码皮肤》/ ***Digital Skin***

铜 / Bronze
67×80×82cm, 135×150×75cm
2006
摄影 / Photo：Ellen Page Wilson

S26《频率之中》/ *In Frequencies*

铜 / Bronze
95×120×115cm
2008
摄影 / Photo：David Kaluza

S27《捕捉梦想》/ *Caught Dreaming*

铜 / Bronze
159×285×153cm
2008
摄影 / Photo：Charles Duprat

S28《精神的风景》/ *Mental Landscapes*

铜 / Bronze
120×170×120cm
2007
摄影 / Photo：Charles Duprat

S29《红场》/ ***Red Square***

铜 / Bronze
76×80×66cm
2007
摄影 / Photo：Ellen Page Wilson

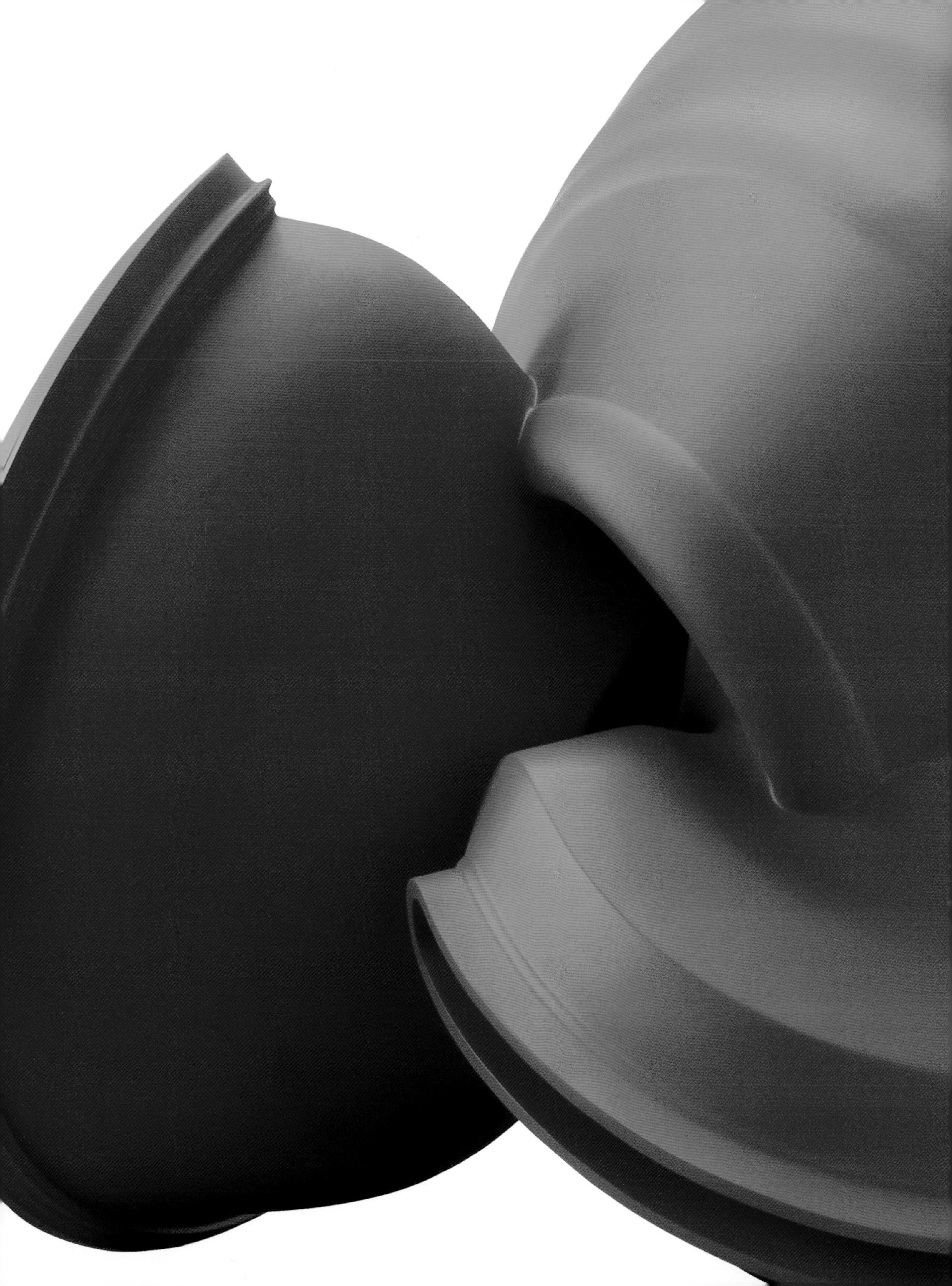

S30《麦科马克》/ *McCormack*

铜 / Bronze
117×130×75cm
2007
摄影 / Photo：Charles Duprat

S31《观点》/ ***Points of View***

铜 / Bronze
107×65×65cm
2007
摄影 / Photo：Charles Duprat

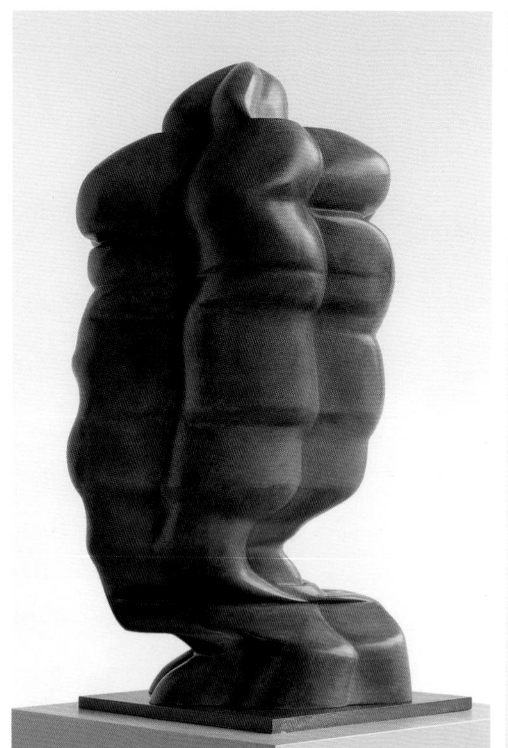

S32《女人头像》/ ***Woman's Head***

铜 / Bronze
87×60×50cm
2007
摄影 / Photo：Charles Duprat

T.C. 2007

S33《建造者》/ *Constructor*

不锈钢 / Stainless
116×73×70cm
2007
摄影 / Photo：Dave Morgan

S34《同伴》/ *Companions*

玻璃钢 / Fiberglass
278×205×294cm
2008
摄影 / Photo：Charles Duprat

S35

石 / Stone
85×60×60cm
2008
摄影 / Photo：Michael Richter

S36《路加》/ ***Luke***

铜 / Bronze
360×192×180cm
2008
摄影 / Photo：Ken Adlard

S37《哈姆雷特》/ ***Hamlet***

木头 / Wood
386×130×100cm
2010
摄影 / Photo：Michael Richter

S38《手肘》/ *Elbow*

木头 / Wood
250×102×429cm
2010
摄影 / Photo：Michael Richter

S39《从此以后》/ *Ever After*

铜 / Bronze
356×138×100cm
2010
摄影 / Photo：Charles Duprat

S40《路加》/ ***Luke***

石 / Stone
120×50×50cm
2010
摄影 / Photo：David Kaluza

S41《碎片》/ *Chip*

木头 / Wood
232×80×80cm
2010
摄影 / Photo：Michael Richter

S42《它是，它不是》/ *It is, it isn't*

铜 / Bronze
242×120×110cm
2010
摄影 / Photo：Charles Duprat

S43《操纵》/ ***Manipulation***

铜 / Bronze
215×240×190cm
2010
摄影 / Photo：Charles Duprat

S44《观点》/ *Points of View*

不锈钢 / Stainless
575×130×130cm
2010
摄影 / Photo：Kevin Todora

S45《聚合》/ *Group*

铁 / Cast iron
62×60×43cm
2011
摄影 / Photo：Michael Richter

S46《对抗》/ ***Versus***

铜 / Bronze
266×285×105cm
2011
摄影 / Photo：Kevin Todora

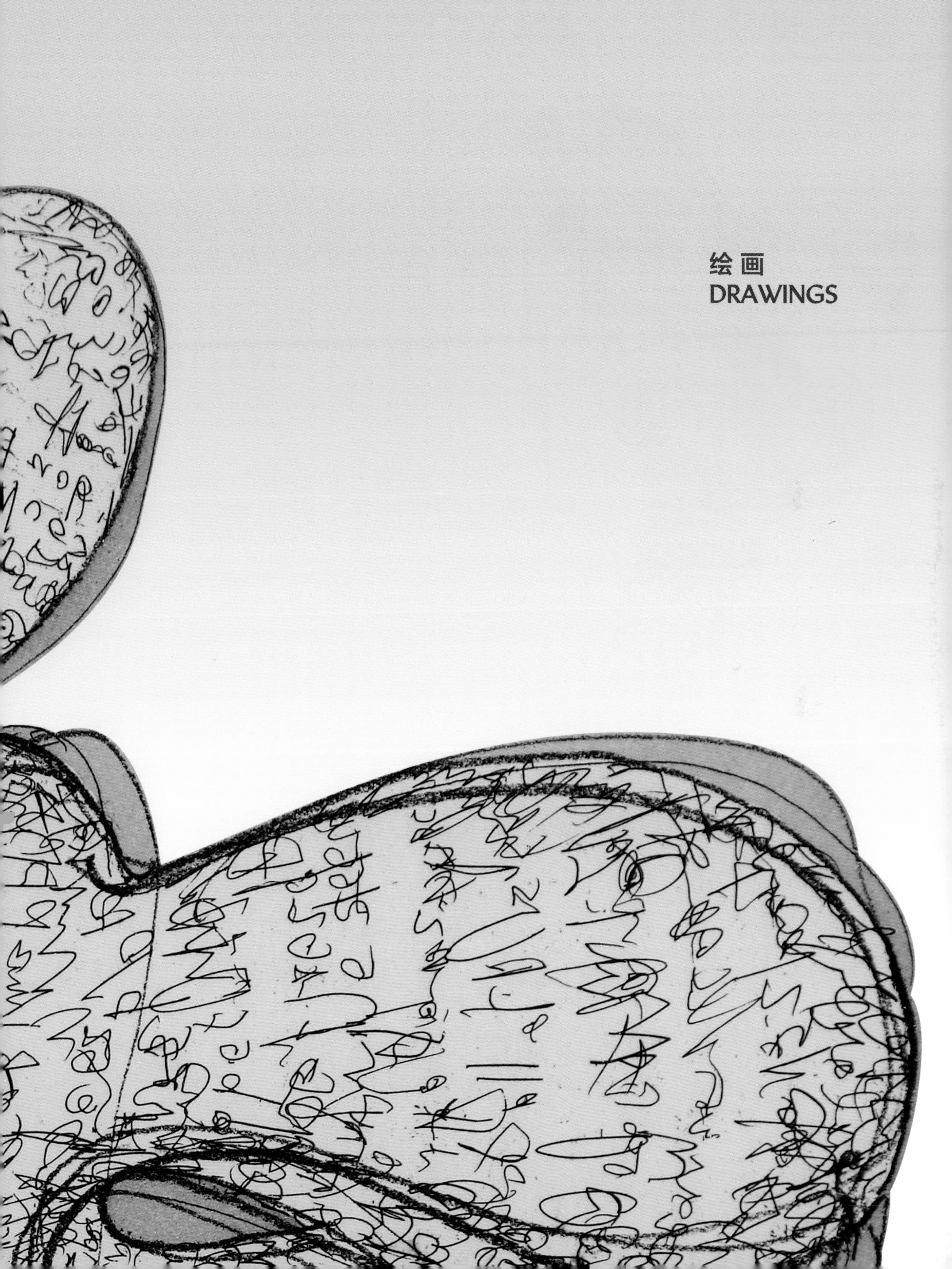

绘画
DRAWINGS

1

D1

纸上水粉 / Gouache on paper
45.2×31.7cm
1990
摄影 / Photo: Michael Richter

D2

纸上铅笔 / Pencil on paper
22.8×31cm
1990
摄影 / Photo: Michael Richter

D3

纸上水粉 / Gouache on paper
45×31cm
1990
摄影 / Photo: Michael Richter

D4

纸上水粉 / Gouache on paper
45×31cm
1990
摄影 / Photo: Michael Richter

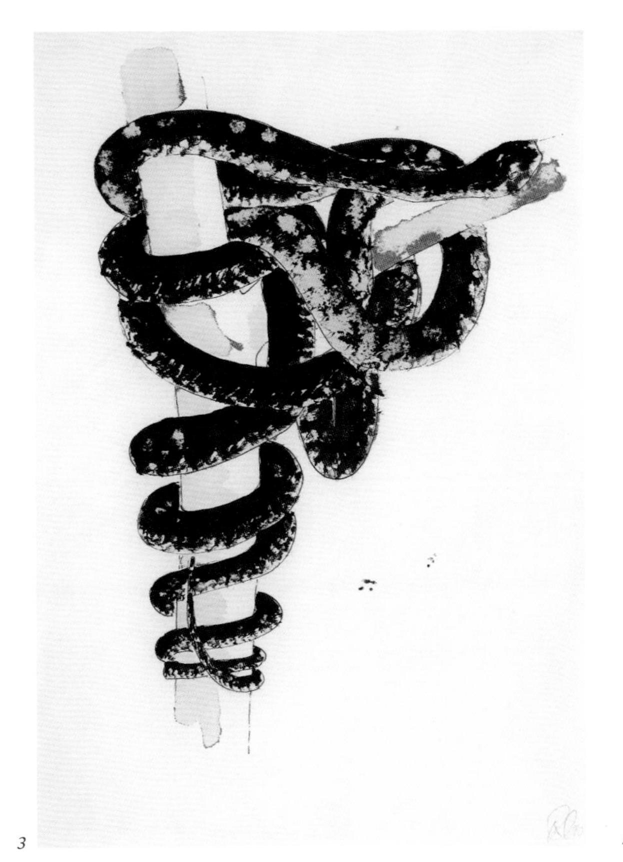

3

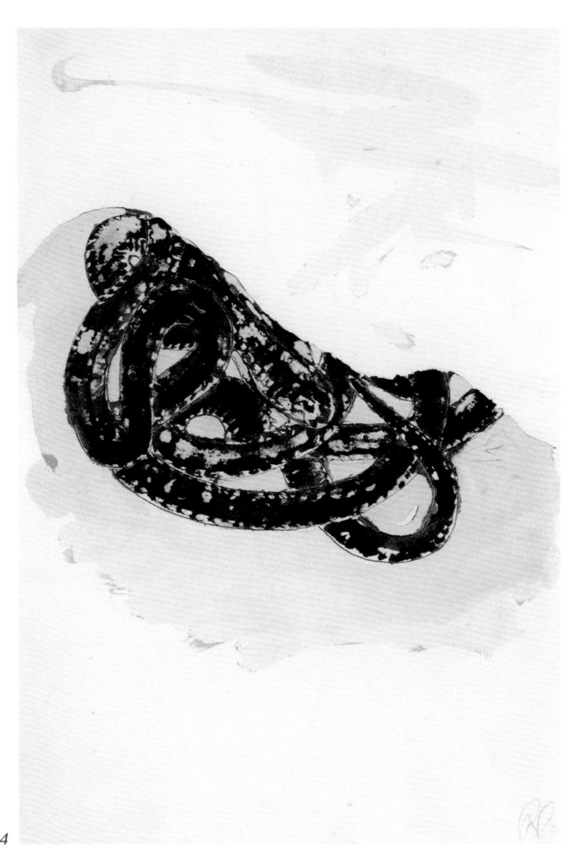

4

2

5

D5

纸上铅笔 / Pencil on paper
29.5×41.5cm
1990
摄影 / Photo: Michael Richter

D6

纸上铅笔 / Pencil on paper
29.5×42cm
2006
摄影 / Photo: Michael Richter

D7

纸上铅笔 / Pencil on paper
29.5×33.5cm
2006
摄影 / Photo: Michael Richter

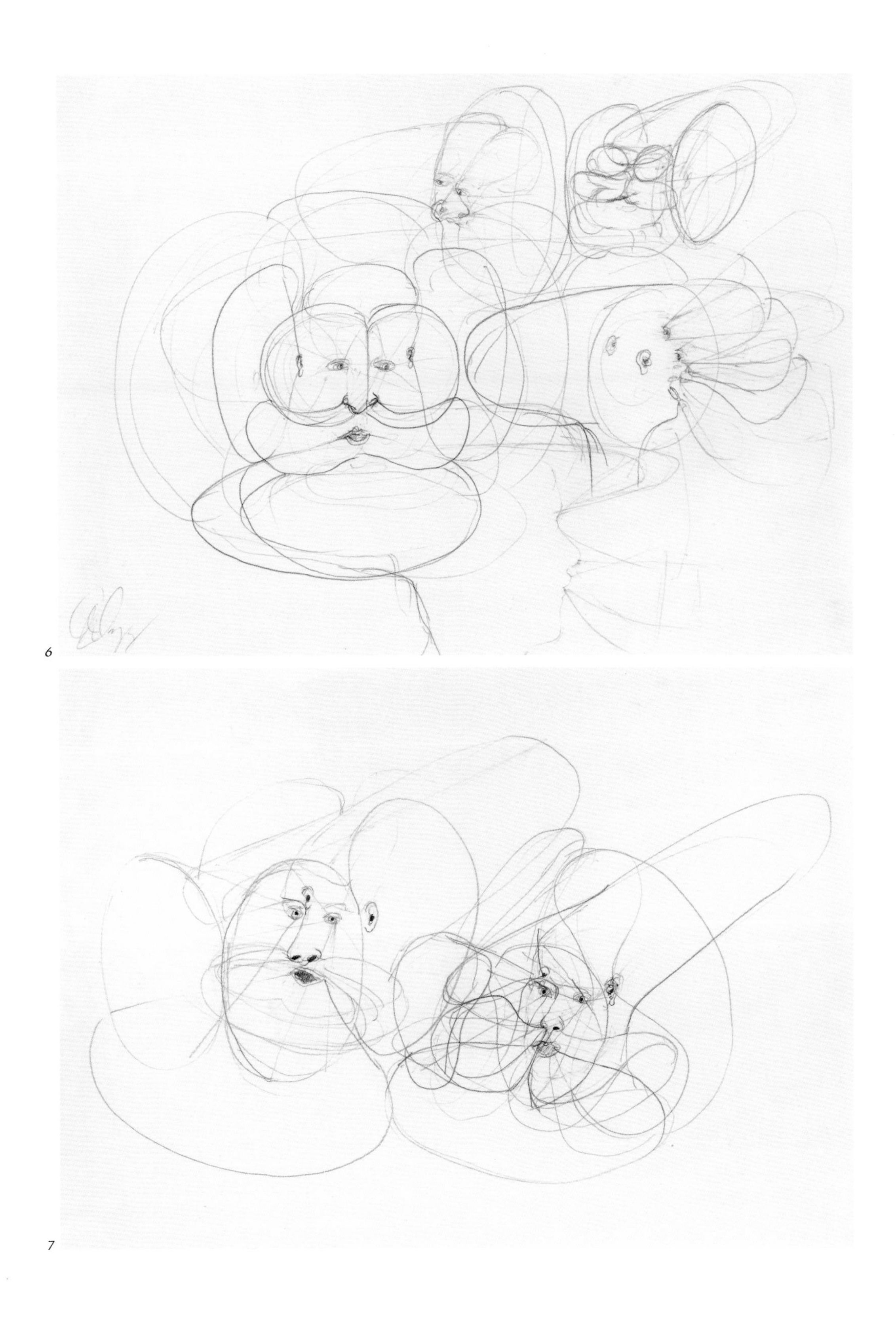

6

7

8

D8

纸上铅笔 / Pencil on paper
48×61cm
2005
摄影 / Photo: Michael Richter

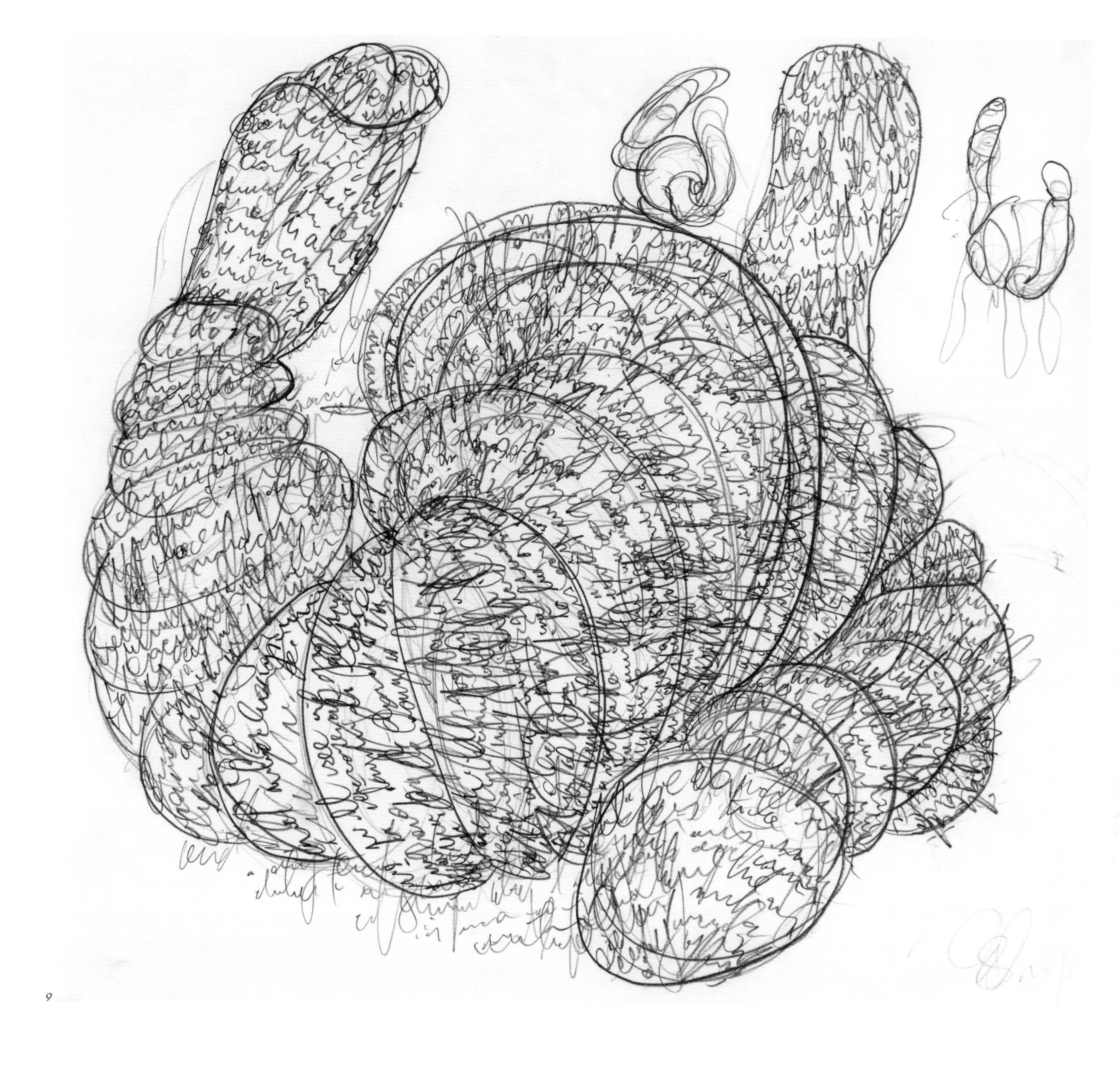

9

D9

纸上铅笔 / Pencil on paper
42×46cm
2005
摄影 / Photo: Michael Richter

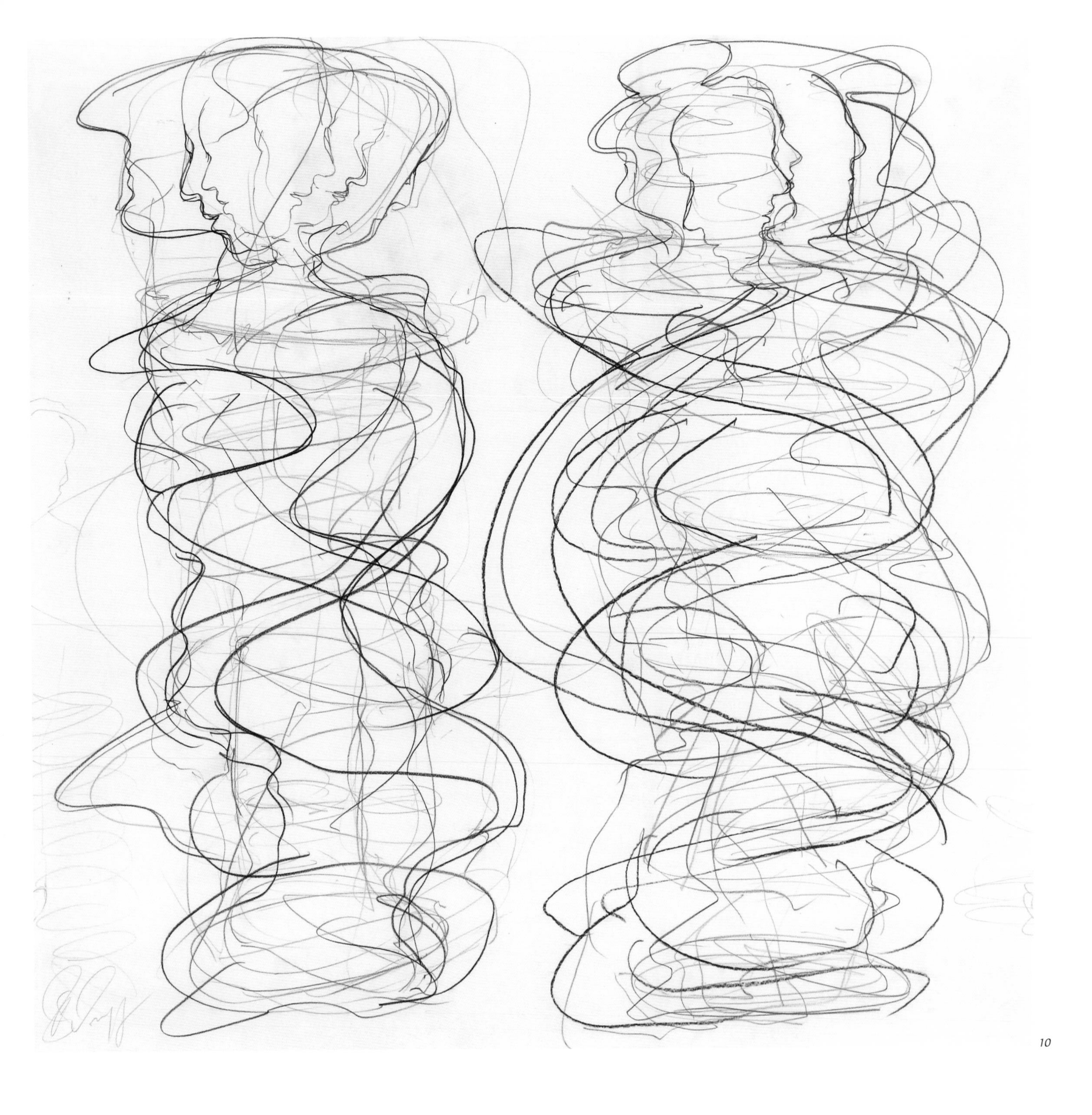

10

D10

纸上铅笔 / Pencil on paper
51.2×52.2cm
2005
摄影 / Photo: Michael Richter

11

D11

纸上铅笔 / Pencil on paper
56.8×49.6cm
1997
摄影 / Photo: David Kaluza

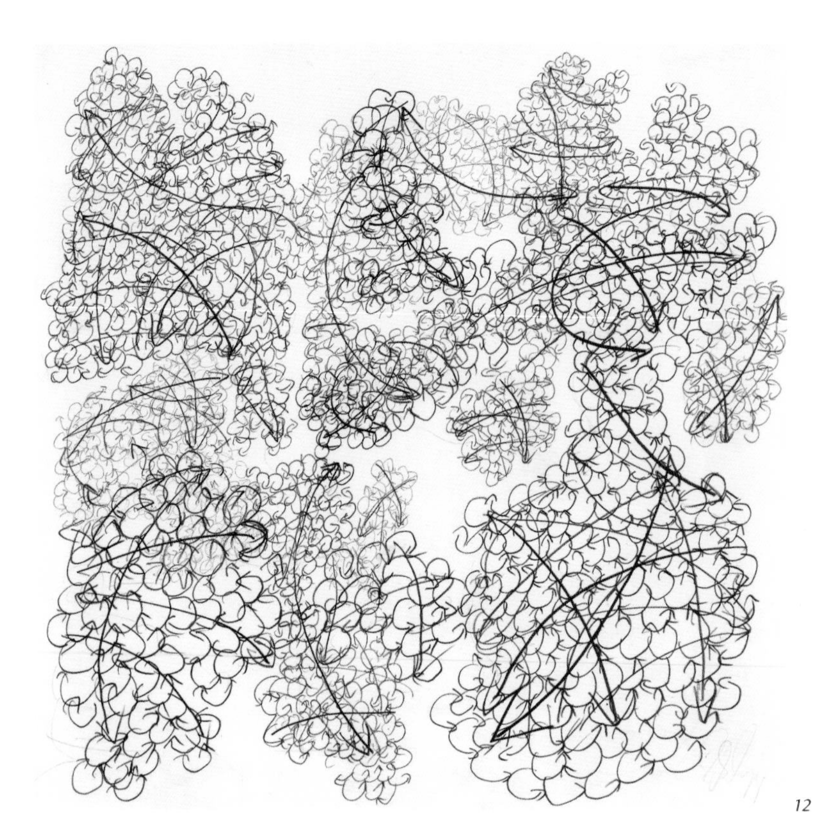

12

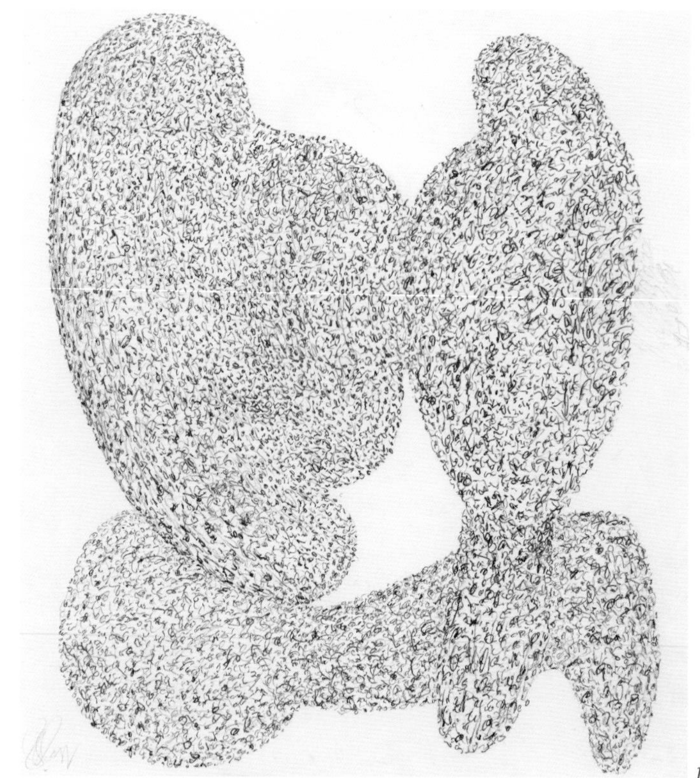

13

D12

纸上铅笔 / Pencil on paper
42.5×43cm
2005
摄影 / Photo: Michael Richter

D13

纸上铅笔 / Pencil on paper
42×39.5cm
2007
摄影 / Photo: Michael Richter

14

D14

纸上铅笔 / Pencil on paper
30×42cm
2006
摄影 / Photo: Michael Richter

D15

纸上铅笔 / Pencil on paper
47.4×36.6cm
2005
摄影 / Photo: Michael Richter

15

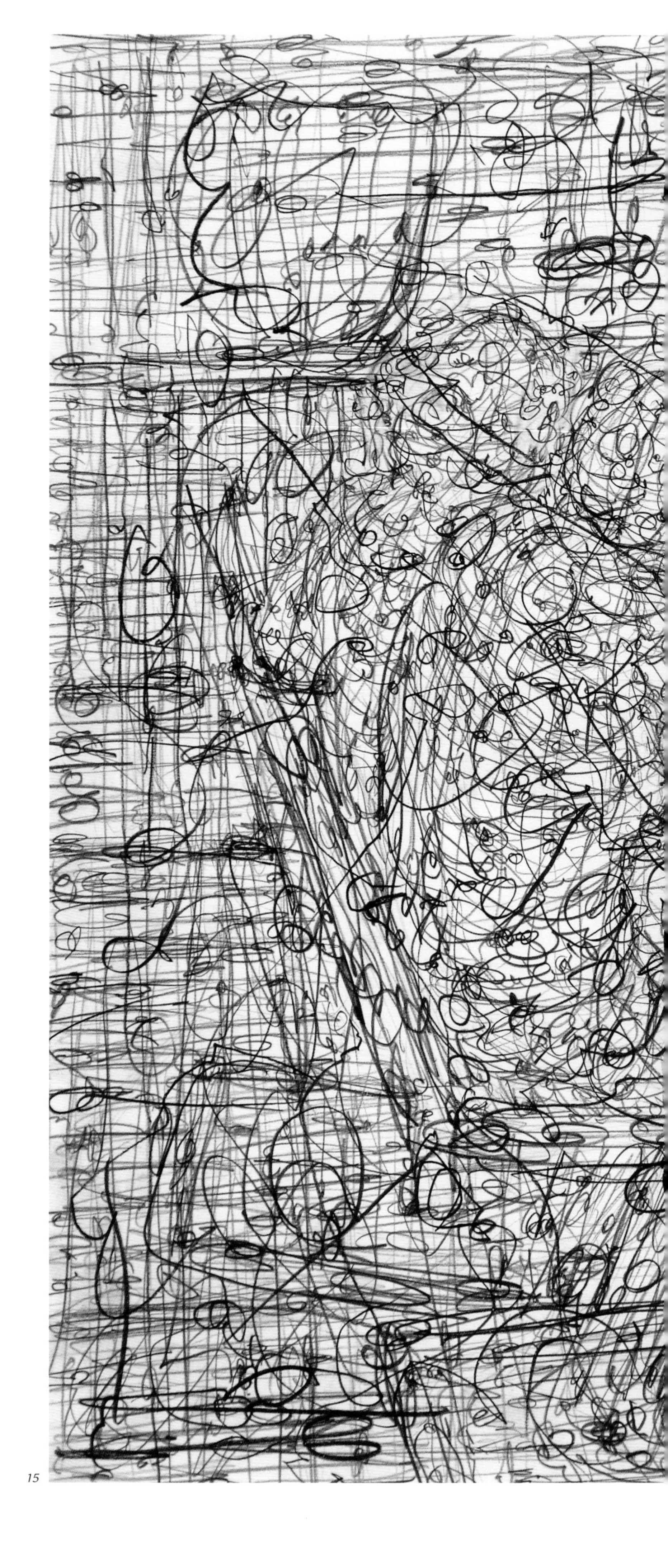

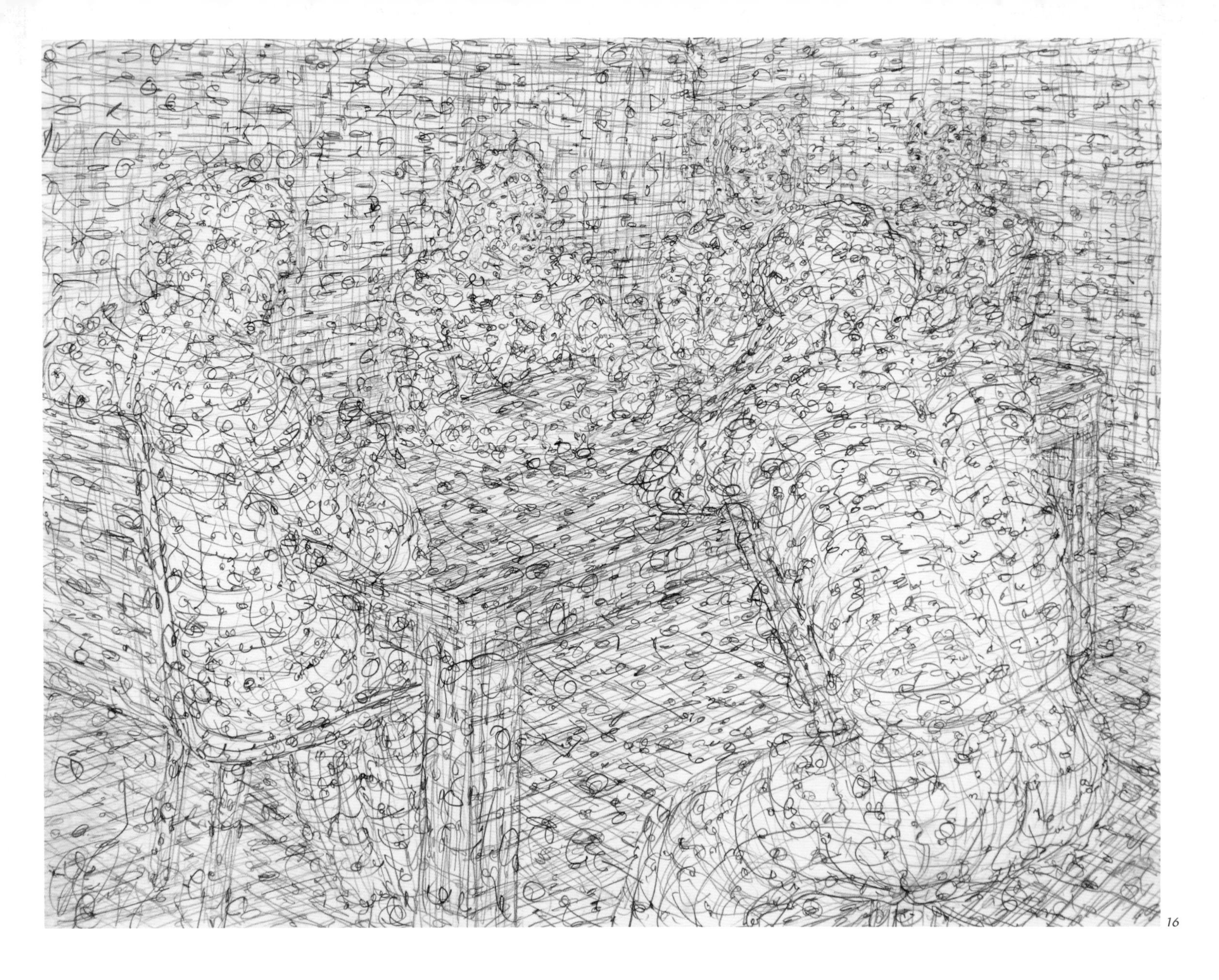

16

D16

纸上铅笔 / Pencil on paper
47.4×36.6cm
2005
摄影 / Photo: Michael Richter

17

D17《古怪空间》/ *Odd Space*

纸上铅笔 / Pencil on paper
43.5×49.5cm
2008
摄影 / Photo: Michael Richter

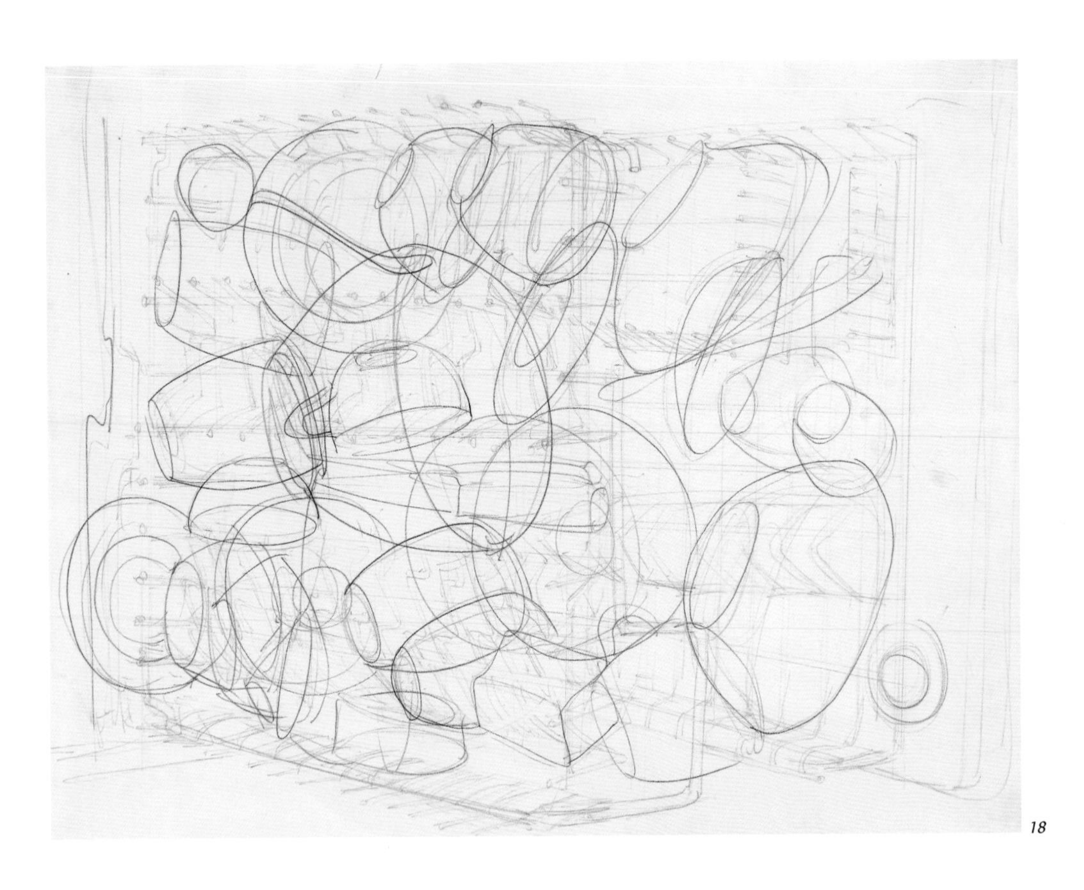

18

D18

纸上铅笔 / Pencil on paper
36.5×47.3cm
2008
摄影 / Photo: Michael Richter

19

D19《储存》/ *In Store*

纸上铅笔 / Pencil on paper
43×51.5cm
2008
摄影 / Photo: Michael Richter

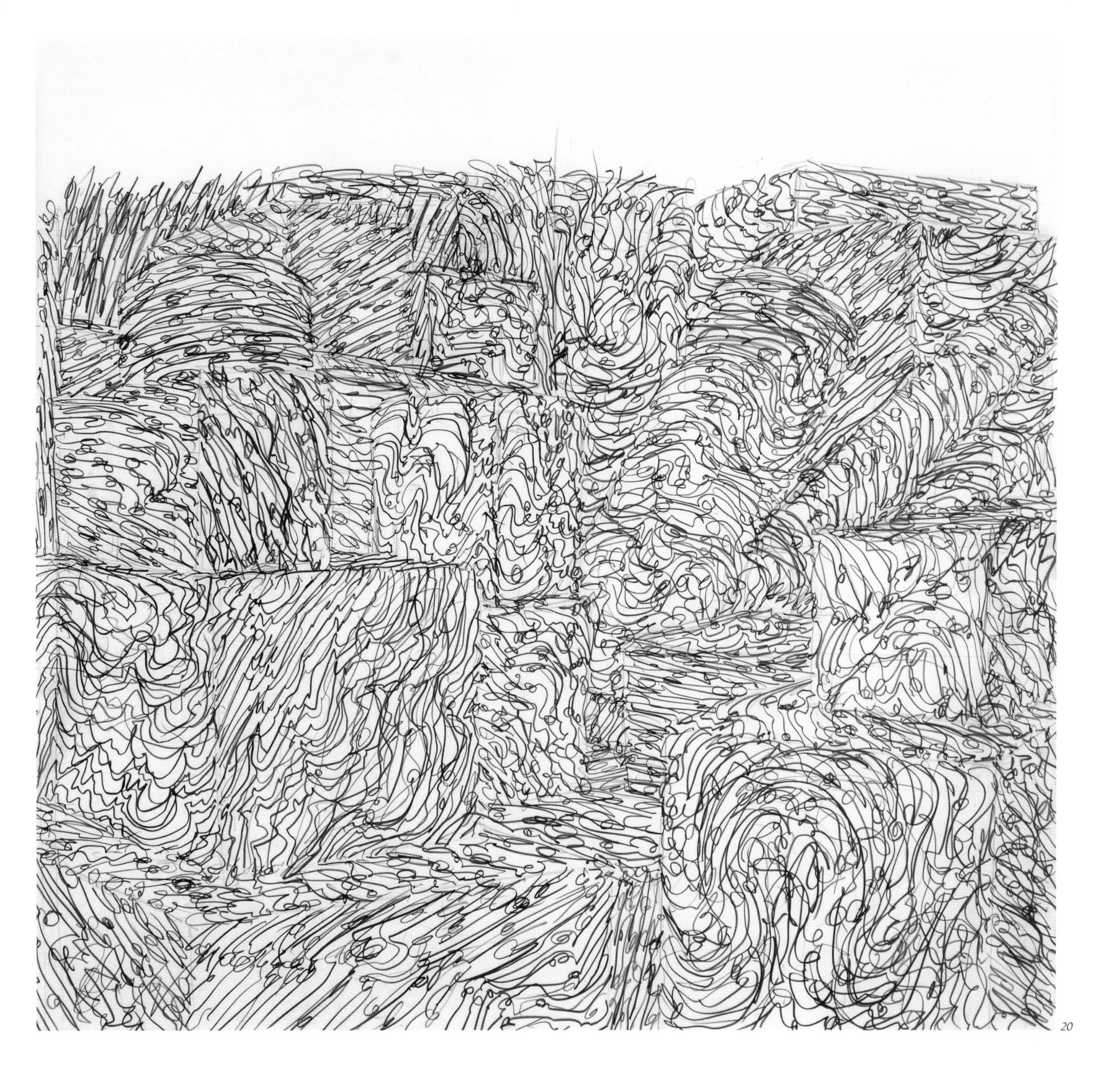
20

D20

纸上铅笔 / Pencil on paper
50×53cm
2009
摄影 / Photo: Michael Richter

21

D21

纸上铅笔 / Pencil on paper
46×57.5cm
2010
摄影 / Photo: Michael Richter

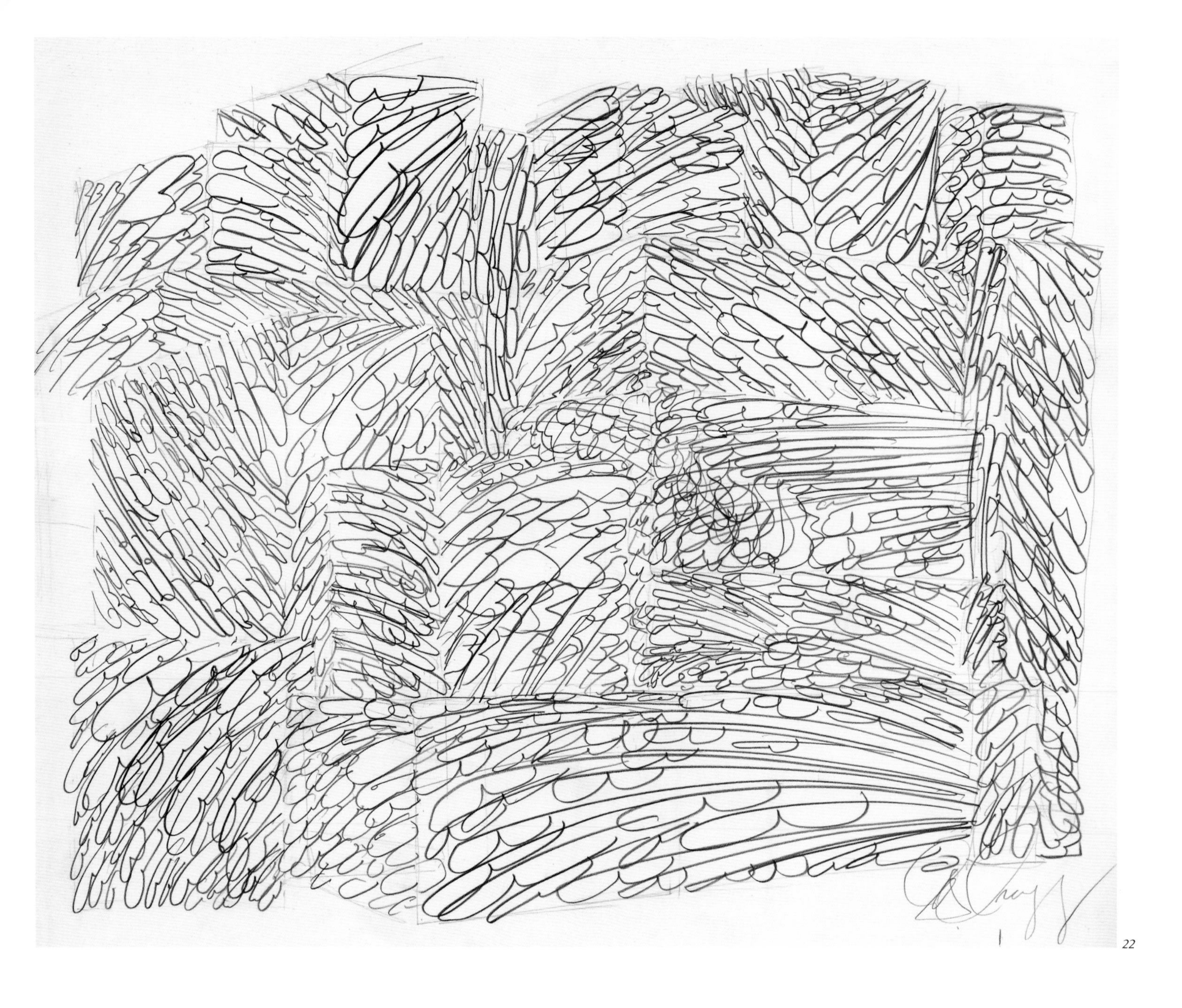

22

D22

纸上铅笔 / Pencil on paper
49.5×60.8cm
2010
摄影 / Photo: Michael Richter

23

D23

纸上铅笔 / Pencil on paper
50.5×44cm
2010
摄影 / Photo: Michael Richter

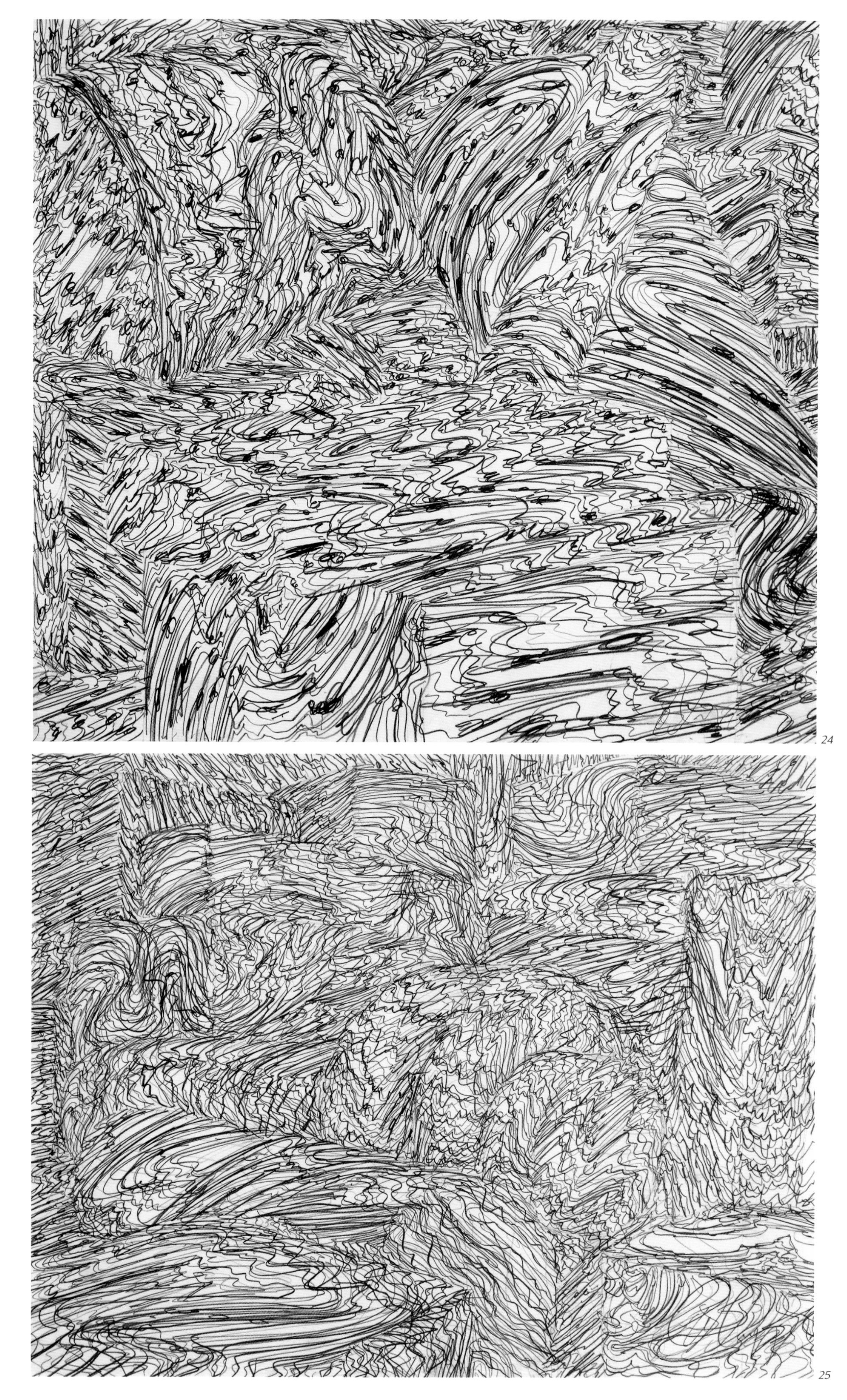

24

25

D24

纸上铅笔 / Pencil on paper
49.5×44cm
2010
摄影 / Photo: Michael Richter

D25

纸上铅笔 / Pencil on paper
57×44cm
2010
摄影 / Photo: Michael Richter

D26

纸上铅笔 / Pencil on paper
43.6×36.1 cm
2010
摄影 / Photo: Michael Richter

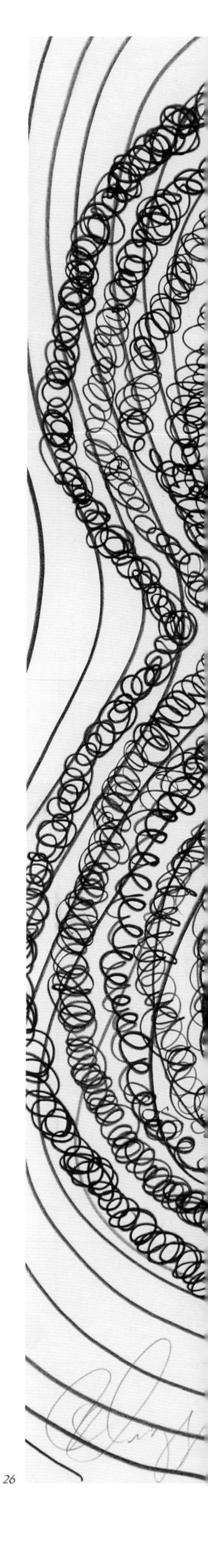

26

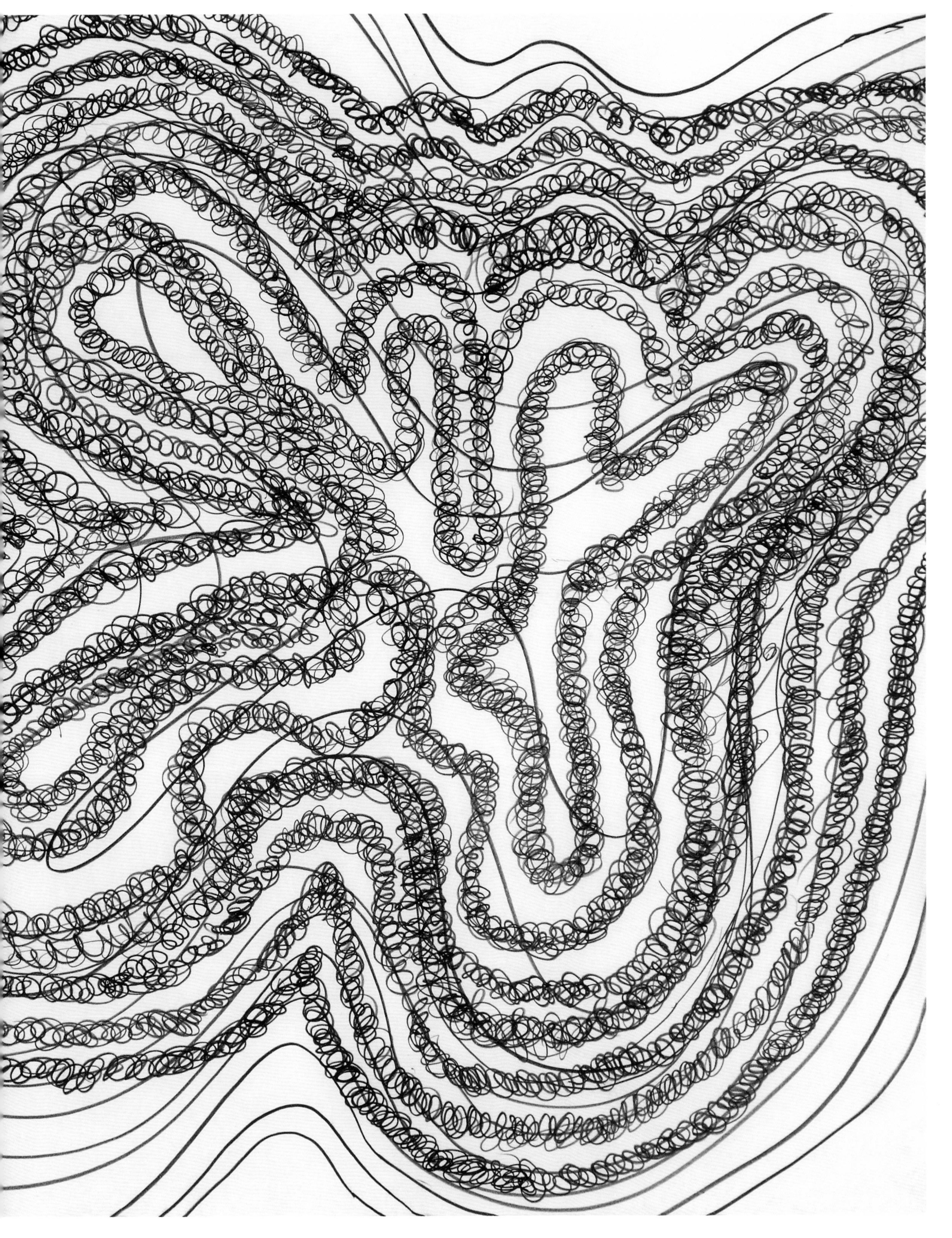

27

28

29

D27

纸上铅笔 / Pencil on paper
46.4×36.1cm
2010
摄影 / Photo: Michael Richter

D28

纸上铅笔 / Pencil on paper
45.1×36cm
2010
摄影 / Photo: Michael Richter

D29

纸上铅笔 / Pencil on paper
49.7×39.8cm
2010
摄影 / Photo: Michael Richter

30

D30

纸上铅笔 / Pencil on paper
33.3×32.1cm
2010
摄影 / Photo: Michael Richter

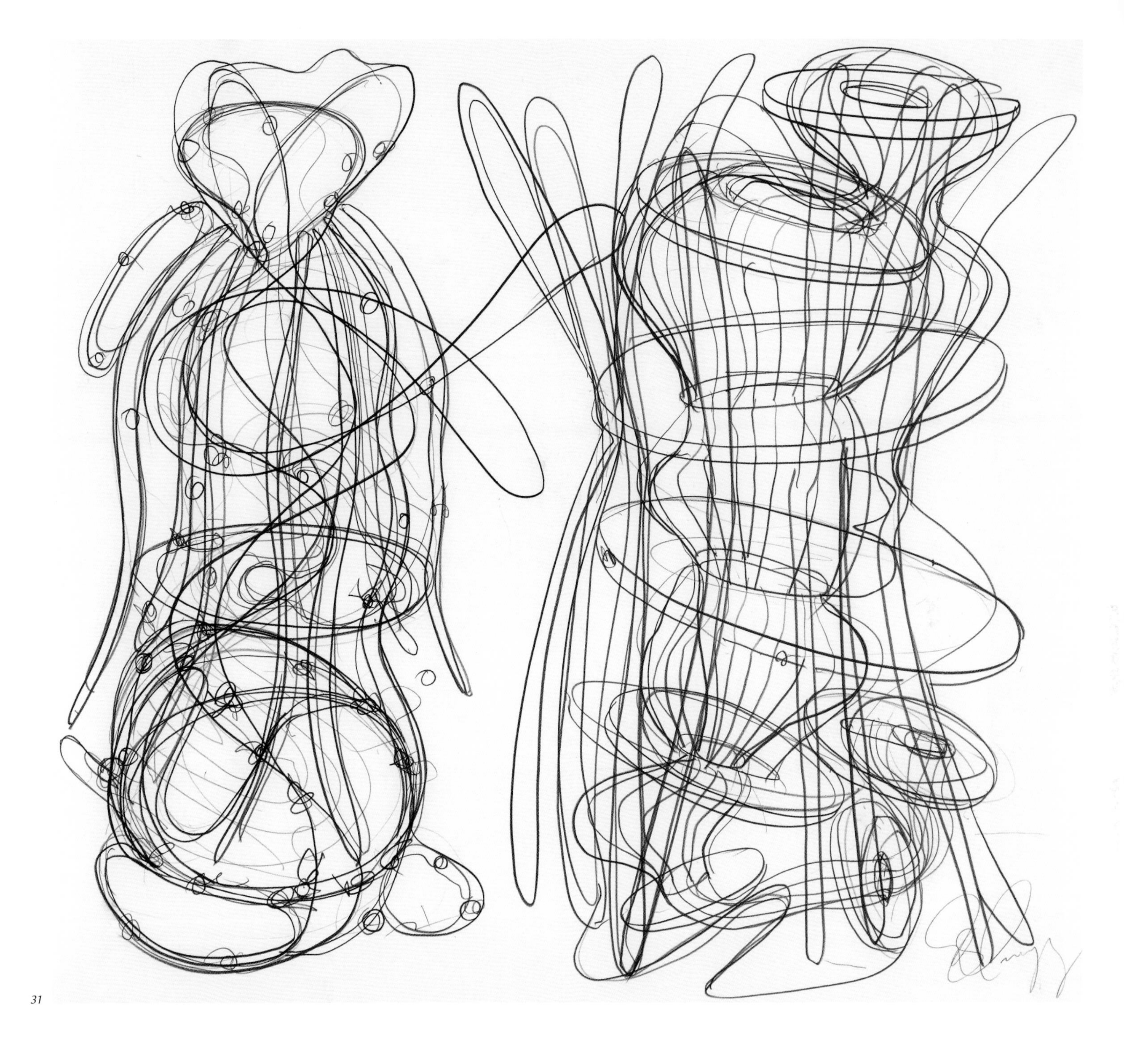

31

D31

纸上铅笔 / Pencil on paper
49.8×55.4cm
2009
摄影 / Photo: Michael Richter

32

D32

纸上铅笔 / Pencil on paper
49.5×56.8cm
2009
摄影 / Photo: Michael Richter

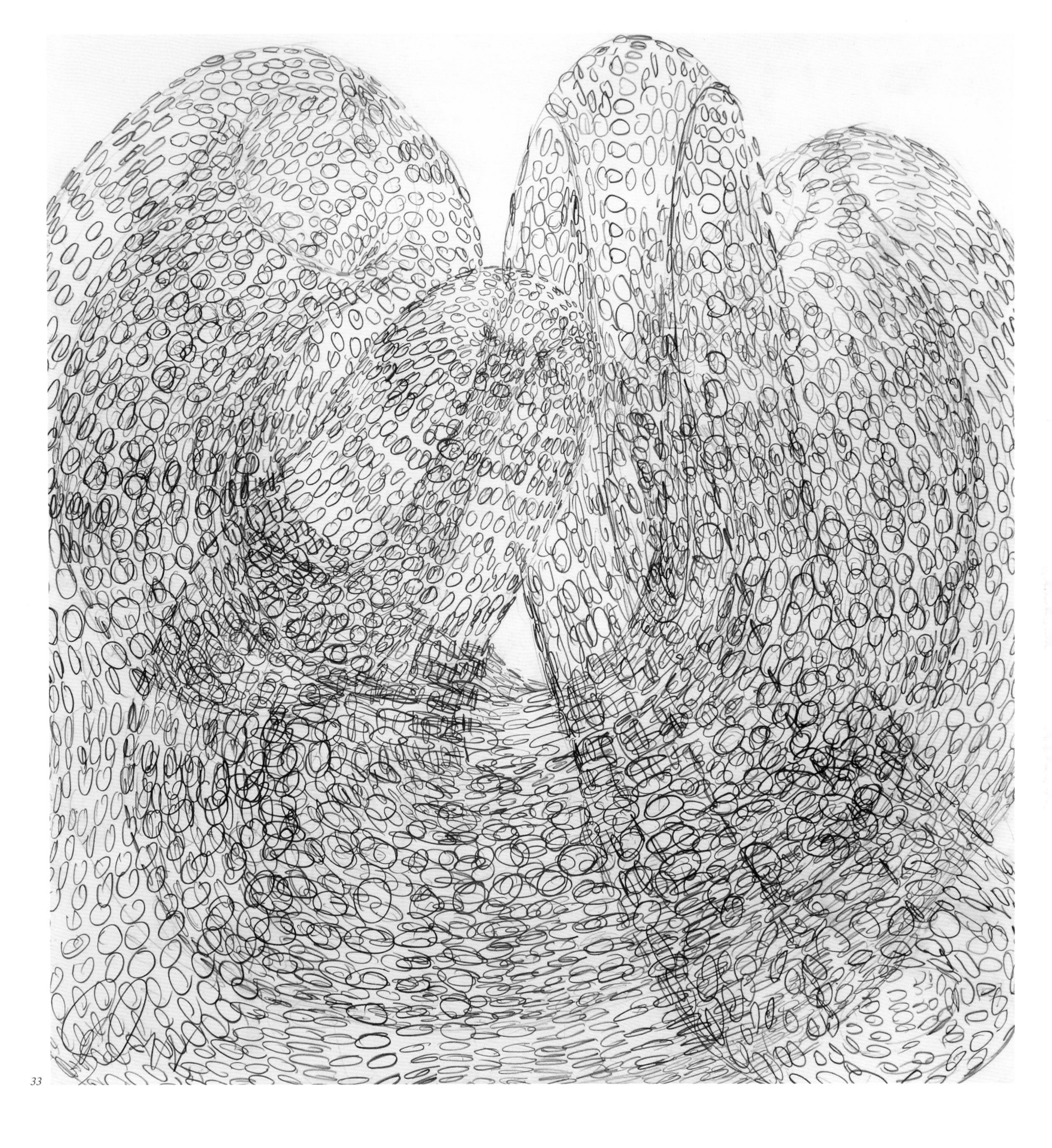

33

D33

纸上铅笔 / Pencil on paper
46.8×44.8cm
2009
摄影 / Photo: Michael Richter

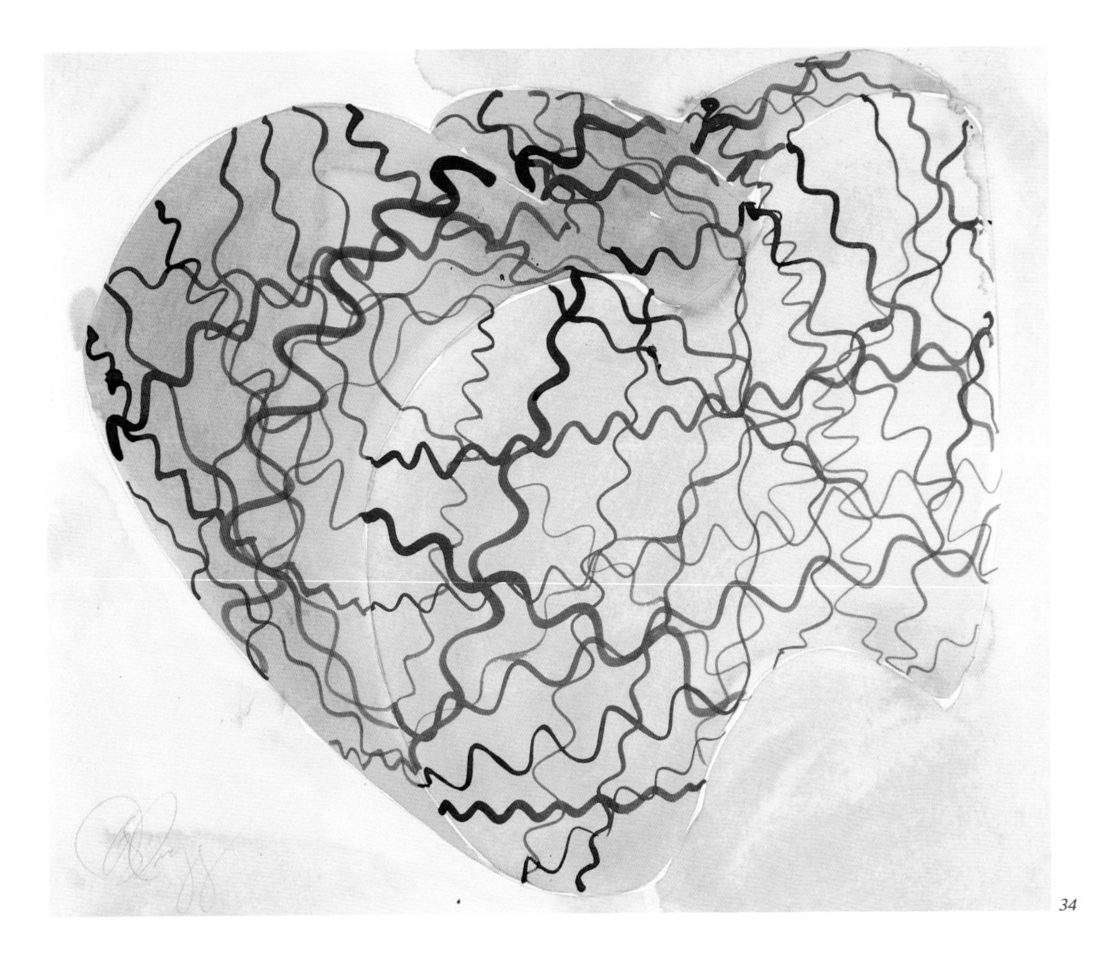

34

D34《波动形式》/ *Wave Forms*

水彩 / Watercolor
41×49.5cm
2007
摄影 / Photo: Christer Hallgren

D35《瓶子》/ *Vessels*

水彩 / Watercolor
53.5×41cm
2007
摄影 / Photo: Christer Hallgren

D36《瓶子》/ *Vessels*

水彩 / Watercolor
53×40.5cm
2007
摄影 / Photo: Christer Hallgren

35

36

D37《自然、本质》/ *Nature, Nature*

水彩 / Watercolor
41.5×55cm
2008
摄影 / Photo: Michael Richter

37

38

D38《自然、本质》/ ***Nature, Nature***

水彩 / Watercolor
41.5×55cm
2008
摄影 / Photo: Michael Richter

D39

水彩 / Watercolor
54×44.5cm
2010
摄影 / Photo: Michael Richter

39

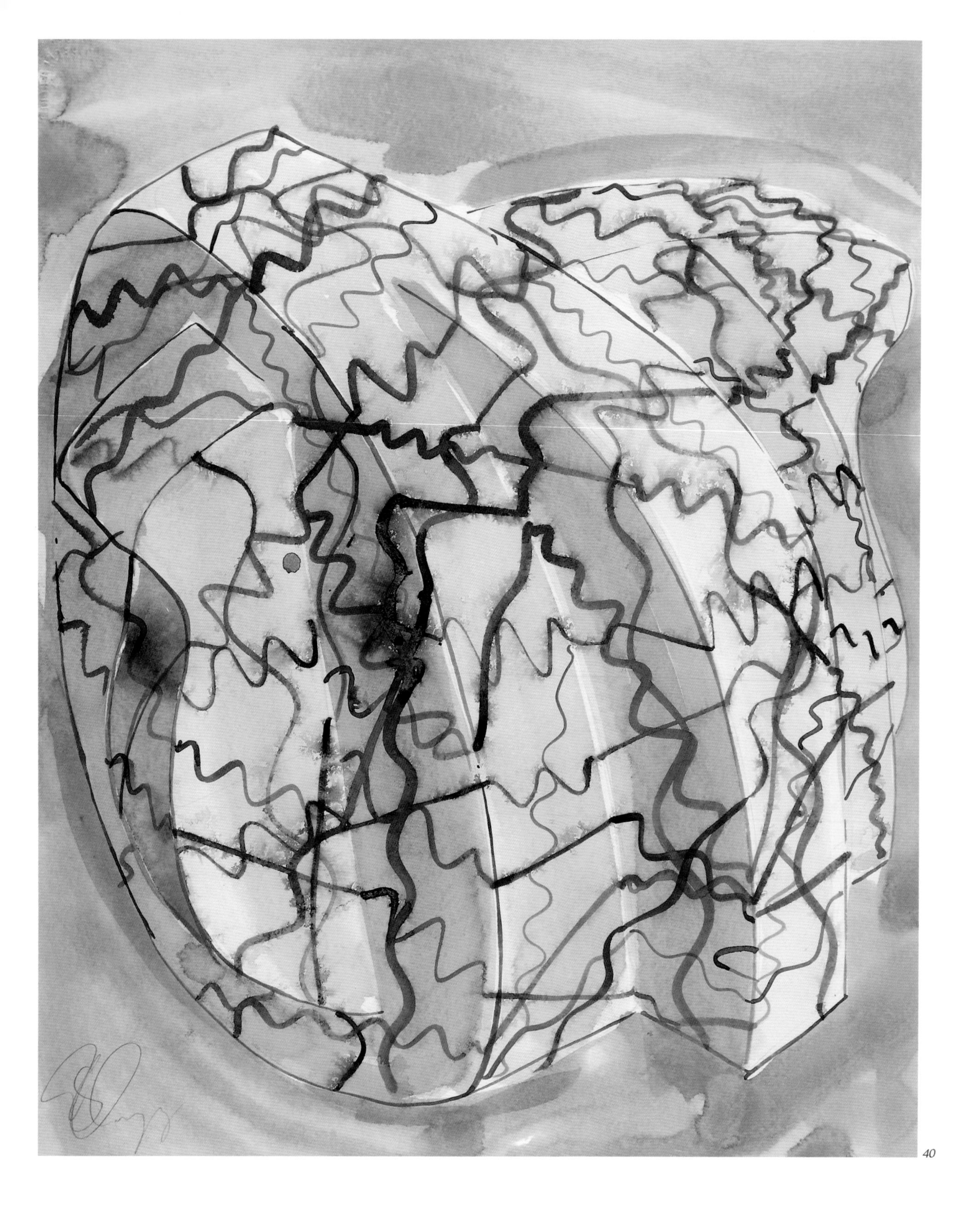

40

D40《共振 1》/ *Resonance 1*

水彩 / Watercolor
62.5×77cm
2009
摄影 / Photo: Michael Richter

D41《共振 2》/ *Resonance 2*

水彩 / Watercolor
62.5×77cm
2009
摄影 / Photo: Michael Richter

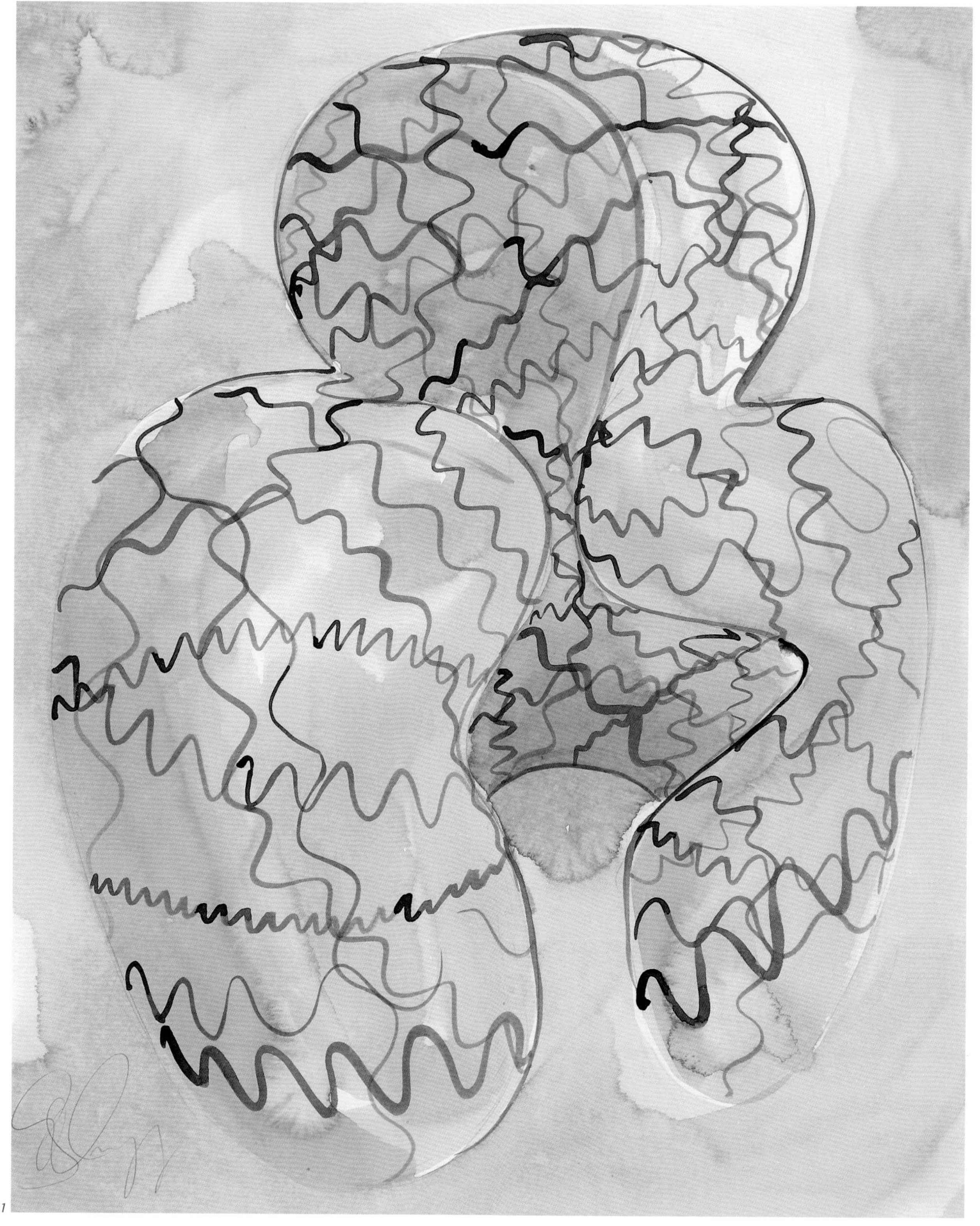

41

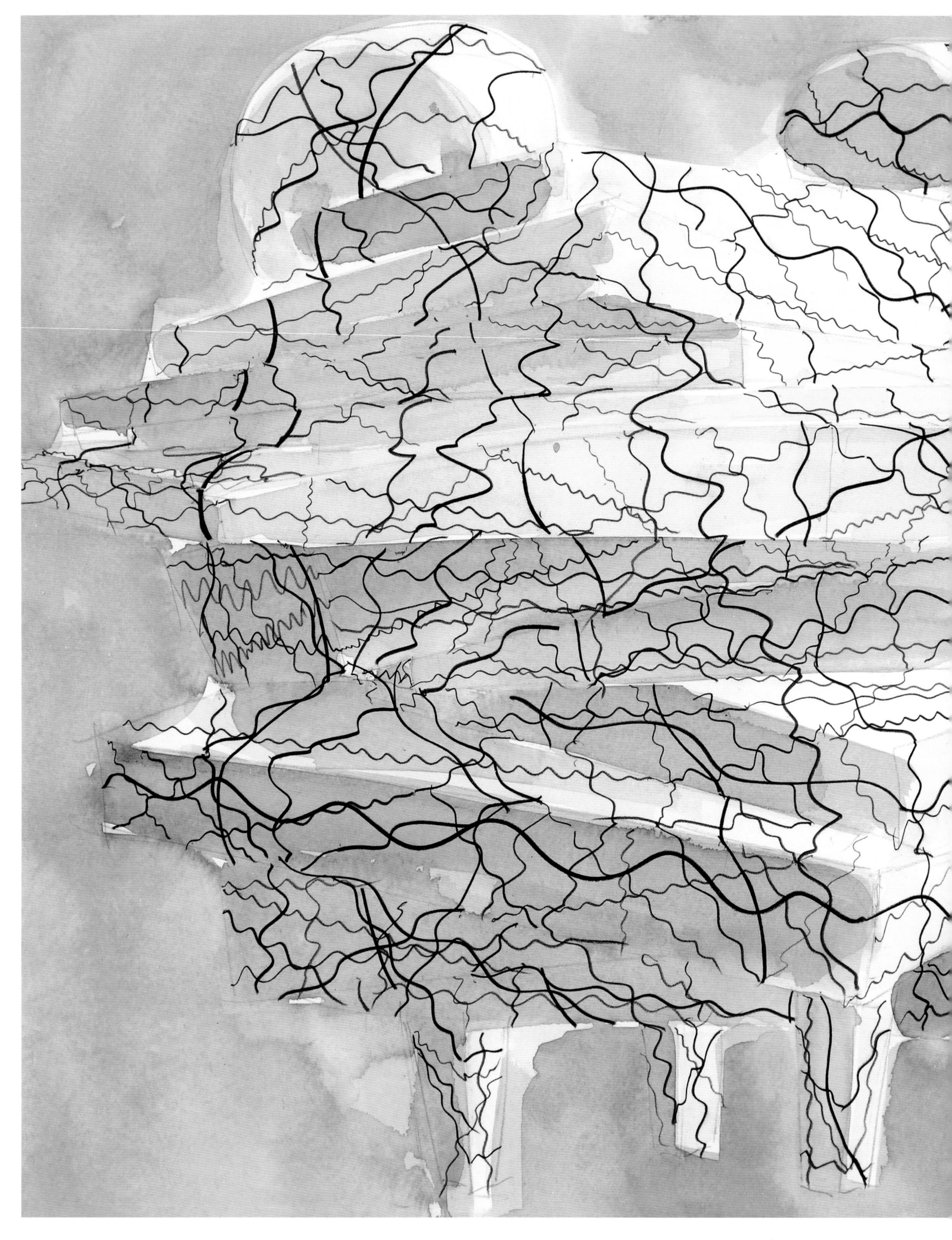

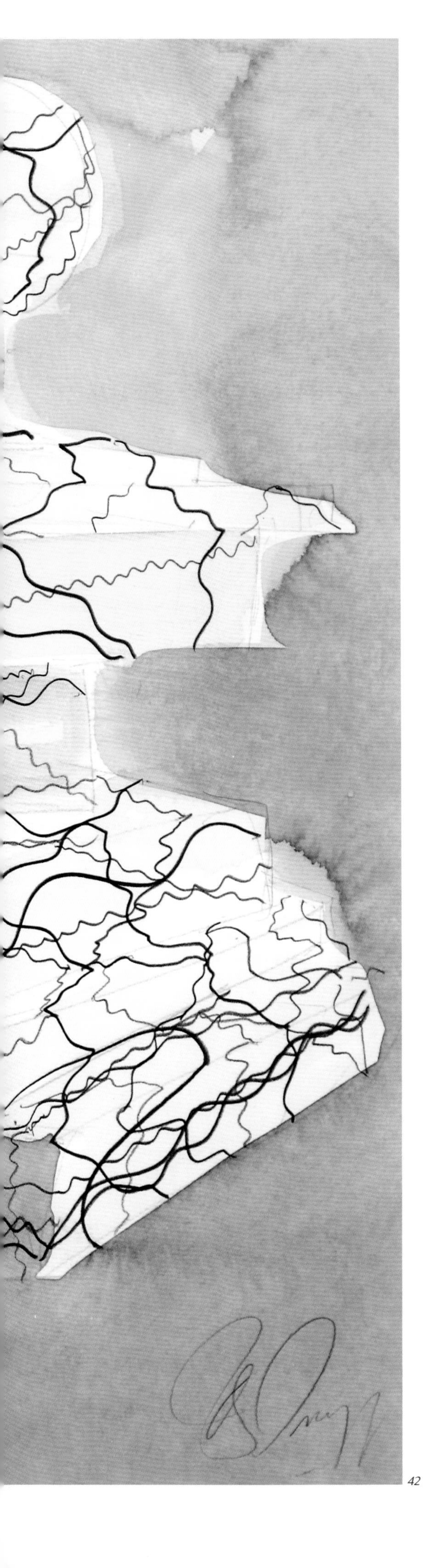

42

D42

水彩 / Watercolor
44.1×50.7cm
2010
摄影 / Photo: Michael Richter

43

D43《绿瓶子》/ ***Vessels***

水彩 / Watercolor
54.5×44.5cm
2010
摄影 / Photo: Michael Richter

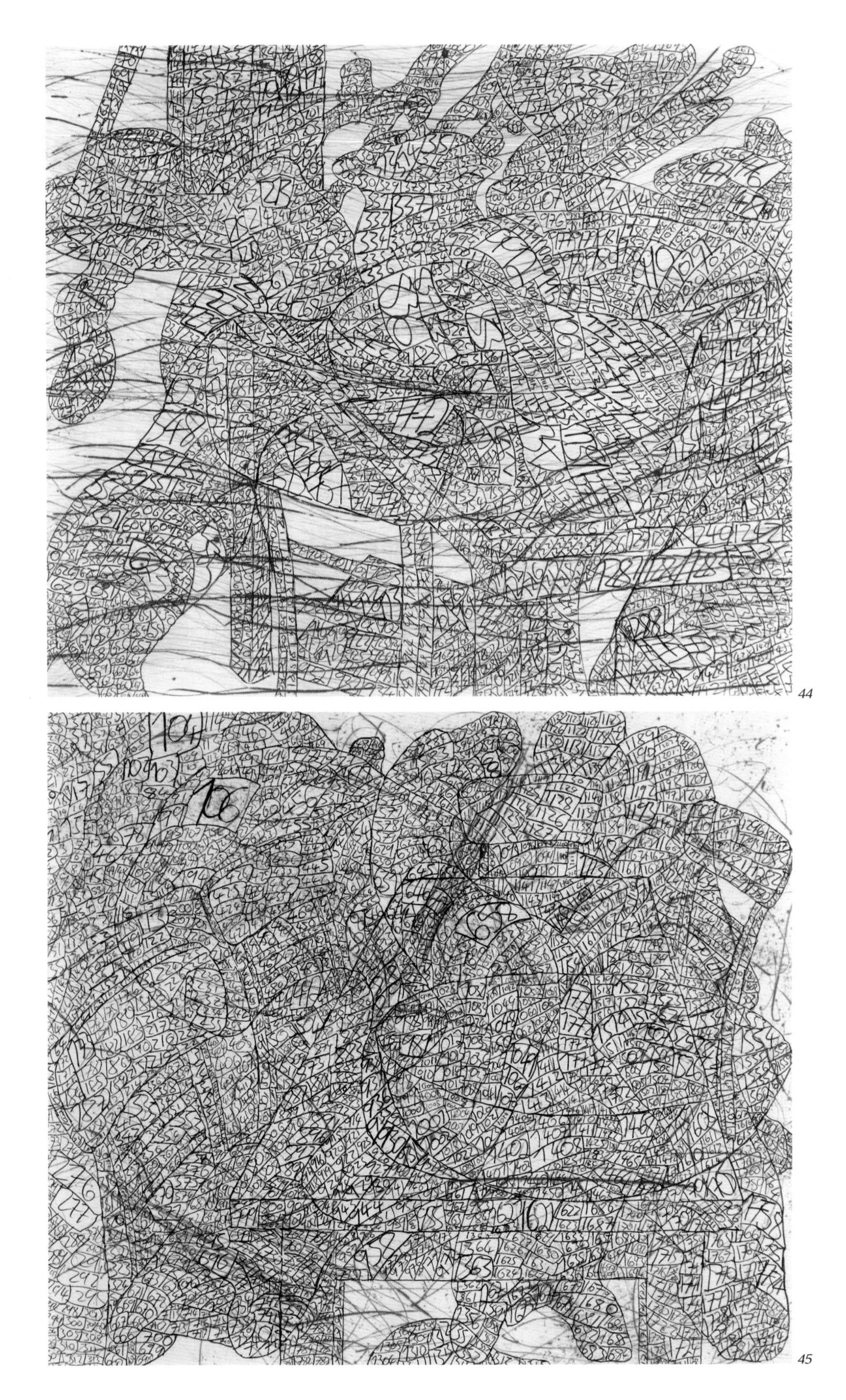
44

45

46

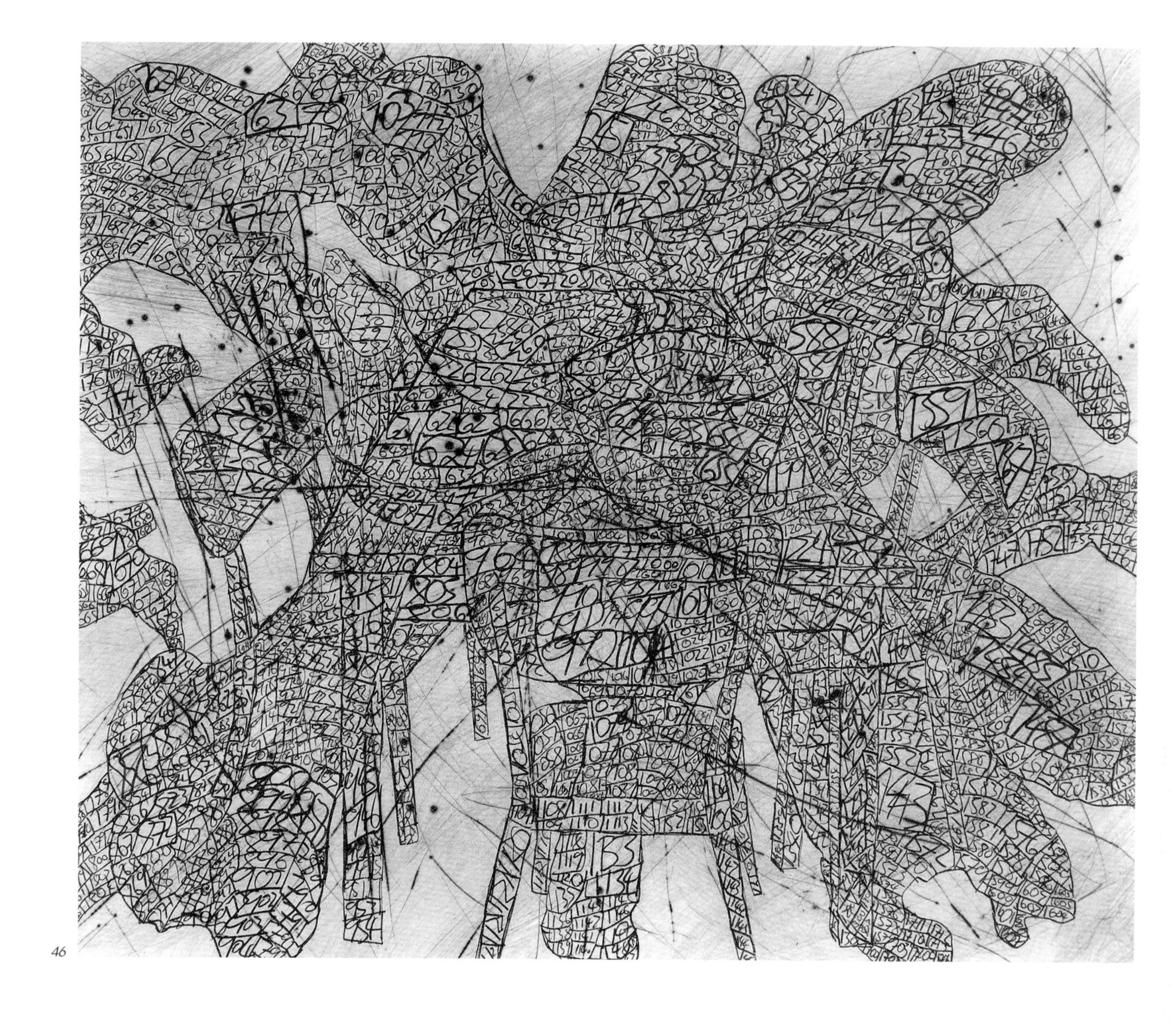

D44 - 46《起居室》/ *Living Rooms*

蚀刻版画 / Etching
41×50cm
2000
摄影 / Photo: Michael Richter

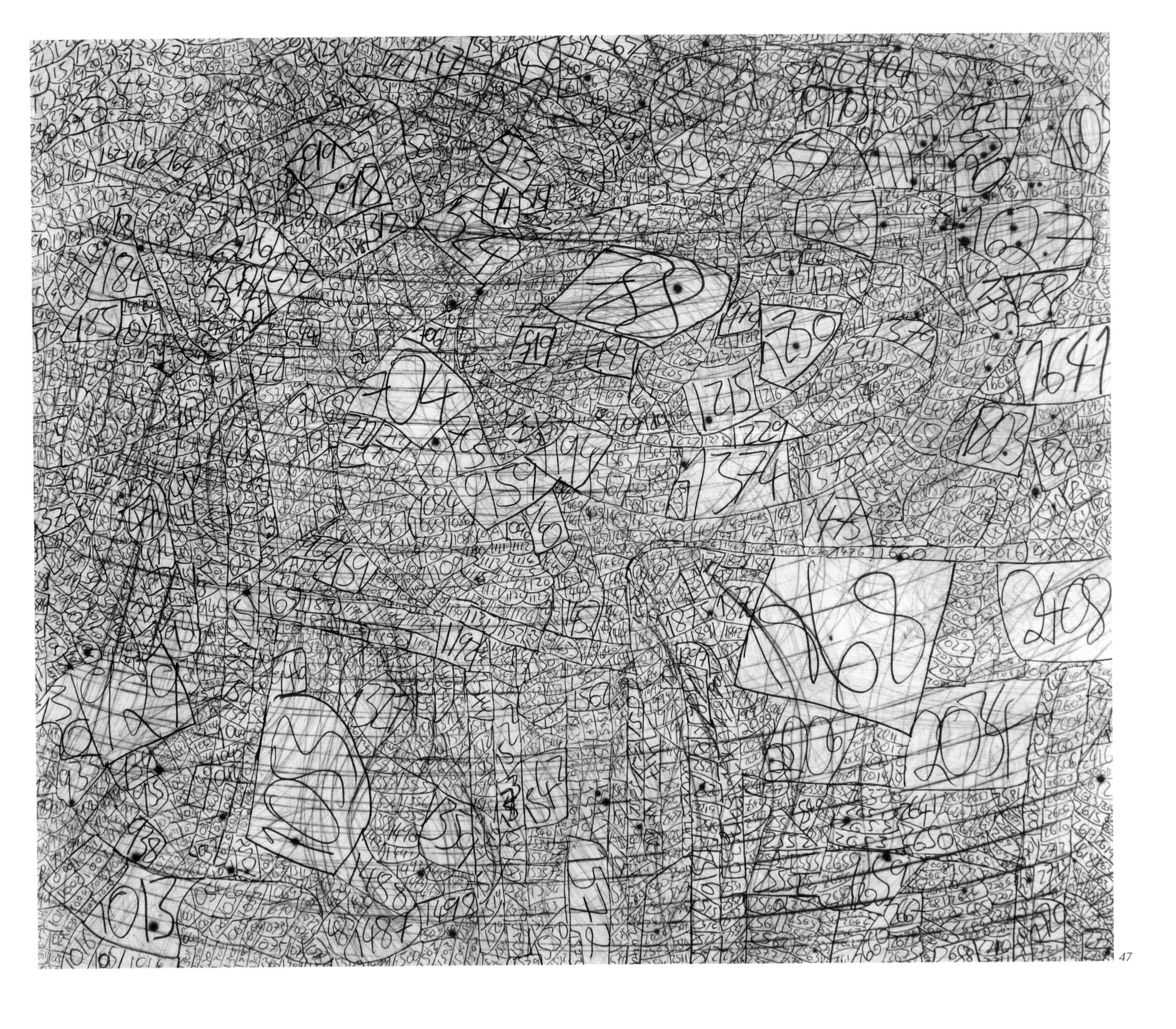

47

D47《起居室》/ *Living Rooms*

蚀刻版画 / Etching
41×50cm
2000
摄影 / Photo: Michael Richter

48

D48

蚀刻版画 / Etching
40×42.5cm
2011
摄影 / Photo: Michael Richter

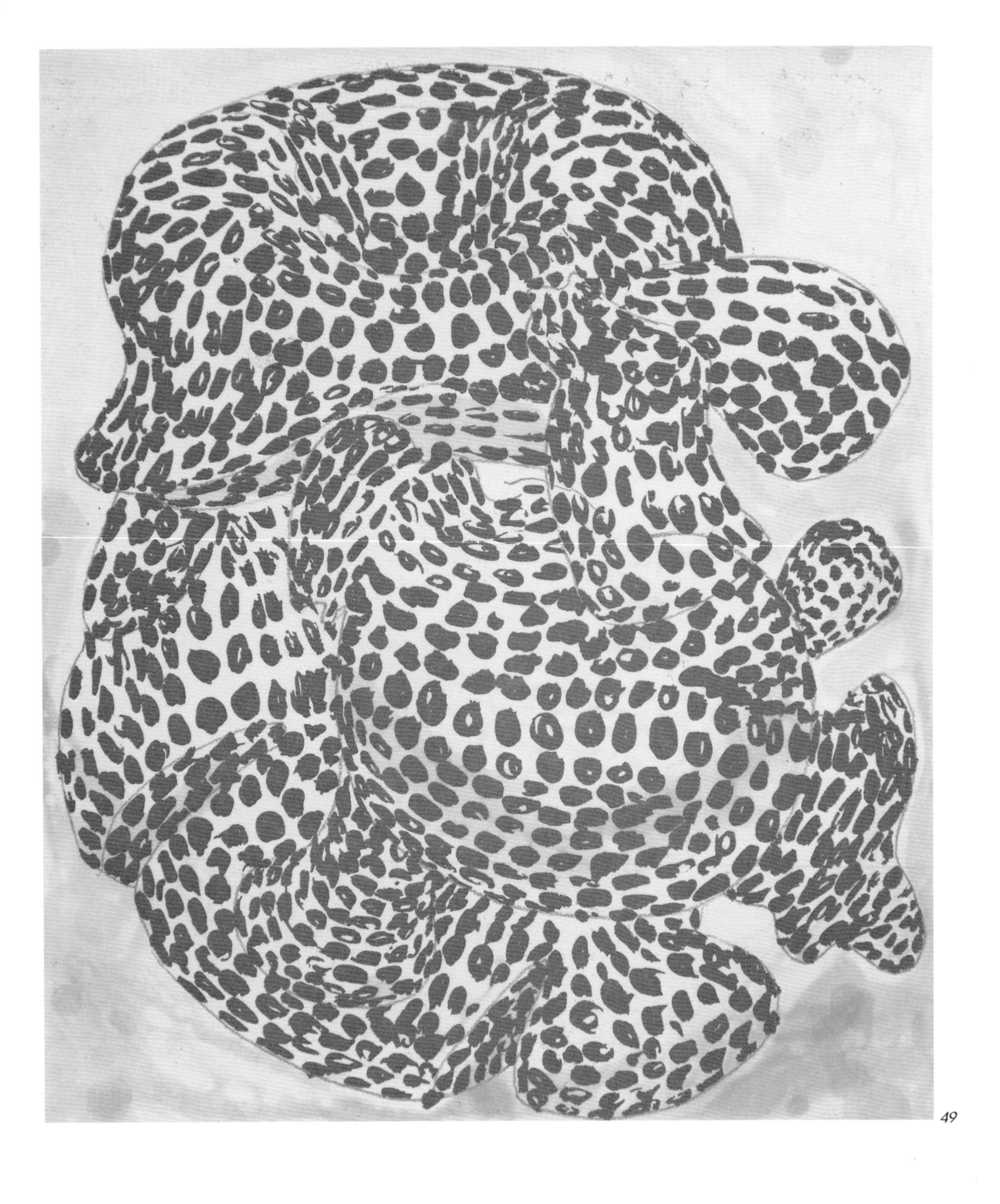

49

D49 - D52《有孔体》/ *Forminifera*

蚀刻版画 / Etching
29×25cm
2000
摄影 / Photo: Michael Richter

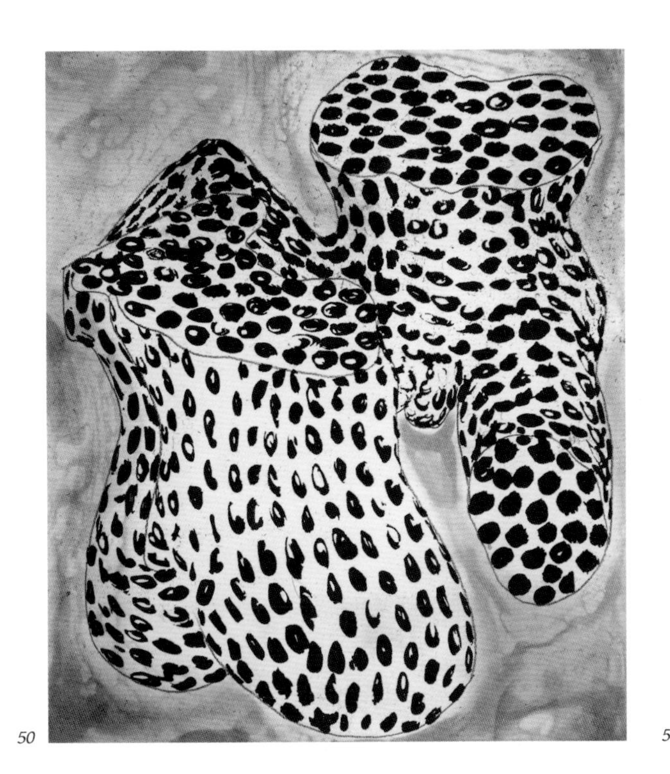
50

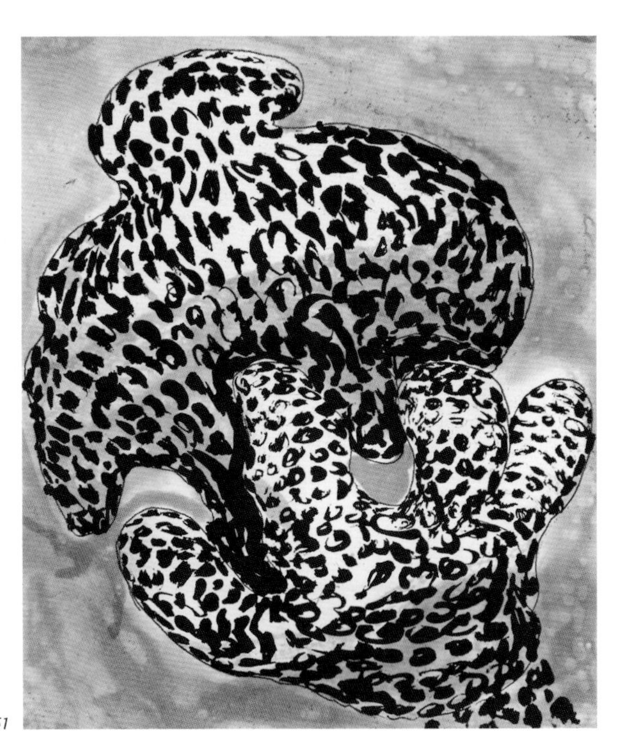
51

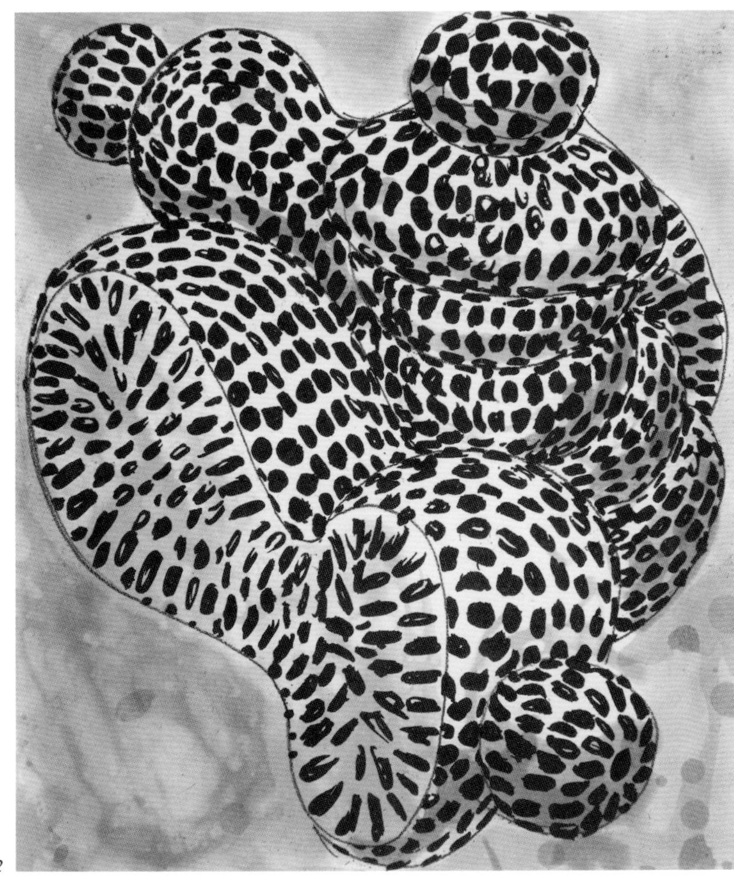
52

53

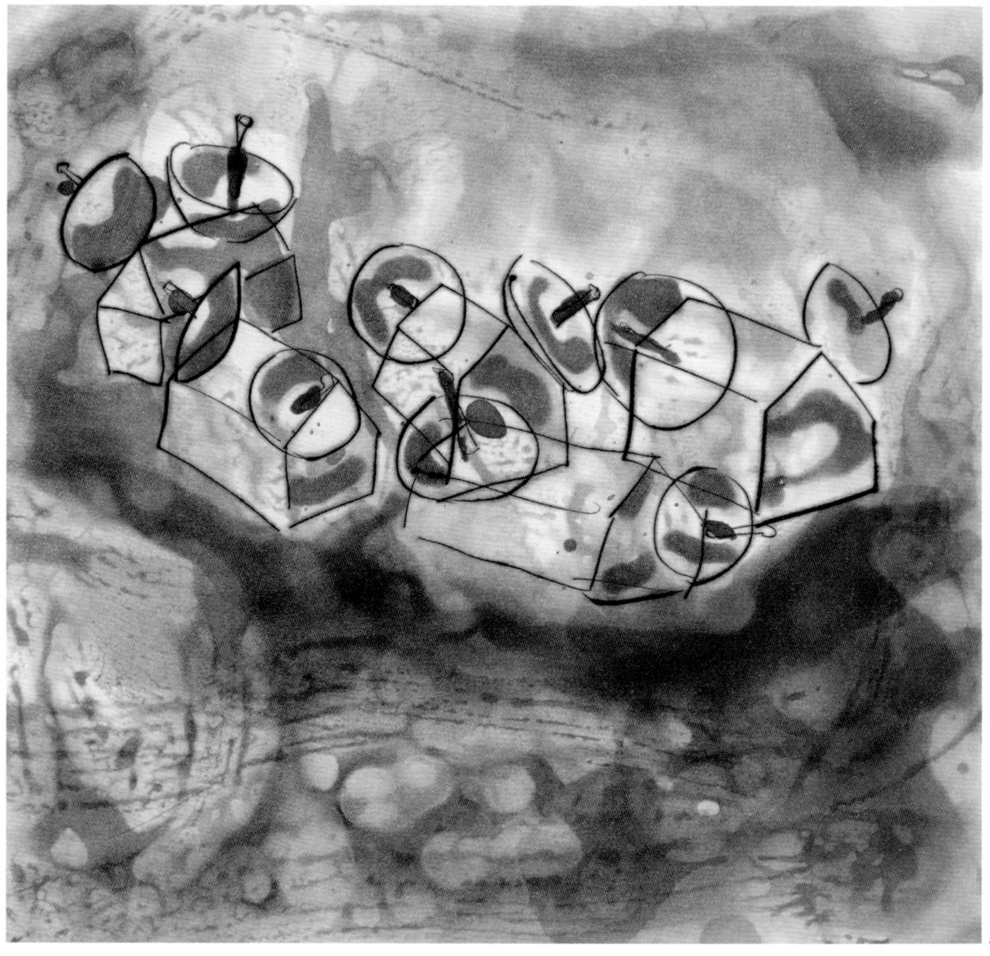
54

D53 - D55《听众》/ ***Listener***

蚀刻版画 / Etching
27×30cm
2000
摄影 / Photo: Michael Richter

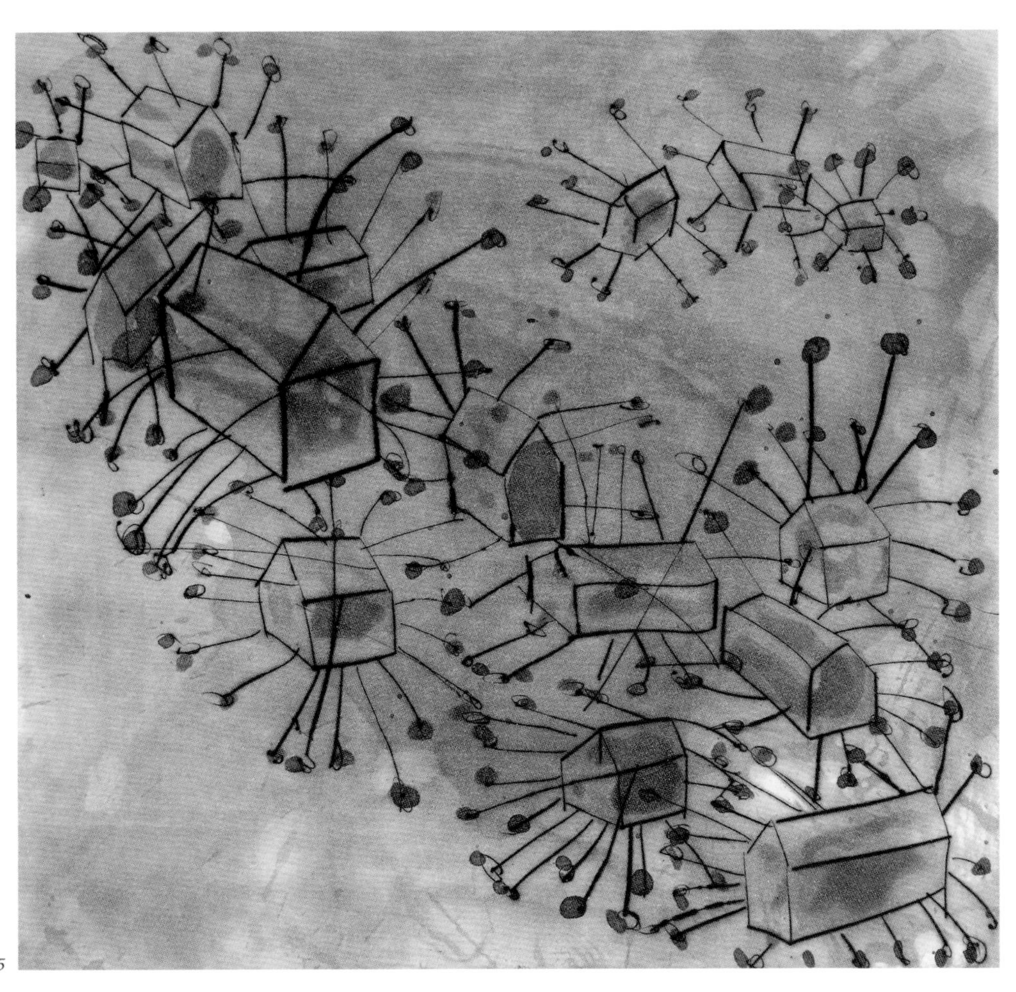

55

56

D56 - D58《静电》/ *Static*

蚀刻版画 / Etching
32×37.5cm
2000
摄影 / Photo: Michael Richter

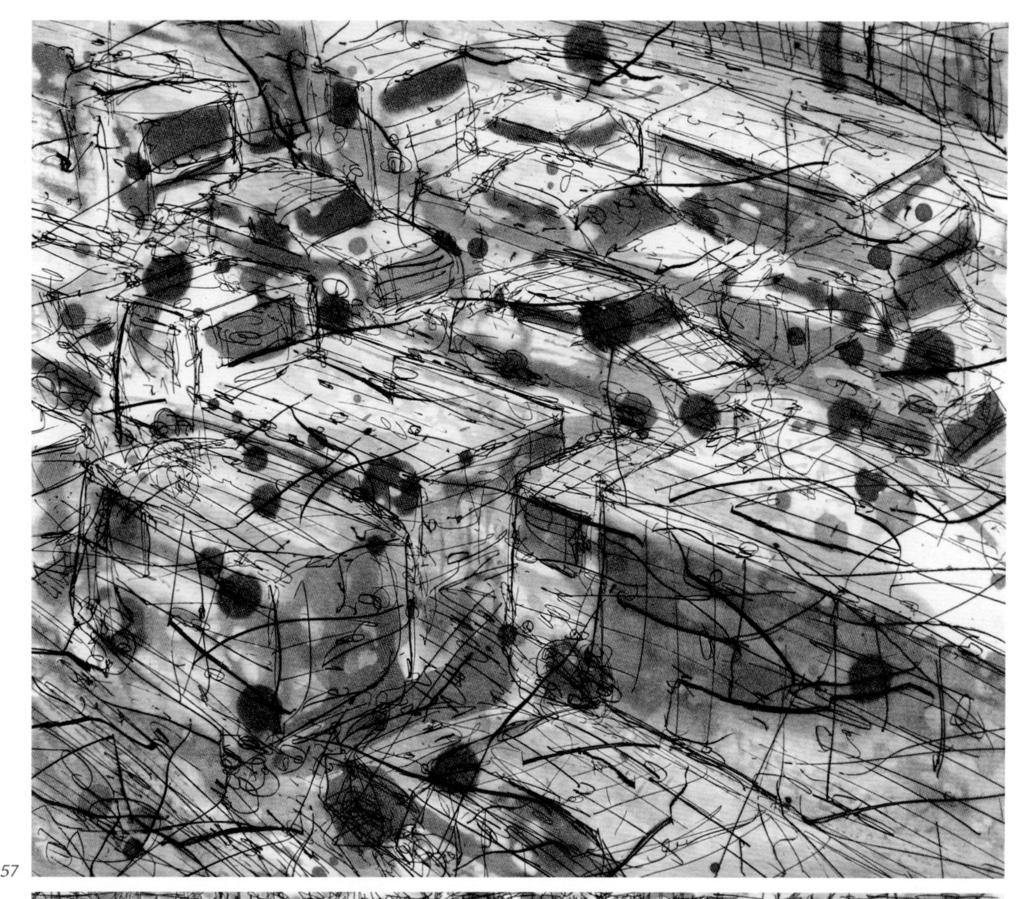

57

58

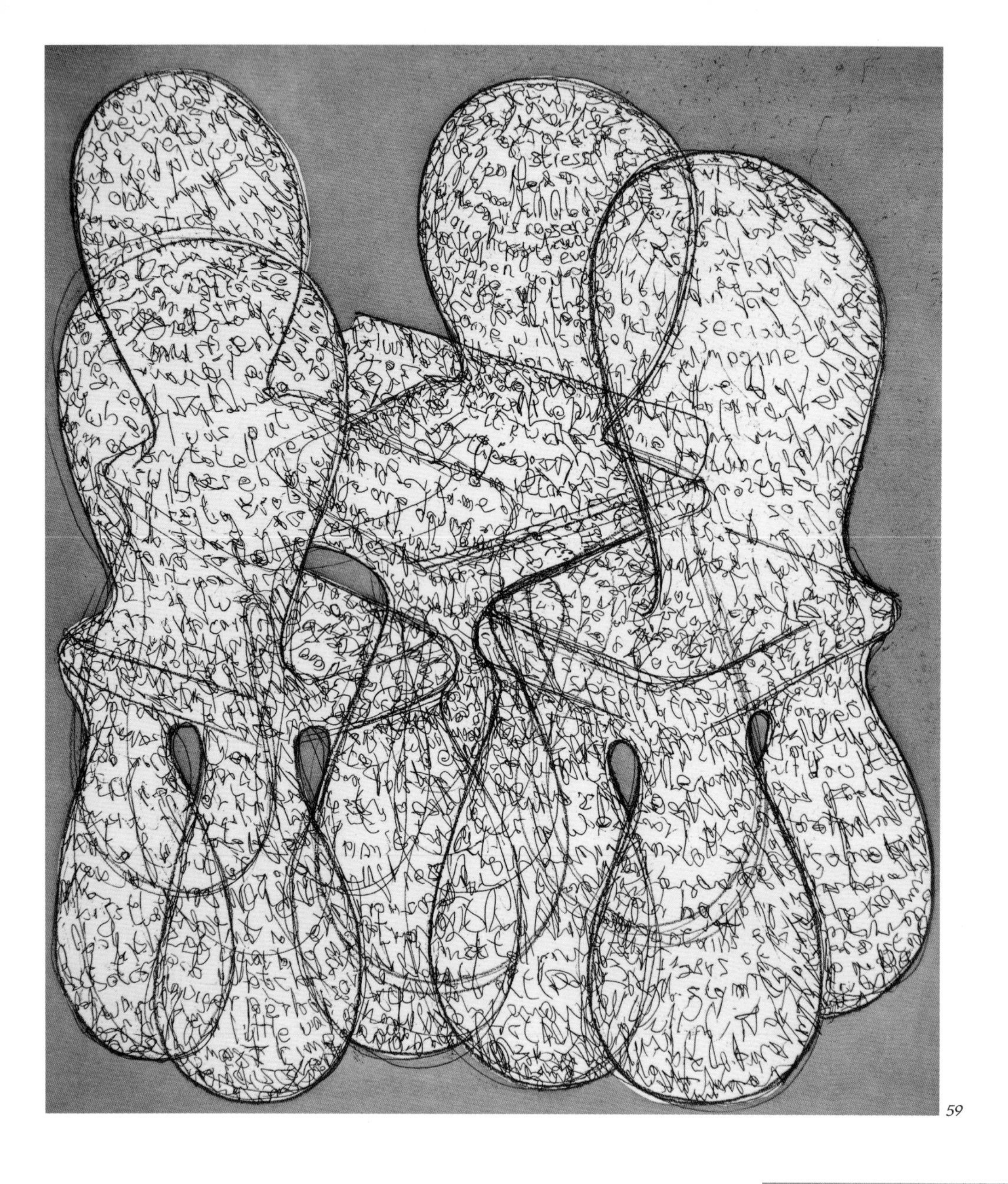

59

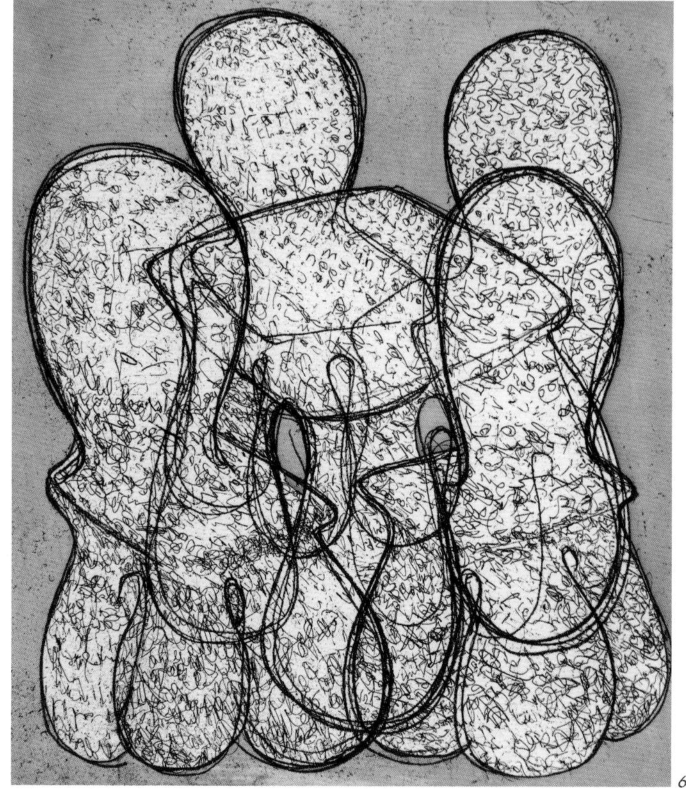

60

D59 - D62《同伴》/ *Companions*

蚀刻版画 / Etching
29×25cm
2000
摄影 / Photo: Michael Richter

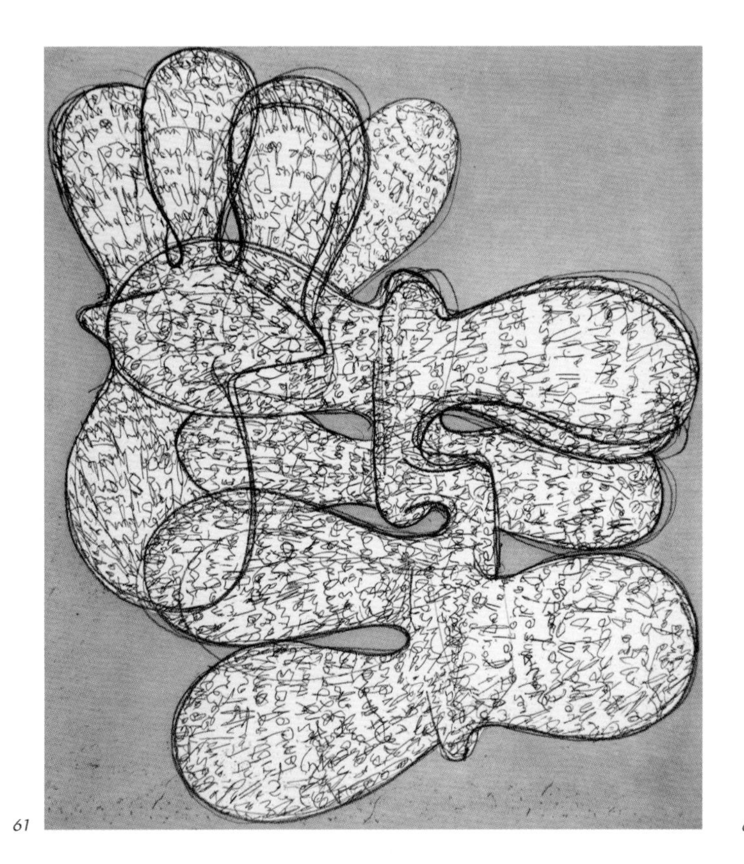

61

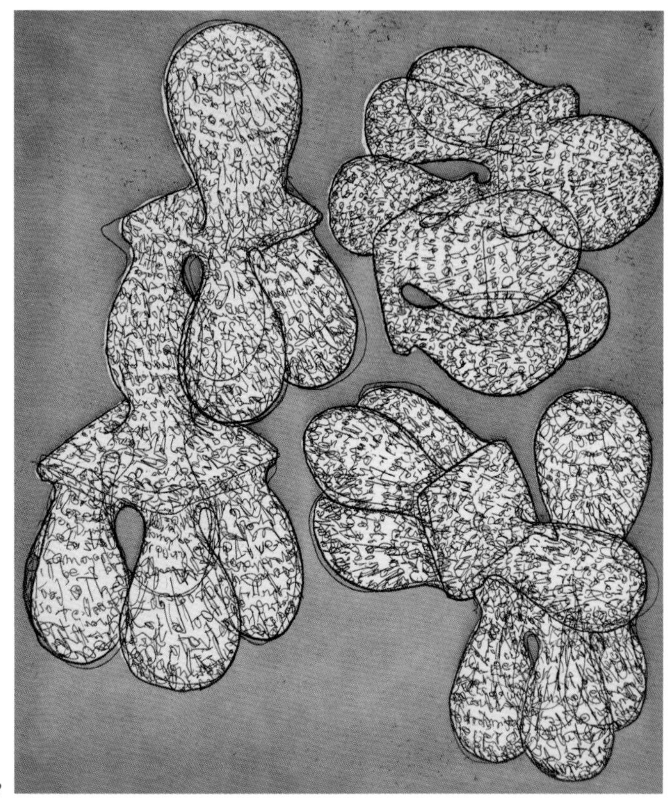

62

63

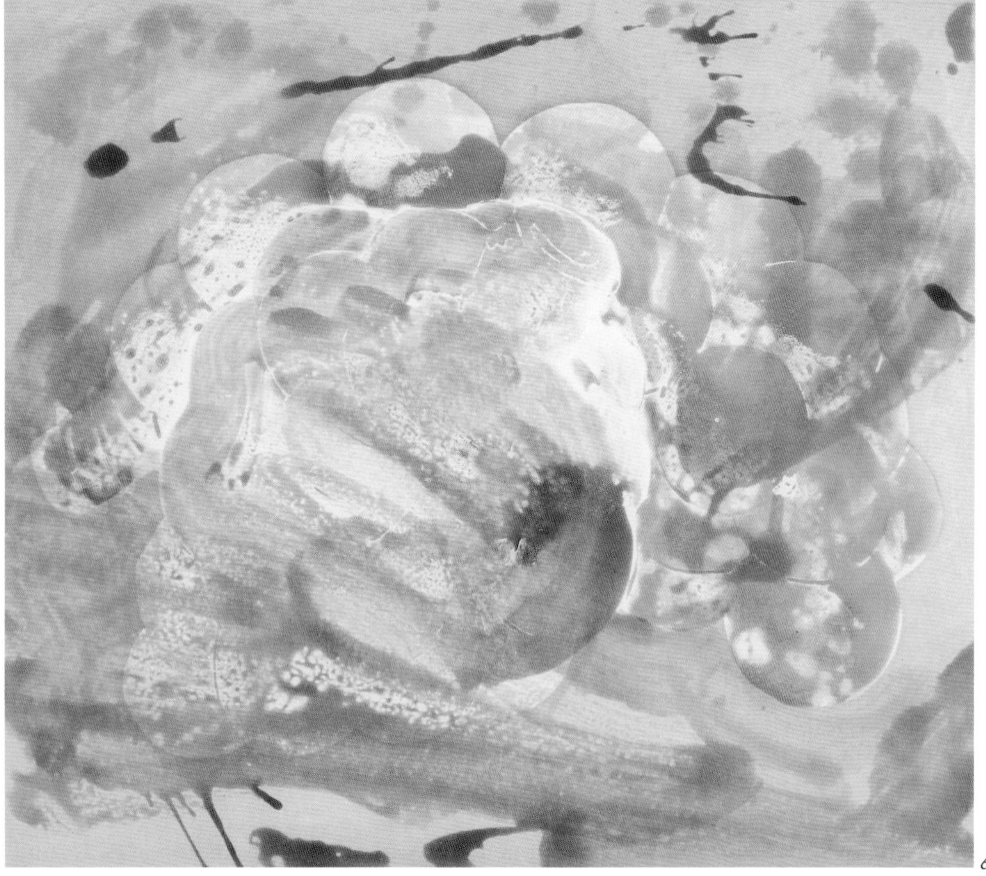

64

D63 - D66《果瓶》/ ***Fruit Bottles***

平版印刷 / Lithography
32.5×38cm
1990
摄影 / Photo: Michael Richter

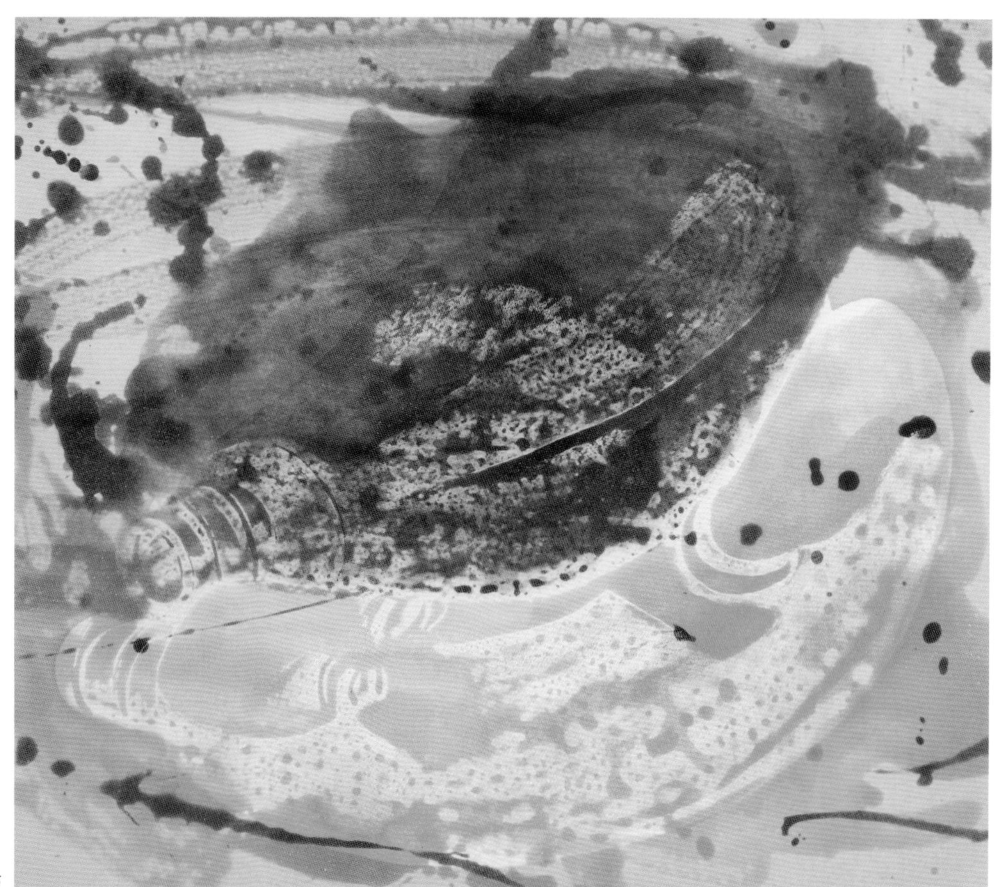
65

66

67

D67《最初时代》/ *First Era*

蚀刻版画 / Etching
29×25cm
1991
摄影 / Photo: Michael Richter

68

D68《最初时代》/ *First Era*

蚀刻版画 / Etching
29×25cm
1991
摄影 / Photo: Michael Richter

69

D69 - D73《最初时代》/ ***First Era***

蚀刻版画 / Etching
29×25cm
1991
摄影 / Photo: Michael Richter

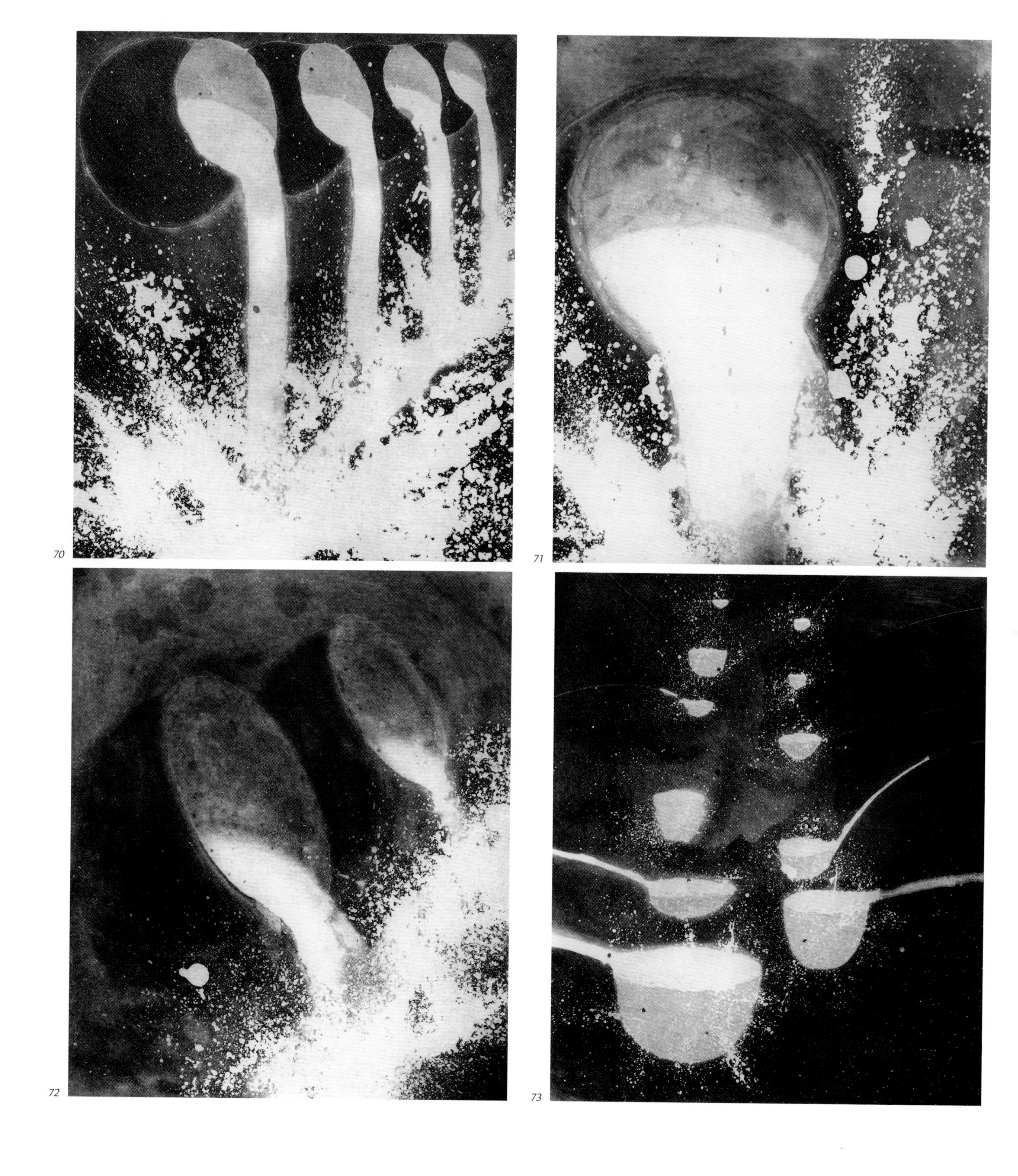

70 71 72 73

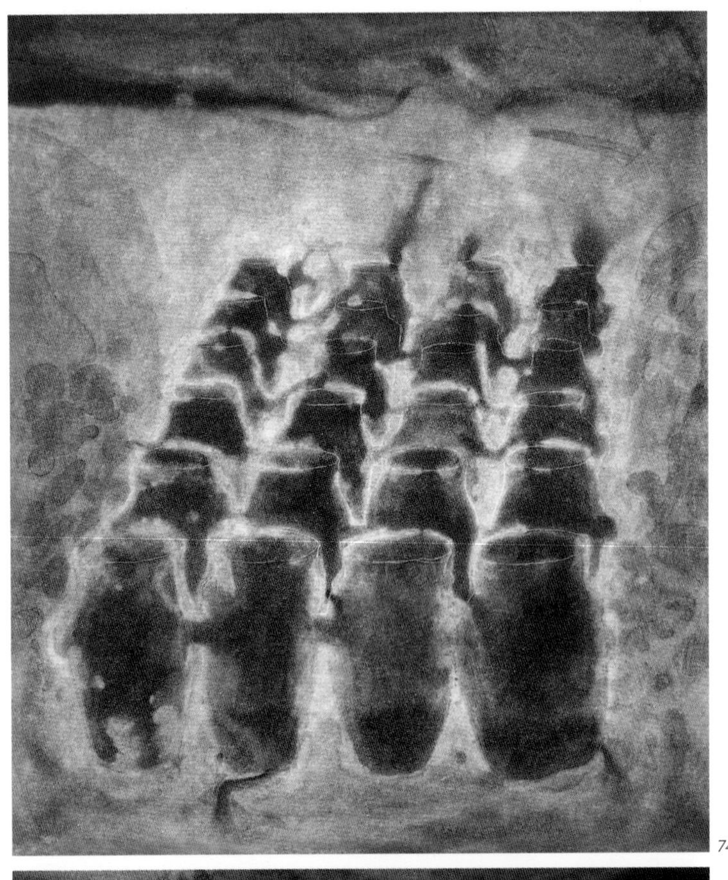
74

75

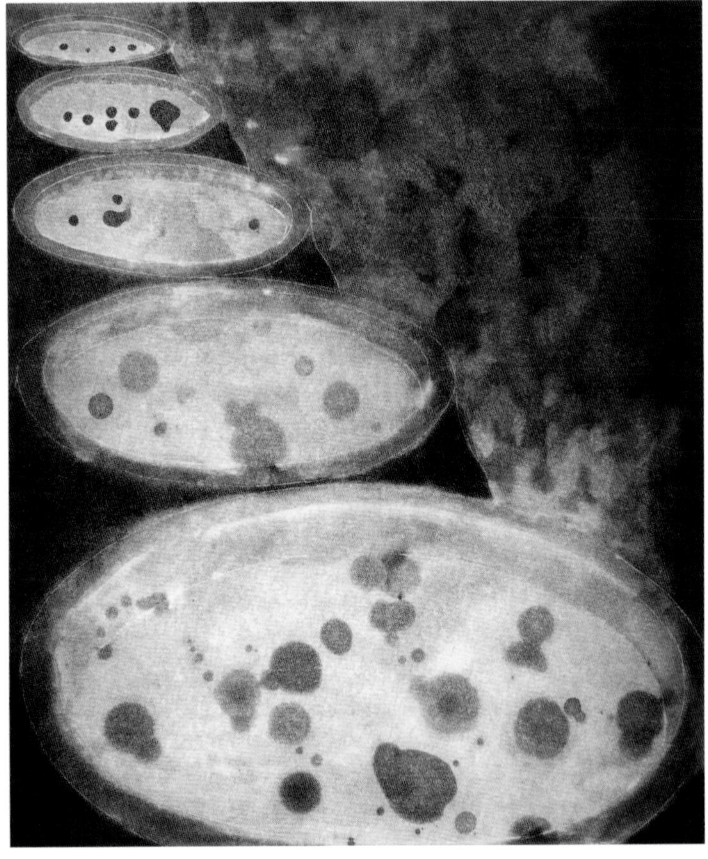
76

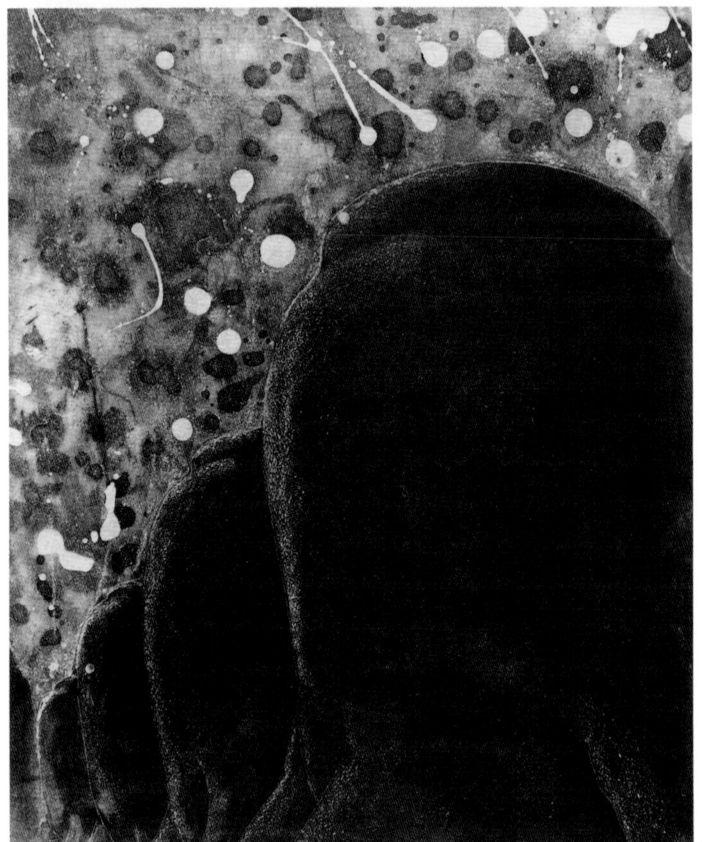
77

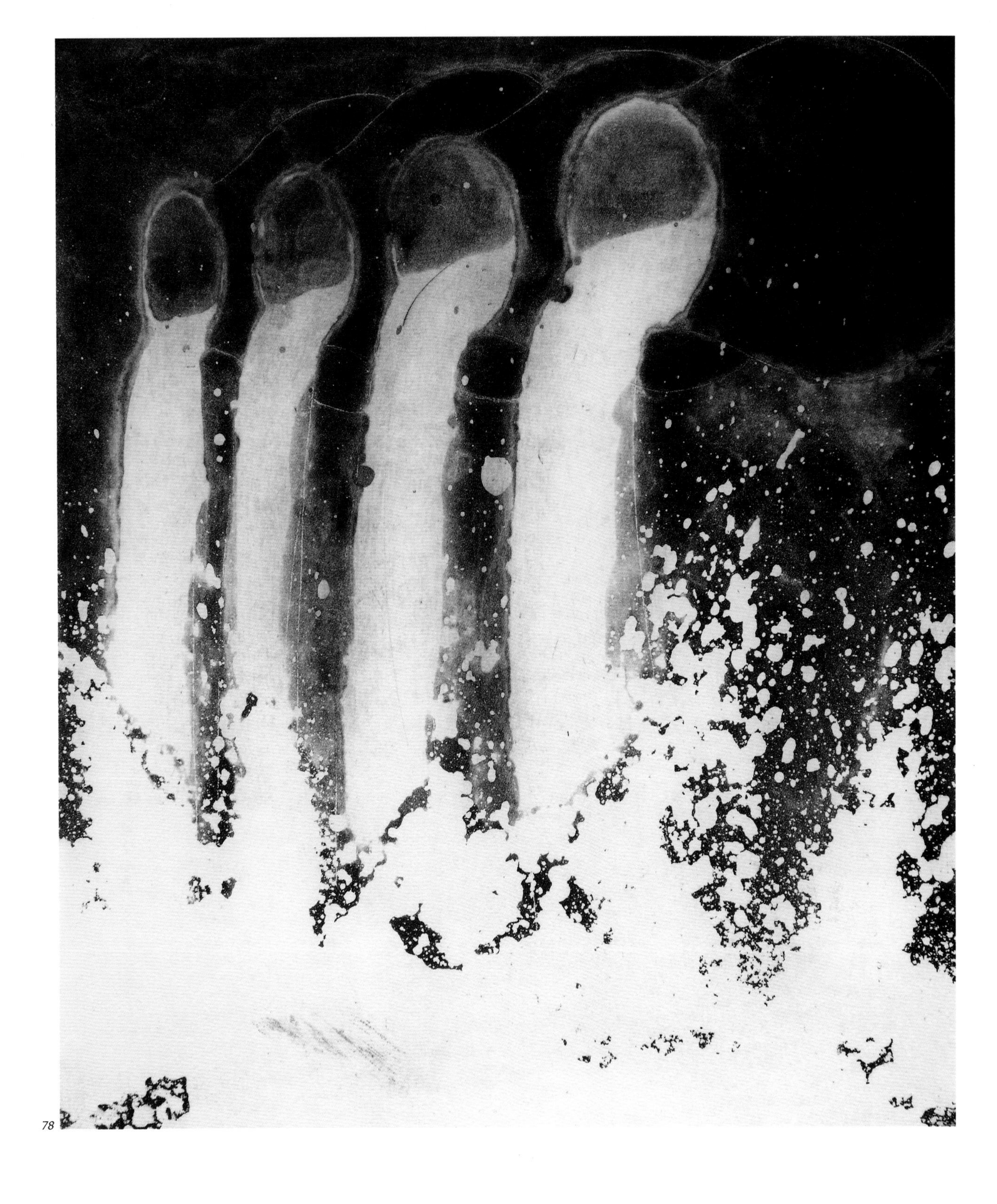
78

D74 - D78《最初时代》/ *First Era*

蚀刻版画 / Etching
29×25cm
1991
摄影 / Photo: Michael Richter

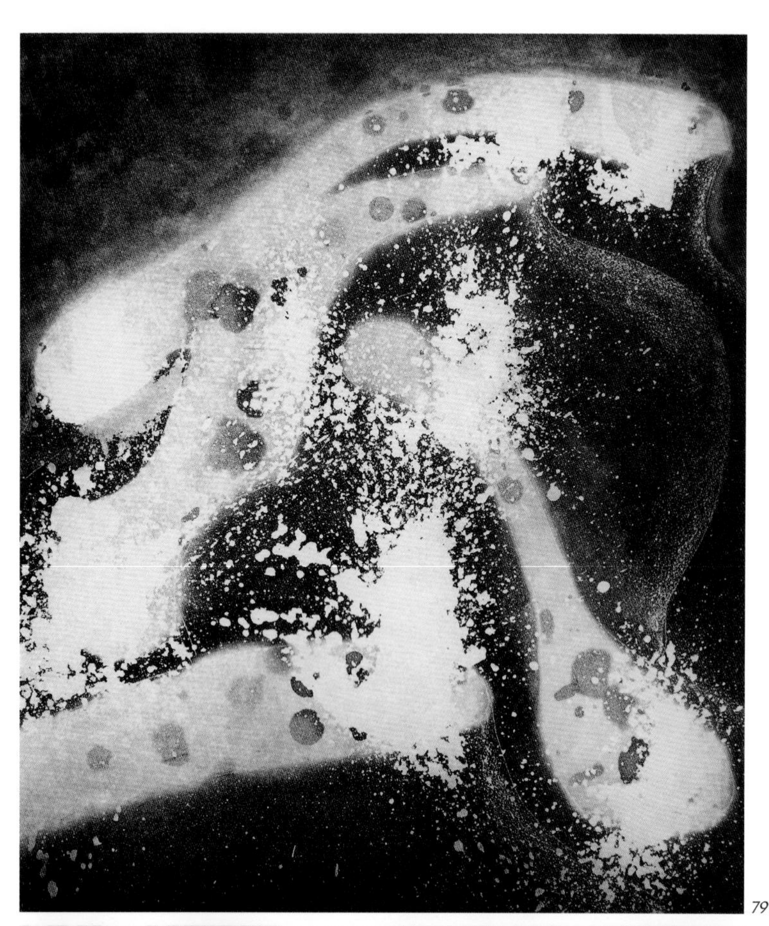
79

80

D79 - D81《最初时代》/ *First Era*

蚀刻版画 / Etching
29×25cm
1991
摄影 / Photo: Michael Richter

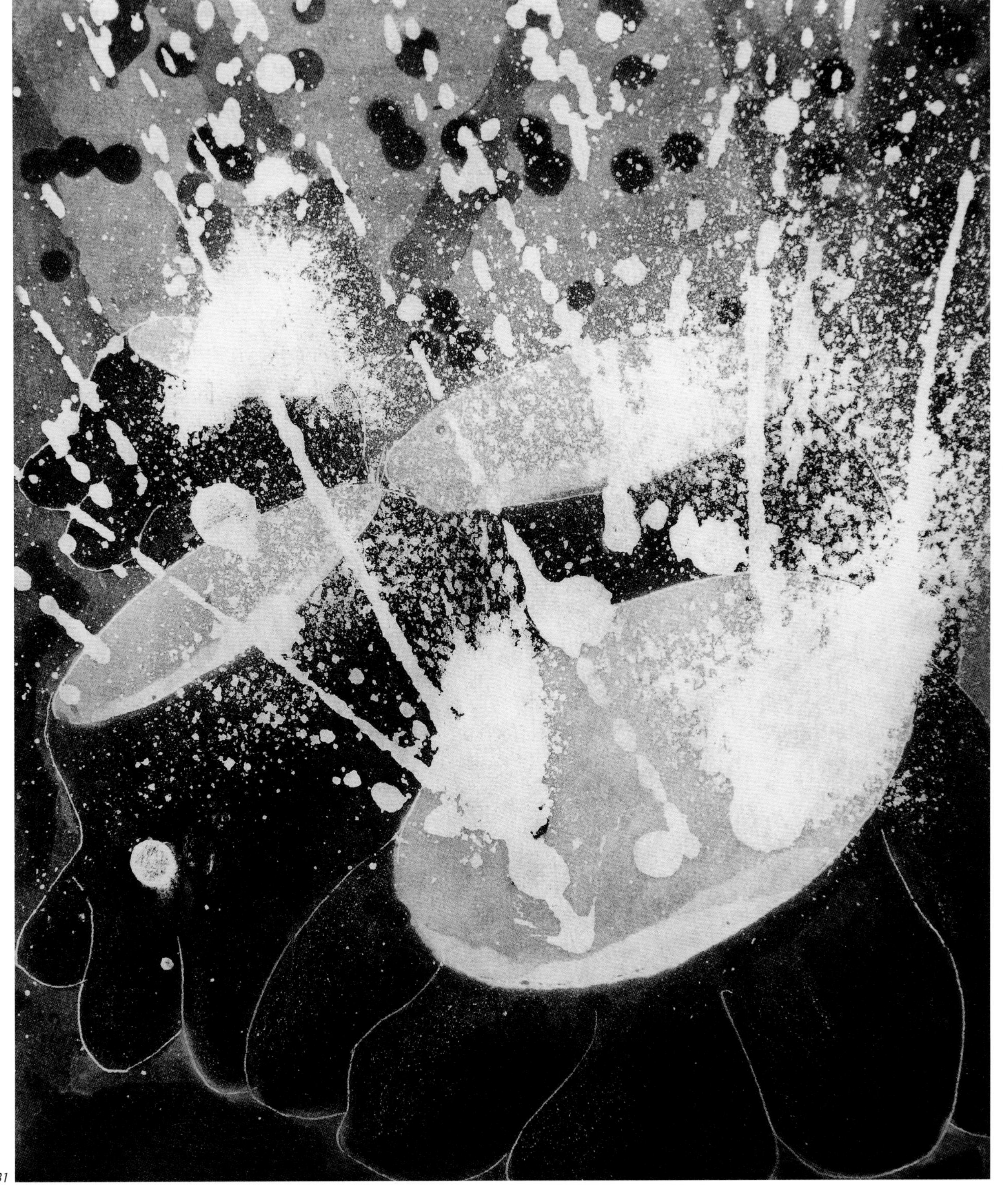

81

D82 - D84《最初时代》/ *First Era*

蚀刻版画 / Etching
29×25cm
1991
摄影 / Photo: Michael Richter

82

83

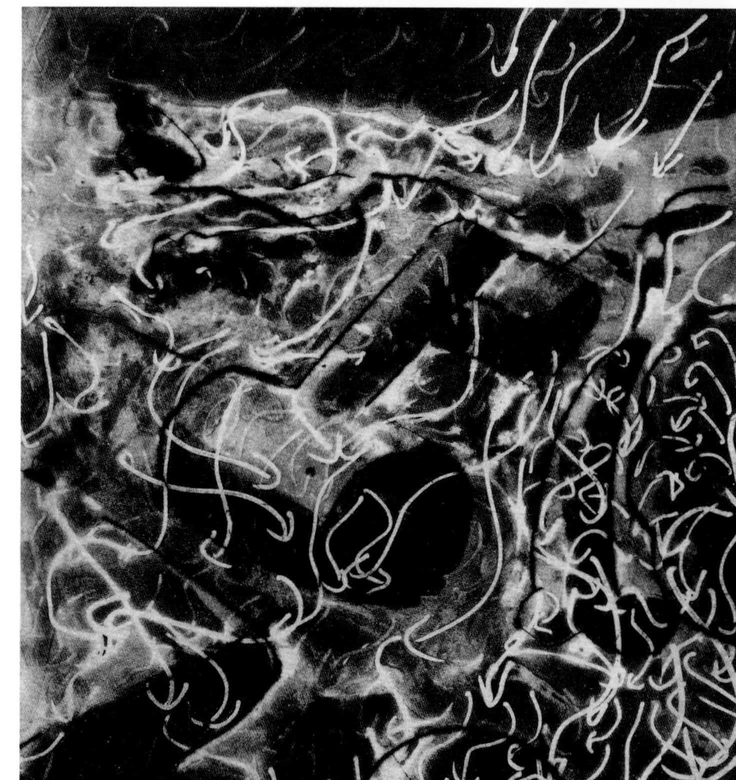
84

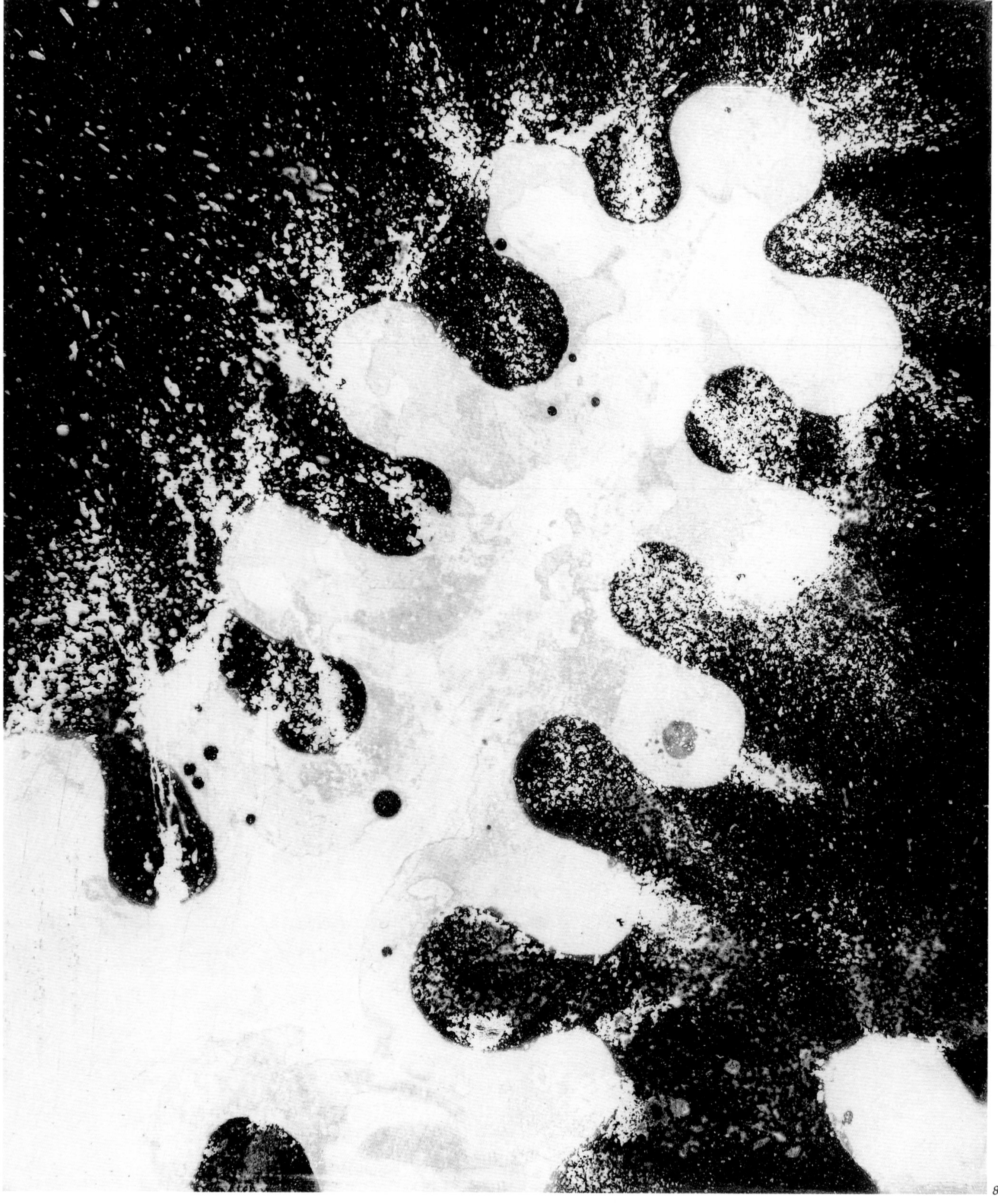

85

86

D85 - 86《最初时代》/ ***First Era***

蚀刻版画 / Etching
29×25cm
1991
摄影 / Photo: Michael Richter

87

D87《最初时代》/ *First Era*

蚀刻版画 / Etching
29×25cm
1991
摄影 / Photo: Michael Richter

88

D88《最初时代》/ *First Era*

蚀刻版画 / Etching
29×25cm
1991
摄影 / Photo: Michael Richter

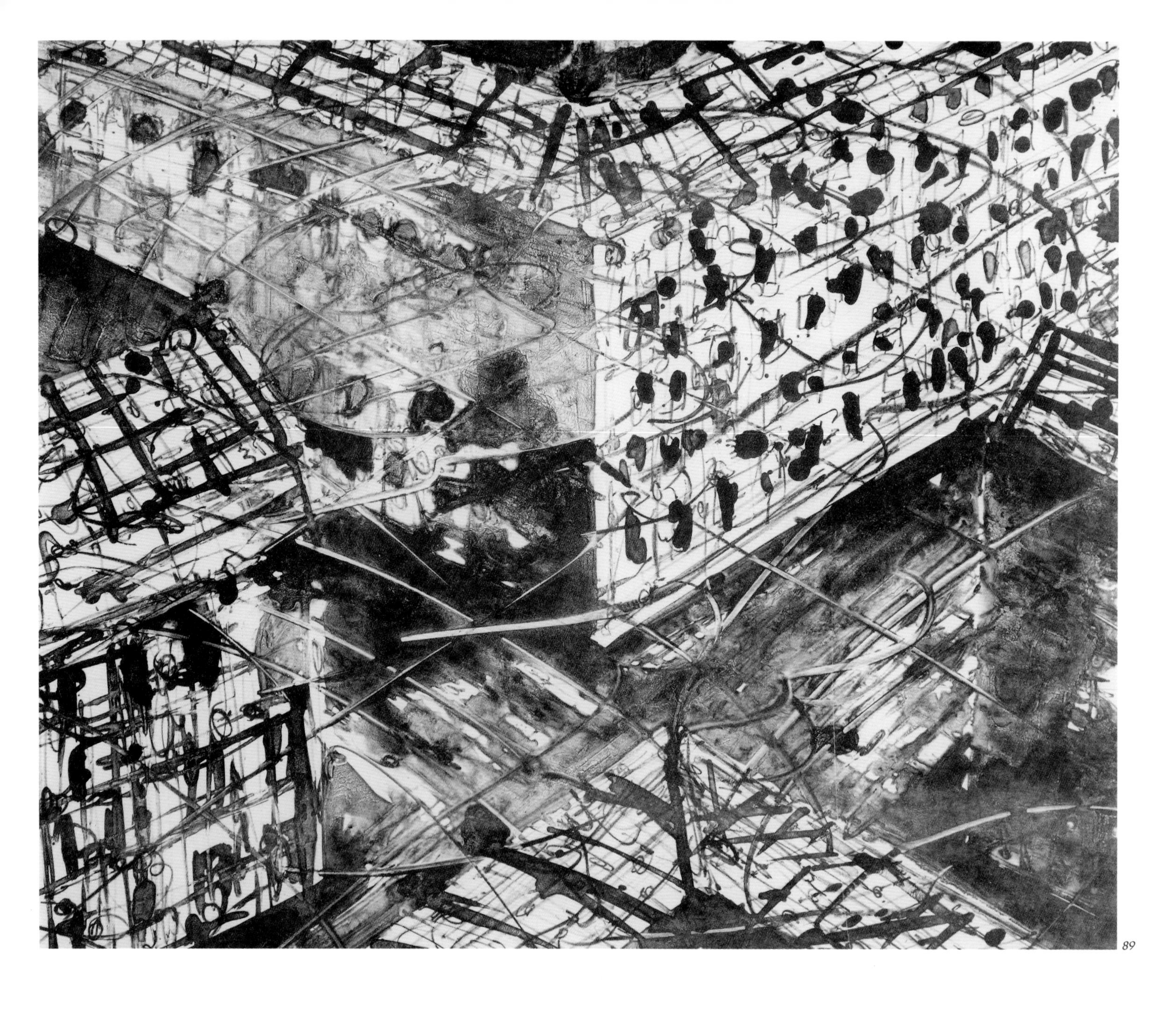

89

D89《浓厚空气 II》/ *Thick Air II*

平版印刷 / Lithography
38×47cm
2003
摄影 / Photo: Michael Richter

90

D90《喧闹的都市》/ *Urban Chatter*

平版印刷 / Lithography
38×47cm
2003
摄影 / Photo: Michael Richter

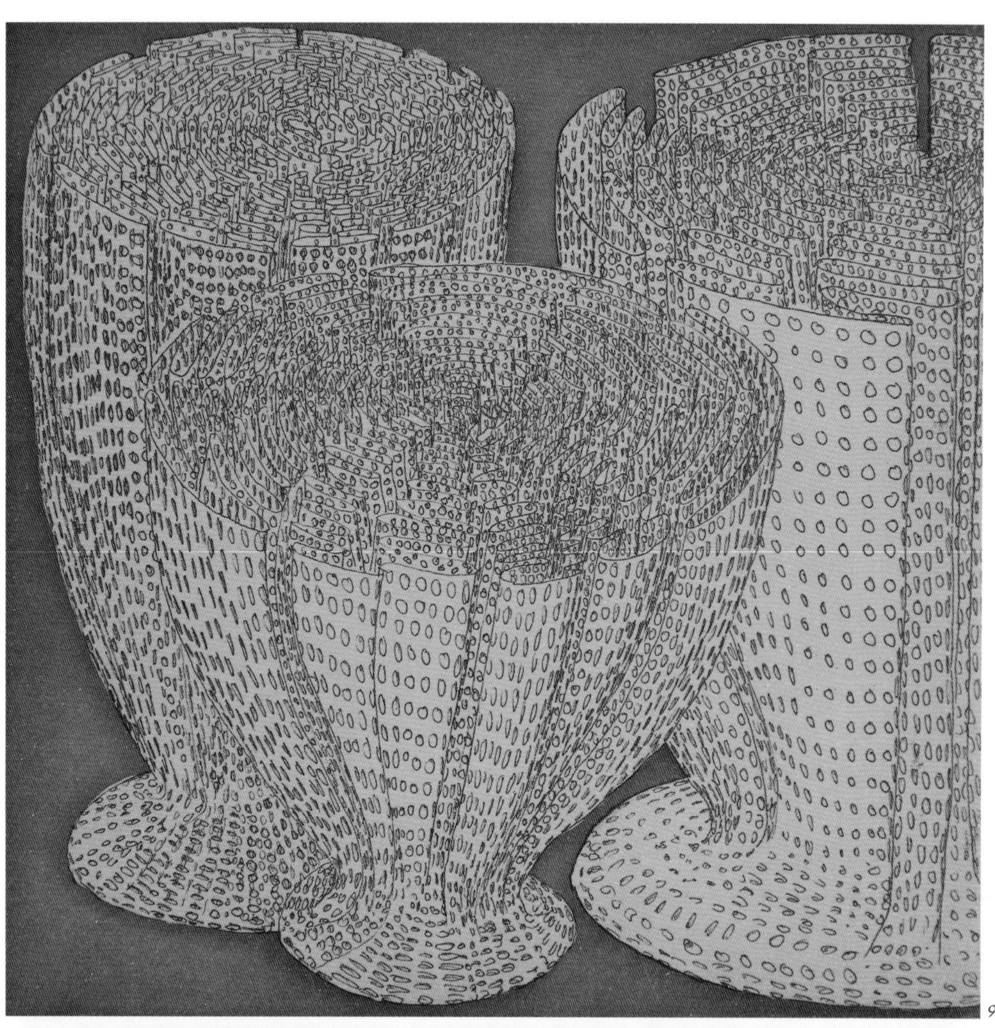

91

92

D91- D94《呼吸者》/ *Breathe*

蚀刻版画 / Etching
22×22cm
1990
摄影 / Photo: Michael Richter

93

94

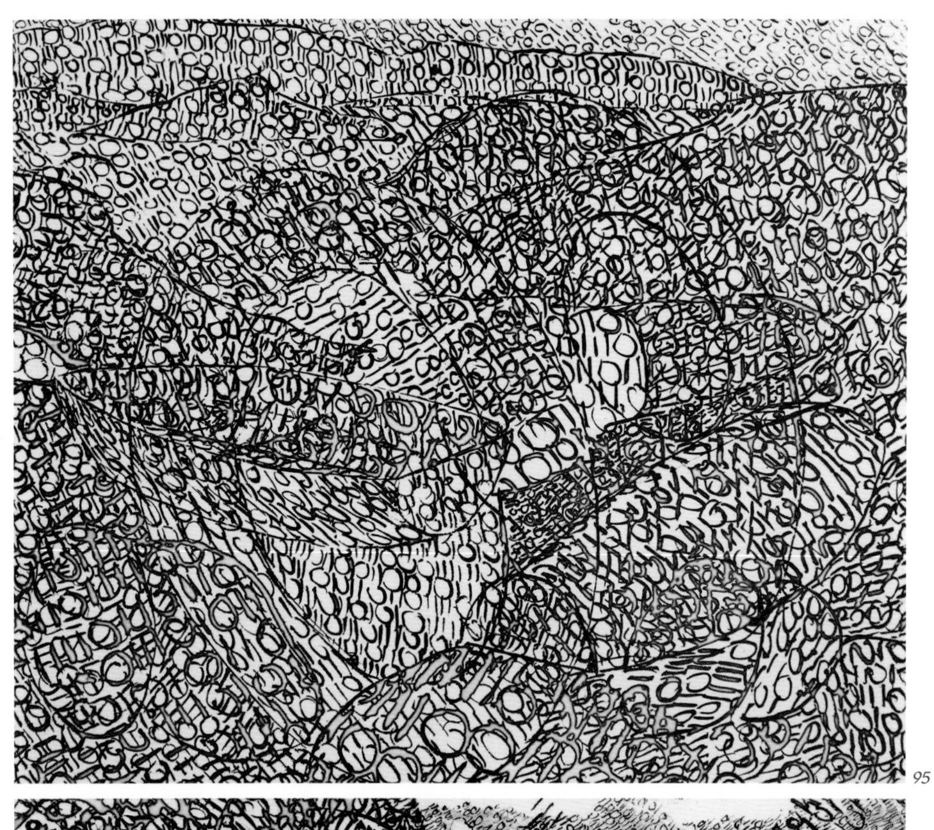
95

96

D95 - D98《自然、本质》/ ***Nature, Nature***

蚀刻版画 / Etching
32×40cm
2007
摄影 / Photo: Michael Richter

97

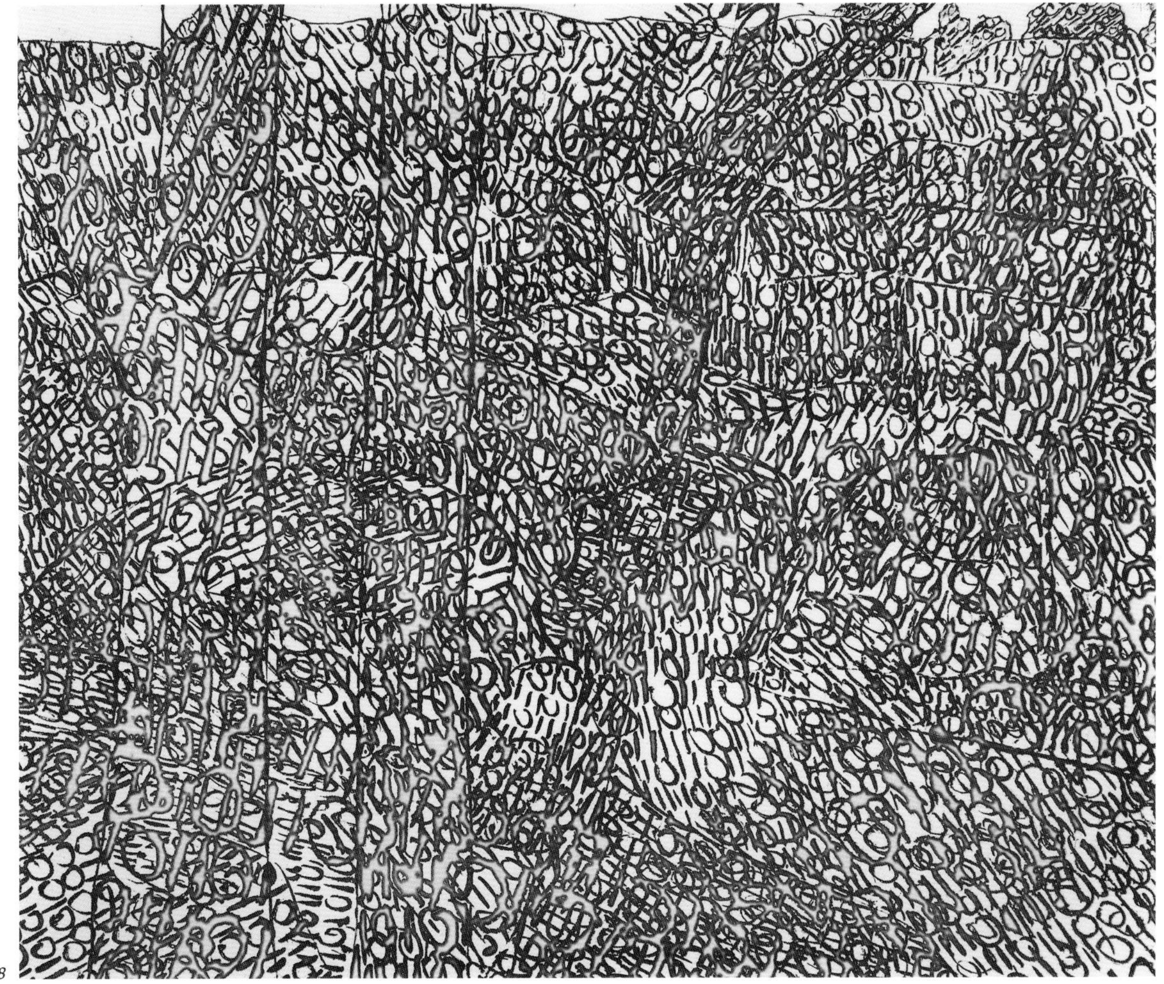
98

99

D99 - D102《操纵》/ *Manipulations*

蚀刻版画 / Etching
32×40cm
2006
摄影 / Photo: Michael Richter

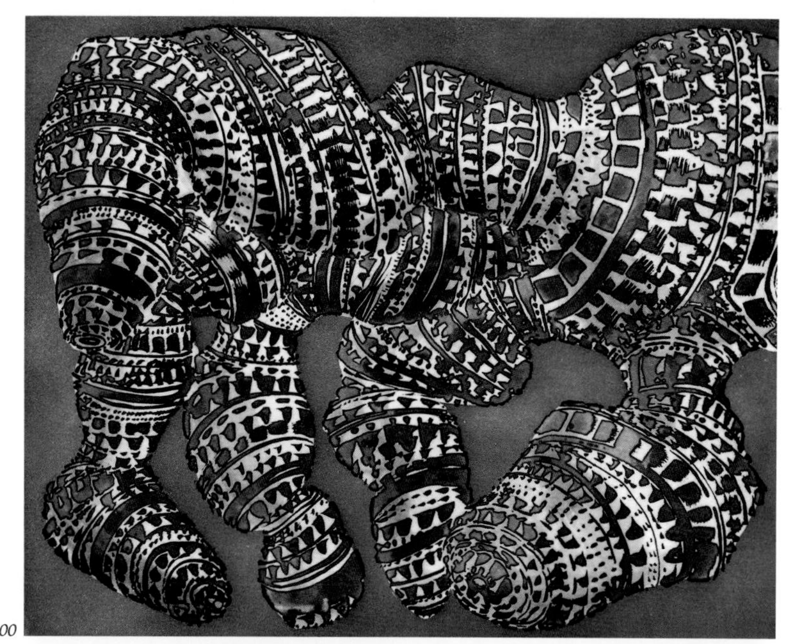
100

101

102

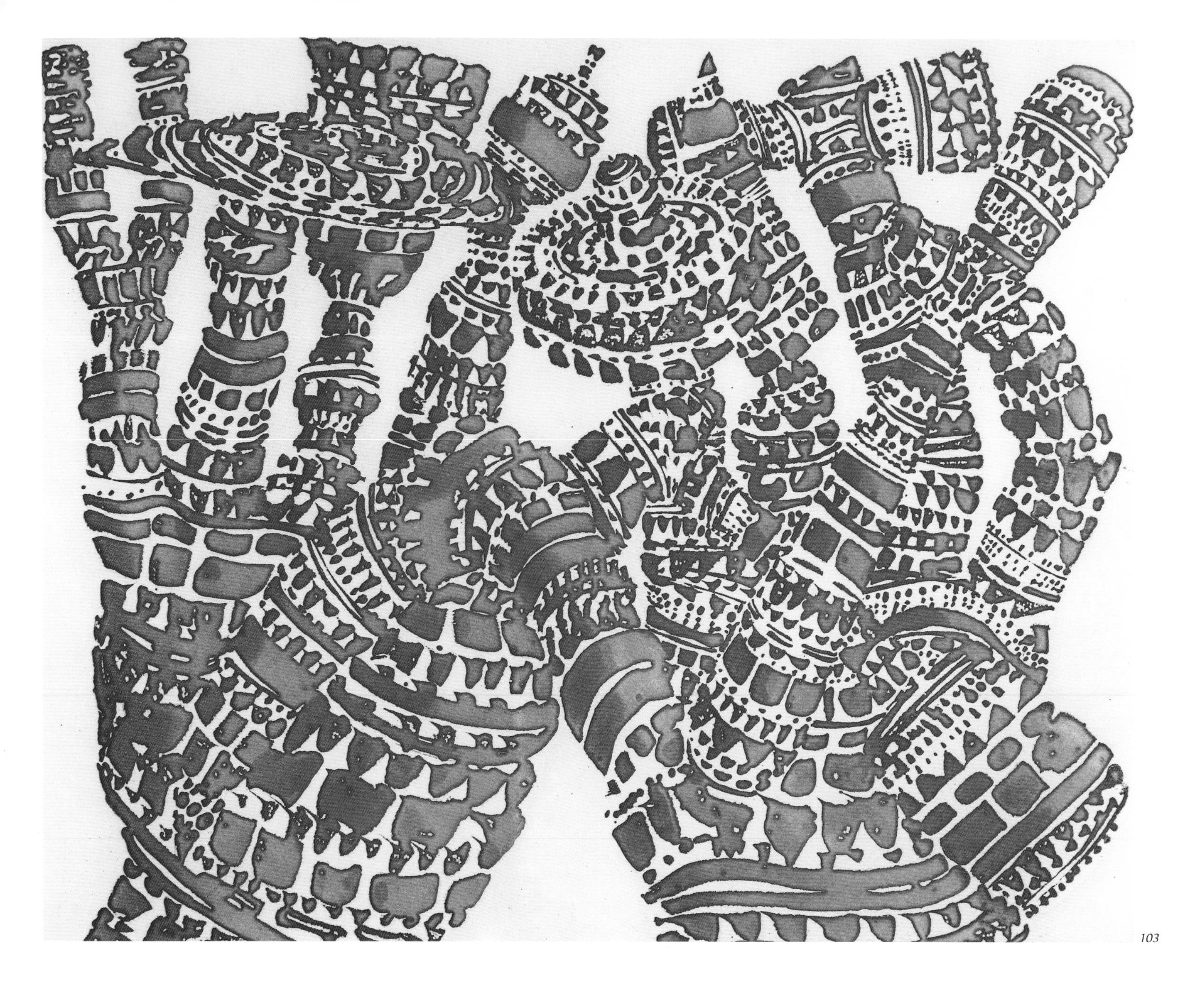

D103《操纵》/ *Manipulations*

蚀刻版画 / Etching
32×40cm
2006
摄影 / Photo: Michael Richter

104

D104《操纵》/ *Manipulations*

蚀刻版画 / Etching
32×40cm
2006
摄影 / Photo: Michael Richter

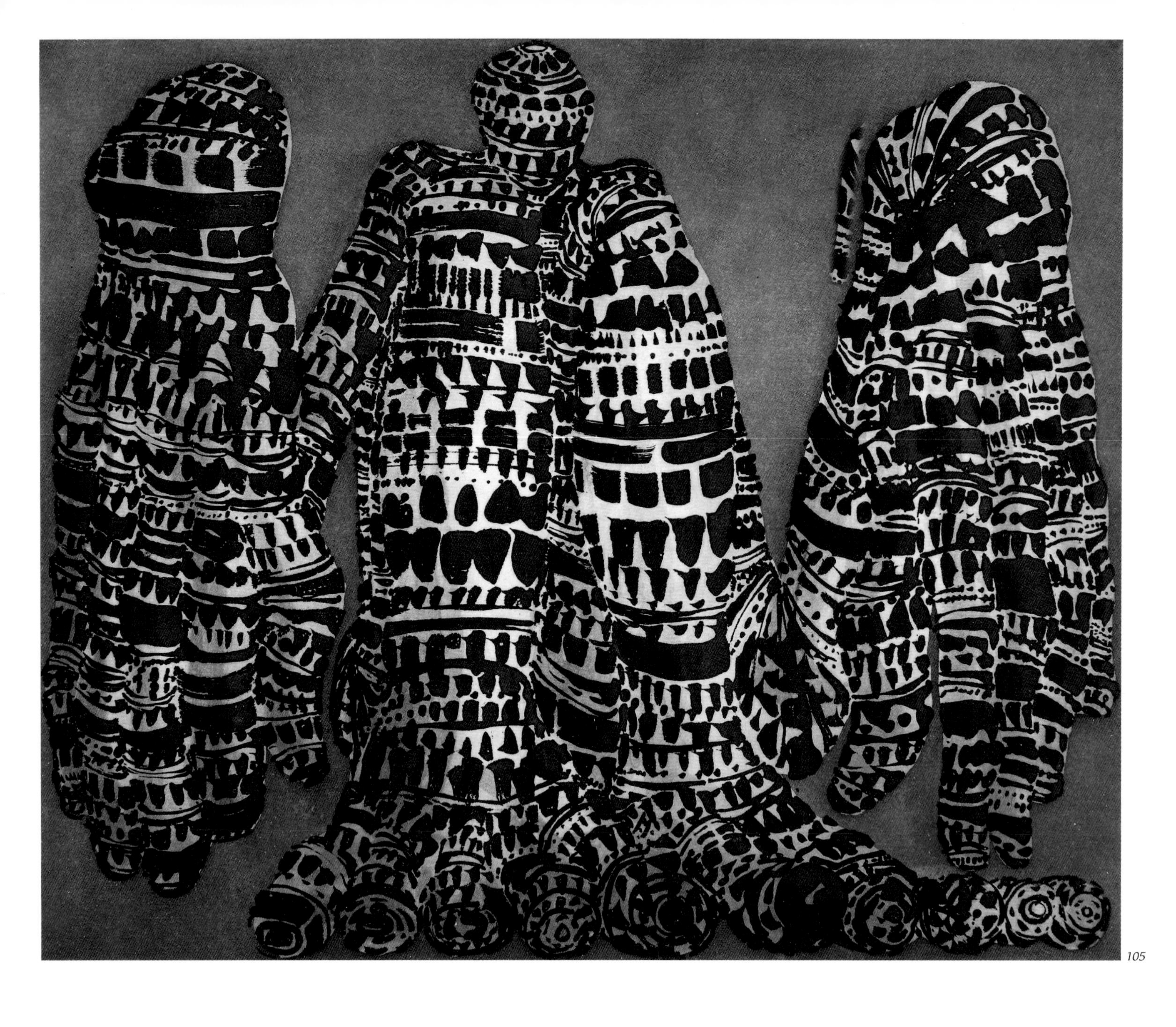

105

D105 - D107《形式密码》/ *Form Codes*

蚀刻版画 / Etching
32×40cm
2006
摄影 / Photo: Michael Richter

106

107

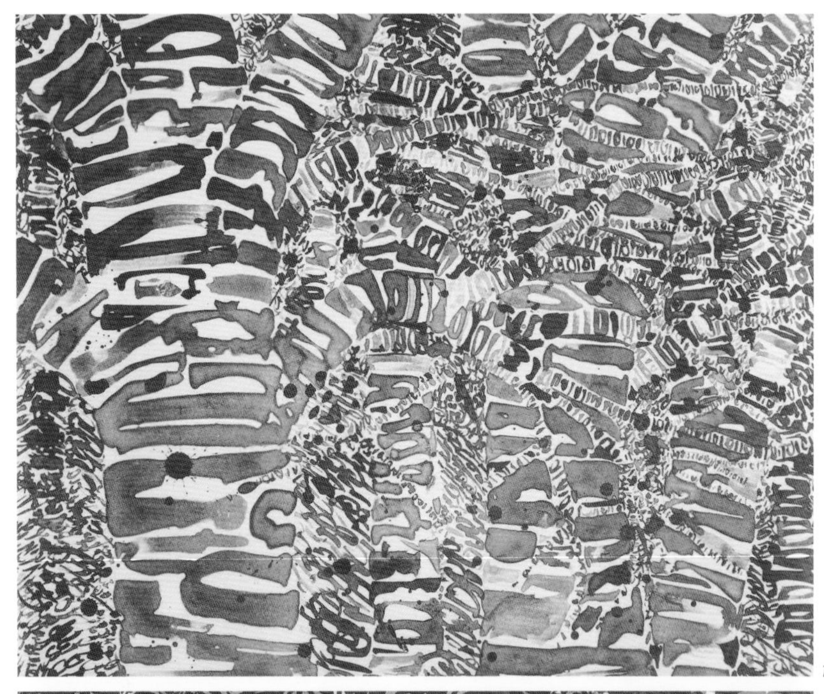

108

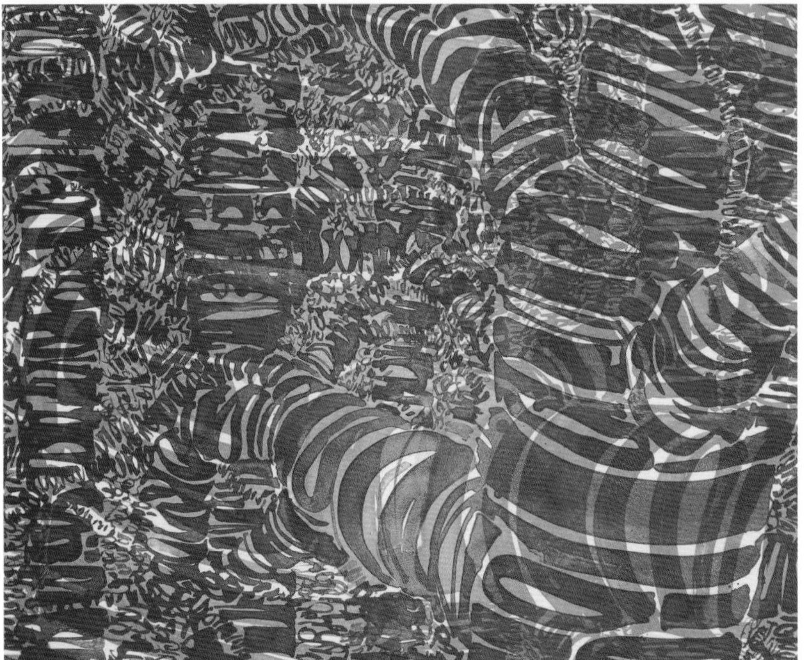

109

D108 - D110《沃尔德奇曼》/ *Waldzimmer*

平版印刷 / Lithography
40.5×50.6cm
2011
摄影 / Photo: Michael Richter

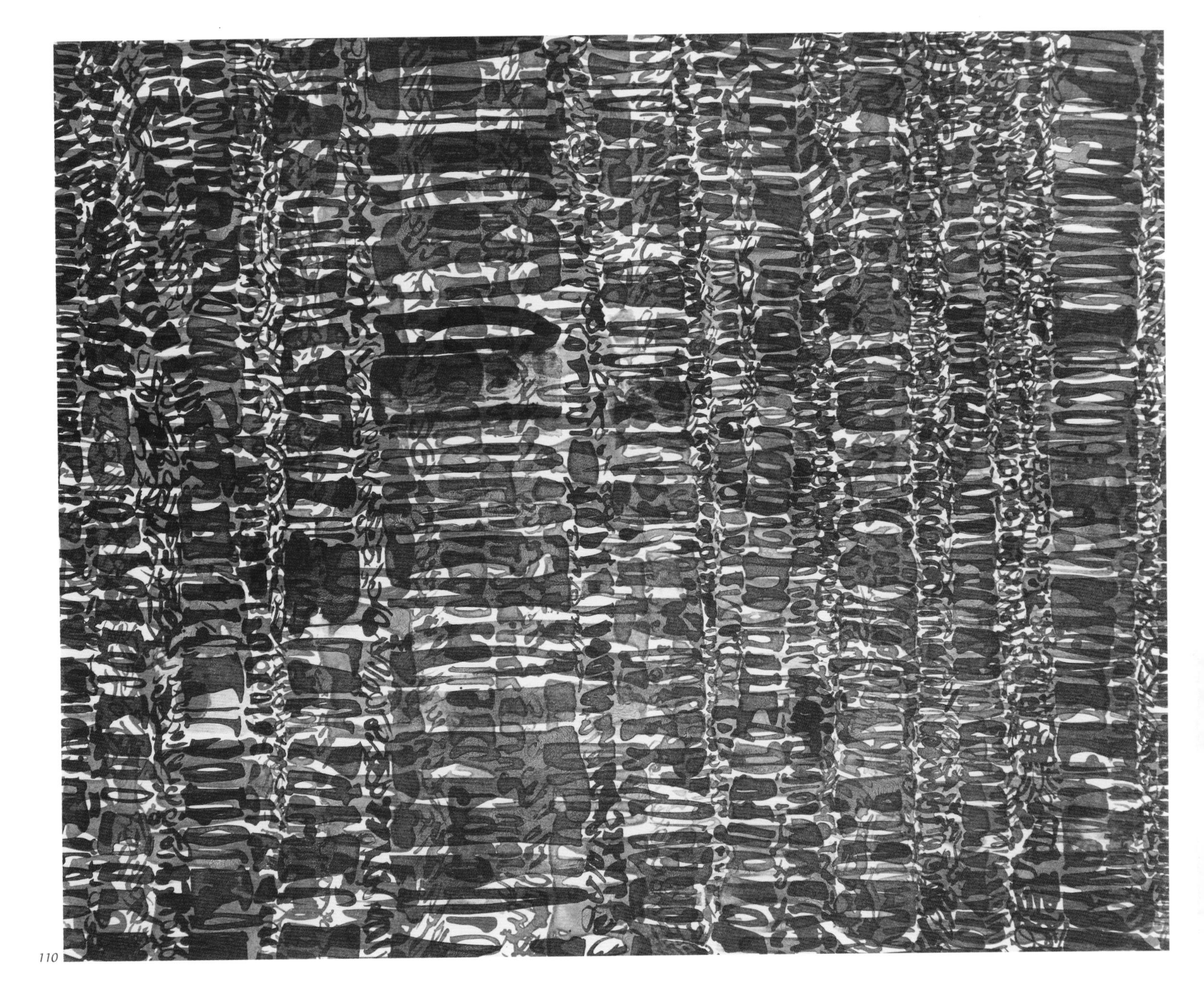

110

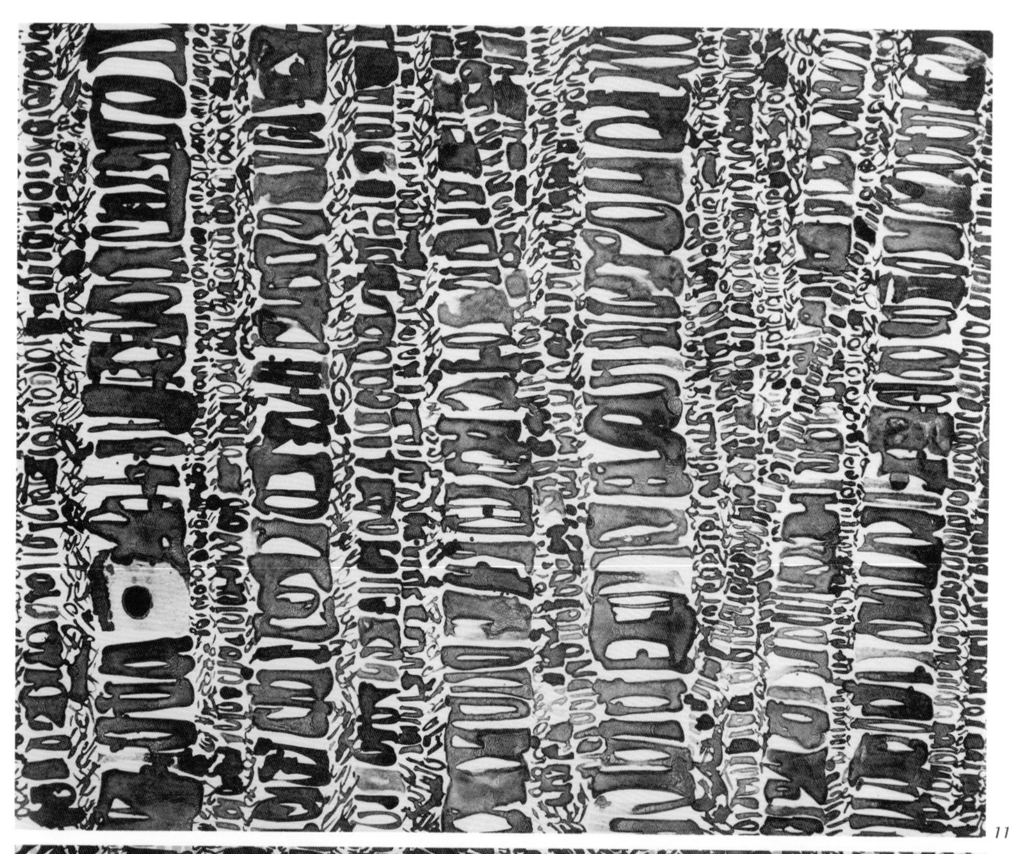

111

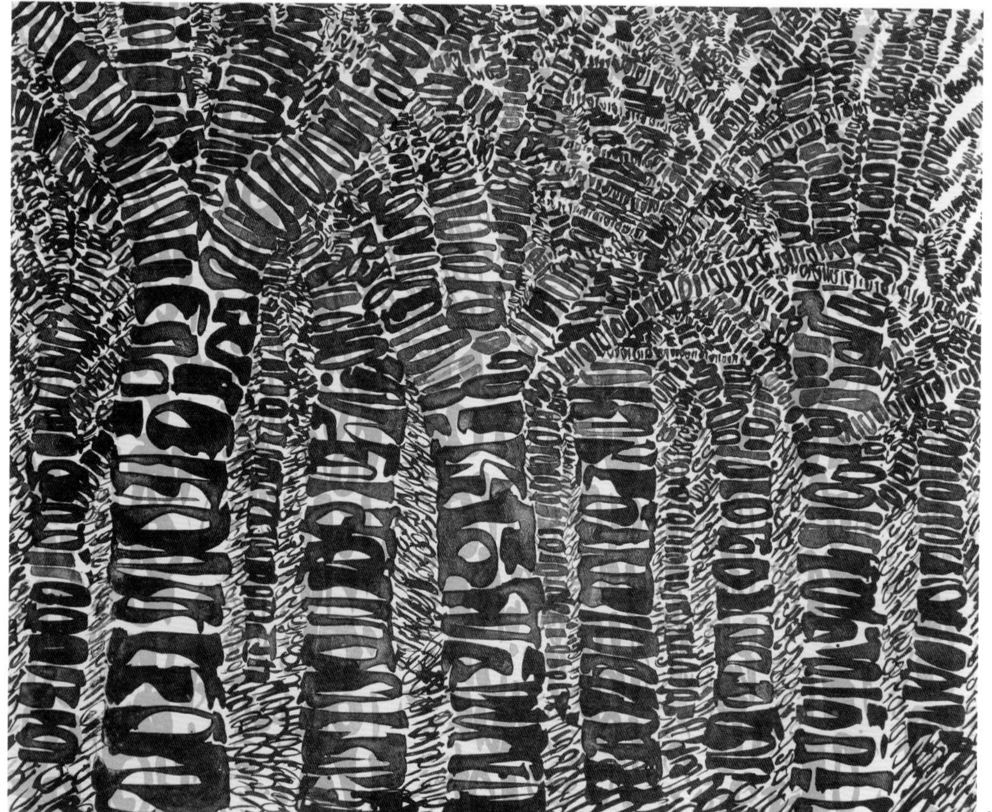

112

D111 - D114《沃尔德奇曼》/ *Waldzimmer*

平版印刷 / Lithography
40.5×50.6cm
2011
摄影 / Photo: Michael Richter

113

114

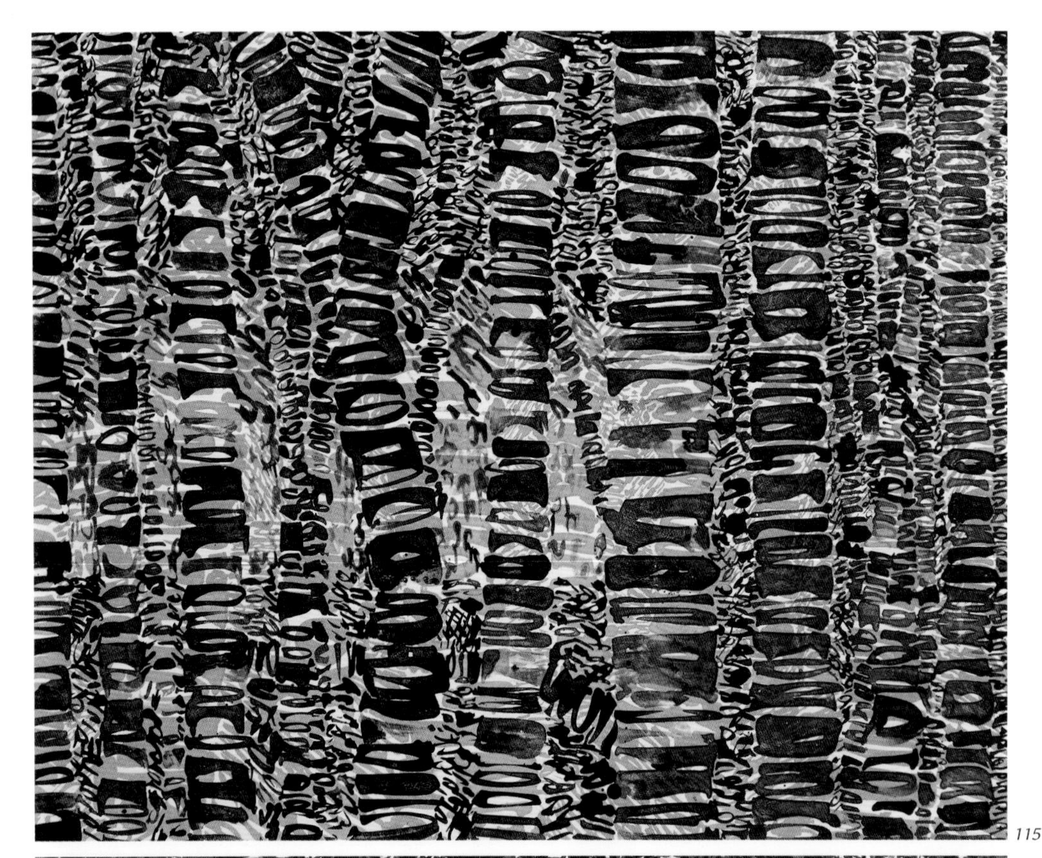

115

116

D115 - D118《沃尔德奇曼》/ *Waldzimmer*

平版印刷 / Lithography
40.5×50.6cm
2011
摄影 / Photo: Michael Richter

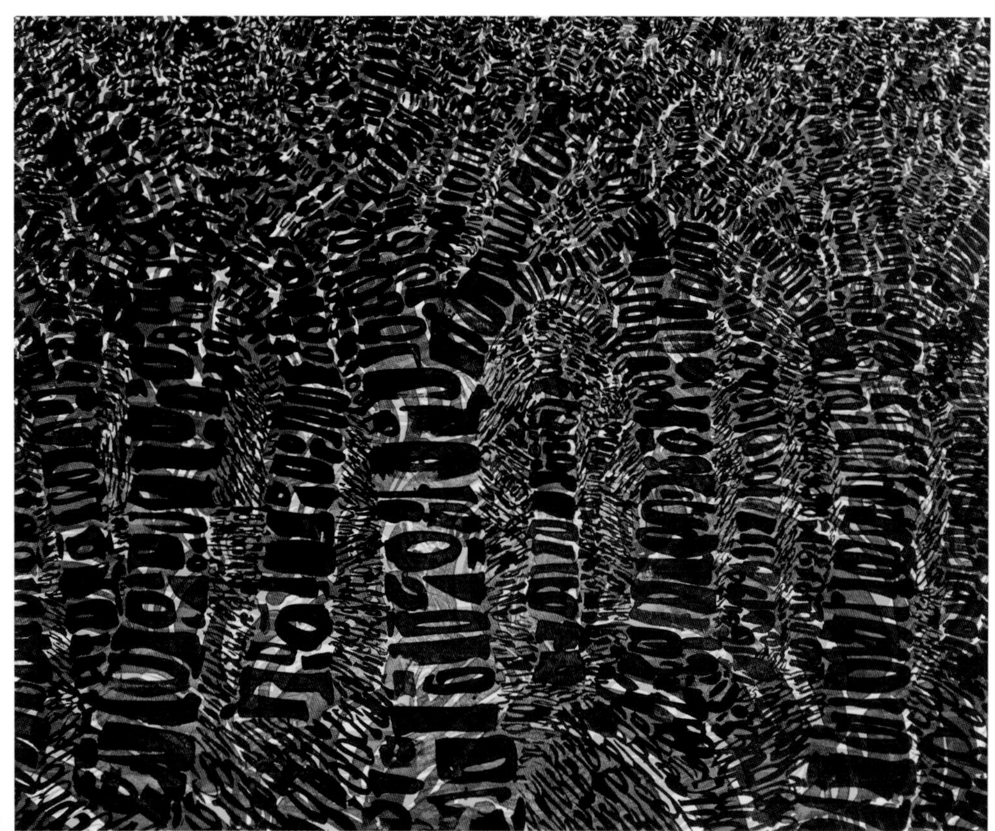
117

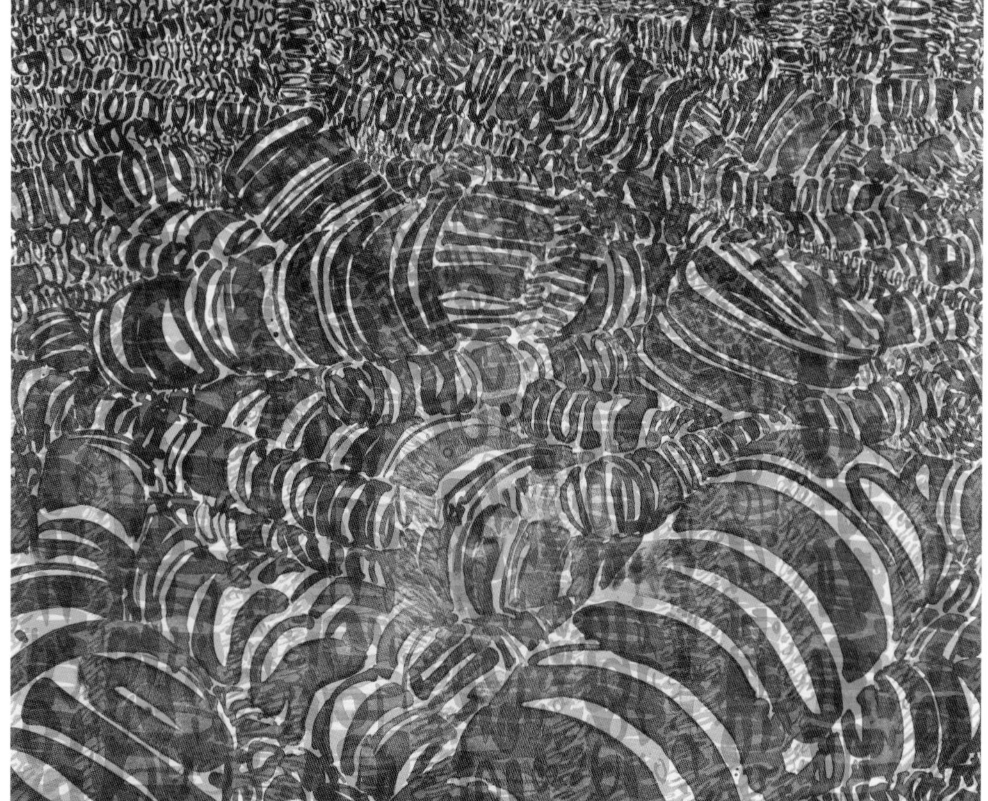
118

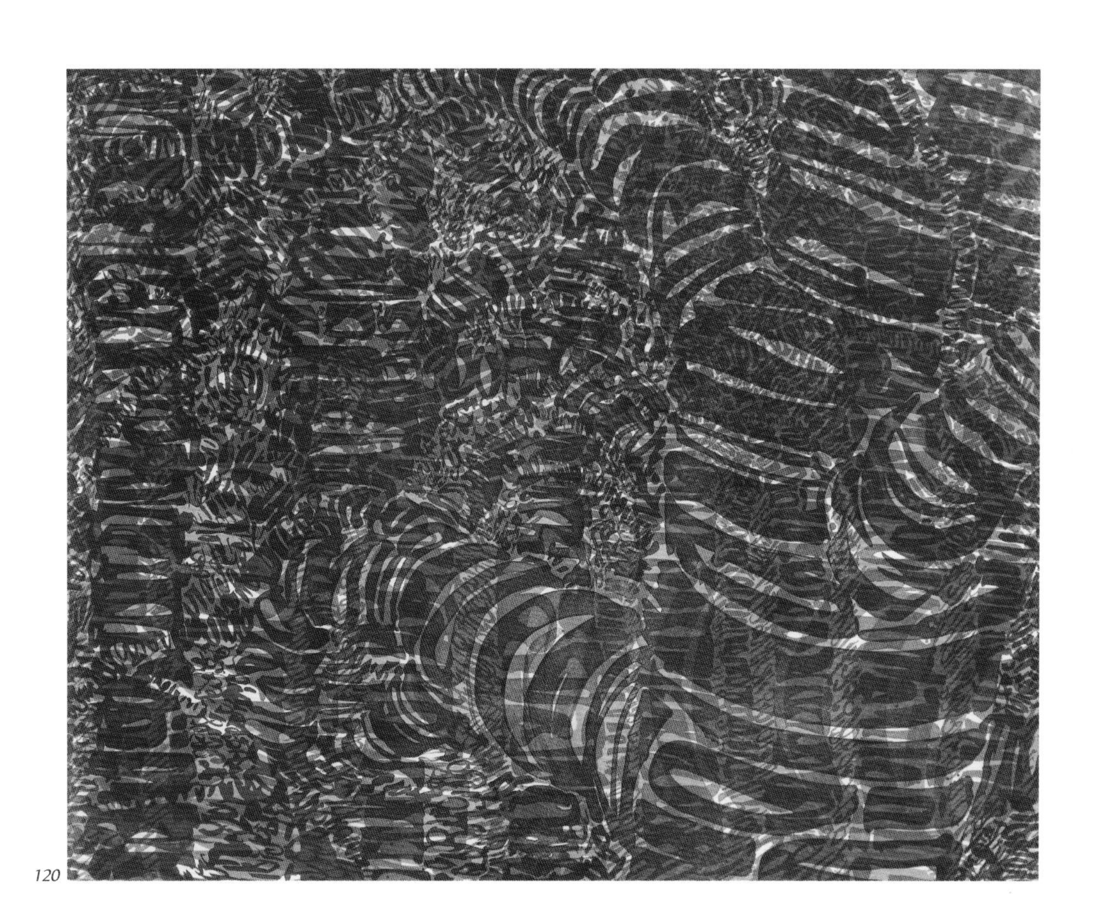

120

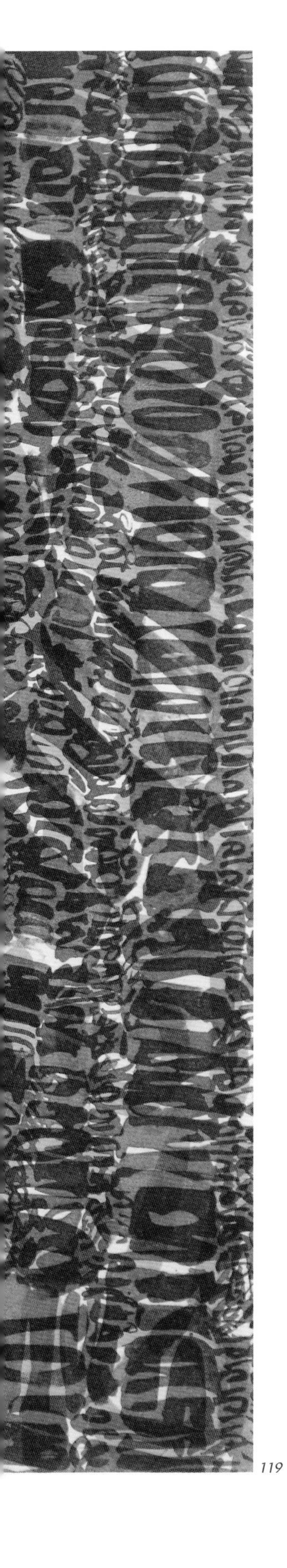

119

D119 - D120《沃尔德奇曼》/ ***Waldzimmer***

平版印刷 / Lithography
40.5×50.6cm
2011
摄影 / Photo: Michael Richter

D121- D123《沃尔德奇曼》/ *Waldzimmer*

平版印刷 / Lithography
40.5×50.6cm
2011
摄影 / Photo: Michael Richter

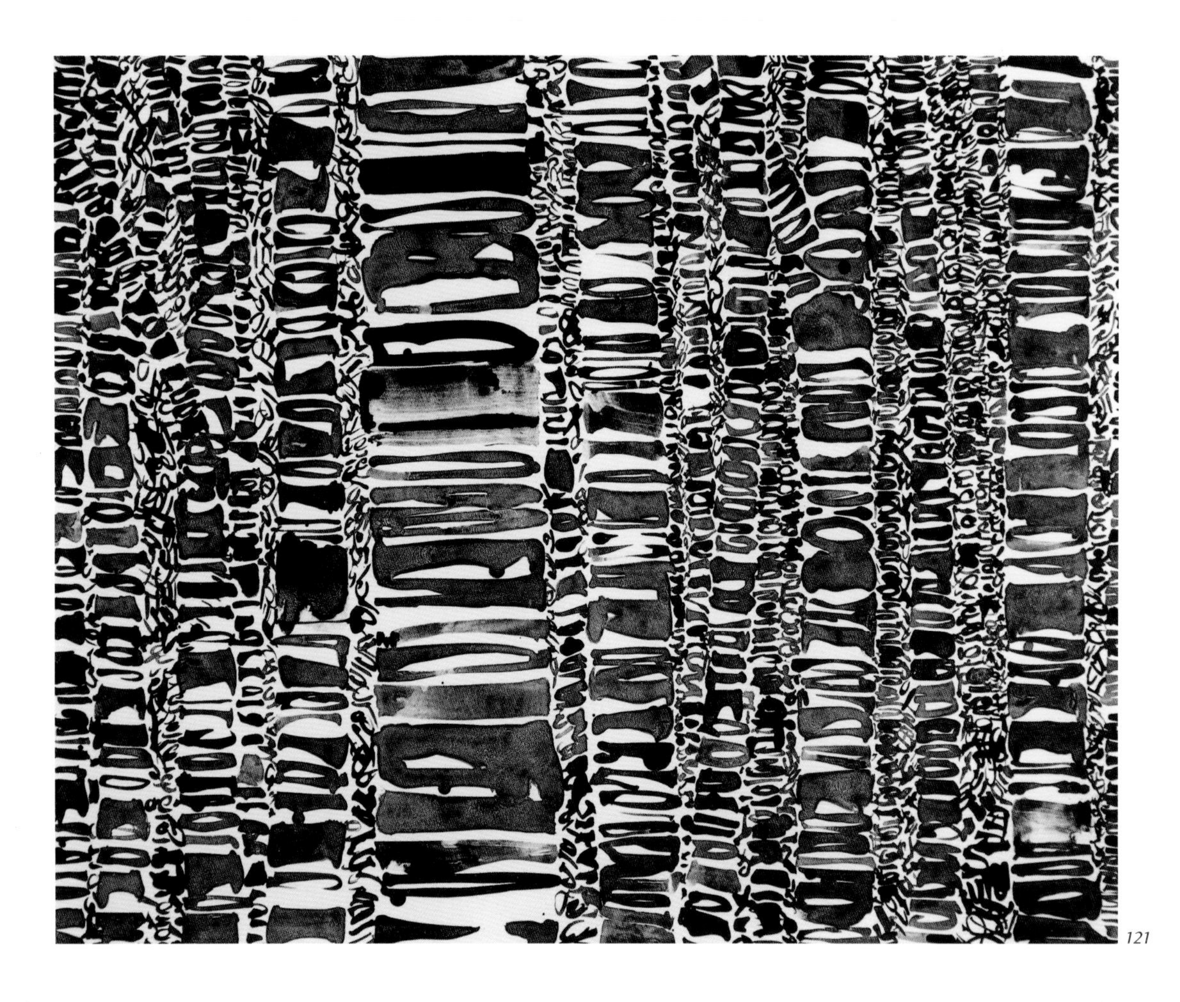

121

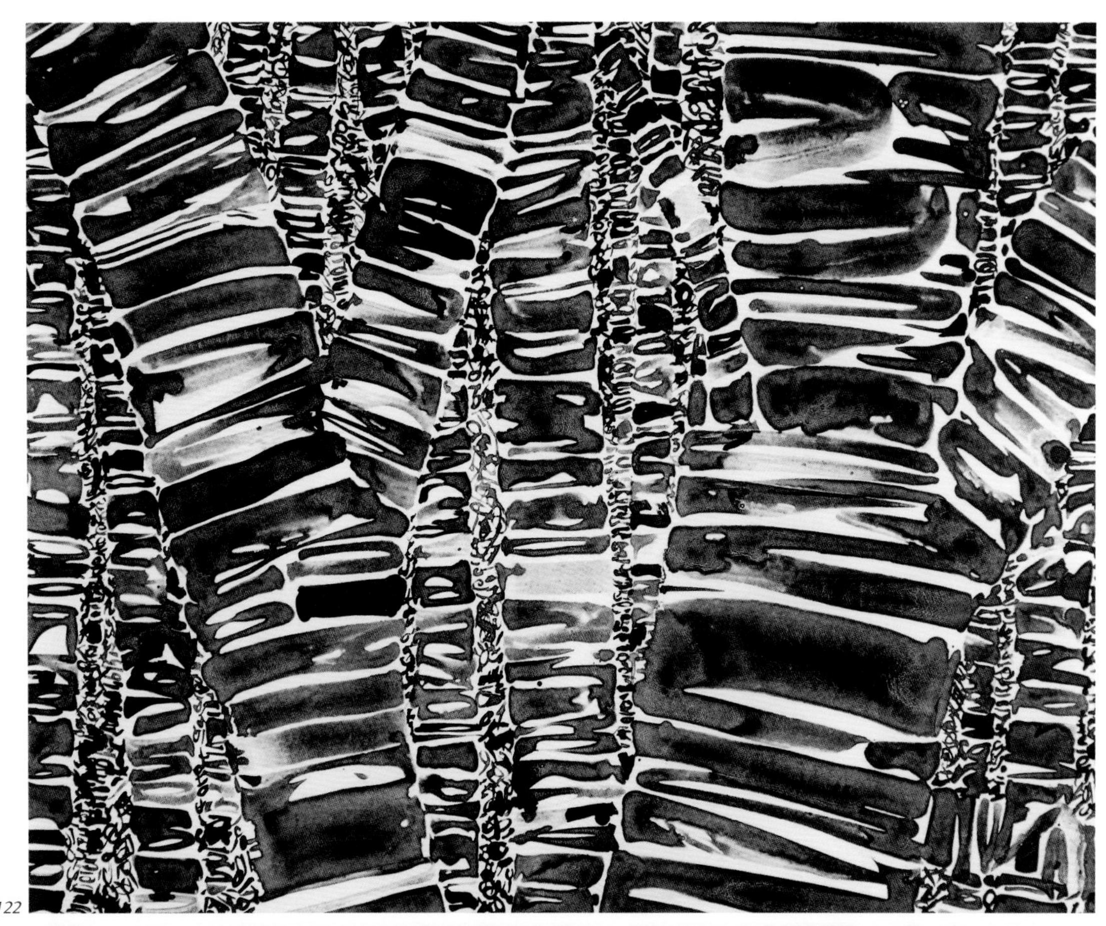
122

123

专文与访谈
ESSAY & INTERVIEW

托尼·克拉格：藉物之思

帕特里克·艾略特

"曾经所有的雕塑都试图模仿和抄袭自然的时代离我们并不遥远。在过去的一百年里，我们向前迈进了很大的一步，只是，在我眼中，我们仍只是站在起跑线上。"

这是建造于二十世纪二十年代，用来修理坦克的一个车库。约在十年前，这栋建筑被改造成现在的样子——一套宽敞的大型工作室。里面有七八个助手忙忙碌碌地雕刻、切割、钻孔、填充、打磨、粘合和抛光。有的助手身穿白色的紧身套装，戴着防尘的空气过滤器。至少有三件相当巨大的雕塑，大约三四米高，已经快要完成；还有一些尚在雏形阶段的作品，放在一边。储藏室里存放着材质各异的早些时候的作品，另外一些作品则正借展在外。克拉格的一场展览不久前刚在巴黎卢浮宫开幕，而他另一场在威尼斯Ca' Pesaro 的展览则刚刚结束；还有一场即将在提洛尔与观众见面，大约一个月之内，他还会有另一场展览在杜伊斯堡开展；夏末时分，美国达拉斯纳什尔雕塑中心会为他组织一场大型展览；而将在爱丁堡举行的展事也已经提上日程。托尼·克拉格是杜塞尔多夫艺术学院的终身院长；约瑟夫·博伊斯、杰拉德·里希特和白南准都曾在这所世界上最享盛名的重要艺术学院之一任教。他还在伍珀塔尔的树林中管理着一个占地三十英亩的雕塑公园：瓦尔德弗莱登雕塑公园。克拉格心中挂念颇多，但我们一起出去吃午饭的时候，他几乎不提及艺术或关于他自己的话题。相反，他谈论诗歌、人口增长、明星、语源学、政治以及人体用酶素分解食物的过程。对克拉格的性格、工作以及言行方式来说，这些都是必不可少的要素。一切都是潜在的灵感来源；任何新鲜的消息、词汇或视觉的东西，都能够让一件雕塑作品在他的头脑里萌芽和生长起来。

克拉格出生于利物浦，不过很快，他的家族就离开了这个城市。他早年的生活漂泊不定：父亲是一位电气工程师，设计航空业所需的零部件，因此，他们全家就随父亲工作地点的变化而不断迁徙。他在波尔顿、苏塞克斯、苏格兰的洛西茅斯以及约维尔都曾居住过一些时间。全家人一直到克拉格大约八岁的时候才安定下来，定居在韦林花园城。他被送去附近小海德海姆的一所寄宿学校就读（碰巧这个寄宿学校离大海德海姆的亨利·摩尔家非常近）。在父亲的鼓励下，克拉格1966年入读中赫特福德学院深造，在那里，他把大部分时间花在了为全国橡胶生产研究会的实验室里，做实验室的研究助理。他帮助一位教授试验了许多种类的橡胶，以期找到一种天然橡胶的抗氧化剂。克拉格是这样评价这些生物化学实验的："相当物质化和雕塑化"。回顾过去，这一切都像是克拉格走向雕塑家之路上的奠基石：创造、实验、把材料压缩或者拉长、观察其中种种要素的作用，并尝试找出原因。为了更好地理解实验，克拉格不厌其烦地用画笔描绘它们，直到点点滴滴积累起来，所绘之图的意义已经远远超过实验本身。克拉格感到绘画的过程令人兴奋，于是，他参加了学校里一个版画工作室的晚间课程。几个月之后，这个版画工作室给了他一份工作，于是借此机会，他离开了实验室。

1969年，克拉格开始在切尔滕纳姆的格罗斯特郡美术学院学习基础课程，这里离他父母在布里斯托尔的家不远，他的父亲在这个城市进行协和式飞机项目的工作。克拉格所学的属于一个传统的课程表，其中包含素描、油画、版画、瓷器与雕塑等课程。接下来的夏天里，他在耶茨值夜班，做金属液压铸造，加工引擎的配件。偶然的机会，他参与了一个物理活动，这给他带来极大的快乐：他要对付那些又大又笨重的工业原料，将它们从一种形式转化成另一种形式。第二年夏天他又在这里工作了一段时间。这段实验室工作的经验，可以从他后来做的雕塑中看到一些影子。

1970年秋，克拉格入读温布尔登艺术学院。他在这里所作的作品是对他之后的艺术创作的预见，尽管除了一些摄影记录之外，这些作品少有存留。1970年底，他在温布尔登的头几个月里做了一系列摄影作品《马铃薯头像》，构成

图1 《自然，本质》，2007 [局部]
Fig.1 *Nature, Nature*, 2007 [detail]

Tony Cragg: Thinking with material

Patrick Elliott

'It's not so long ago that all sculpture tried to imitate, to copy nature. We've come a long way in the last hundred years, but in my view we're still right at the beginning.'

It was built in the 1920s as a garage for mending tanks. Converted about ten years ago, the building is now a vast suite of studios. In it, seven or eight assistants are busy carving, cutting, drilling, filing, sanding, gluing and polishing. Some of the assistants are dressed in white body suits, with integrated air filters to keep out the dust. At least three very big sculptures, three or four metres tall, are nearing completion while others, which are at an earlier stage of production, are kept aside. Storage rooms contain earlier pieces in various different materials, and other works are out on loan. An exhibition of Cragg's work has just opened at the Louvre in Paris, another has just closed at the Ca'Pesaro in Venice, another is about to open in the Tyrol and another will open in Duisburg in a month or so; there is a major show to be organised for the Nasher Sculpture Centre in Dallas in late summer; and the Edinburgh show is forthcoming. Tony Cragg is director of one of the world's great art academies, the Kunstakedemie in Düsseldorf, where Joseph Beuys, Gerhard Richter and Nam June Paik taught, and administrative duties are constant. He also runs a thirty-acre sculpture park set in a forest in Wuppertal: the Skulpturenpark Waldfrieden. Cragg has plenty on his mind, but when we go out for lunch, he scarcely mentions art or himself. Instead, he talks about poetry, population growth, the stars, etymology, politics and the processes by which the body breaks food down using enzymes. This is all integral to Cragg's personality, work and modus operandi. Everything is a potential source of inspiration; any new bit of information, verbal or visual, could help a sculpture germinate and grow inside his head.

Cragg was born in Liverpool but his family moved away almost immediately. His early life was peripatetic: his father was an electrical engineer, designing components for the aircraft industry and the family moved according to his changing place of work. There were periods living in Bolton, Sussex, Lossiemouth in Scotland, and Yeovil. Stability came when the family settled in Welwyn Garden City, when Cragg was about eight years old. He was sent to a nearby boarding school at Little Hadham (coincidentally very close to Henry Moore's home at Much Hadham). Encouraged by his father, in 1966 he enrolled at the Mid-Hertfordshire College of Further Education where he spent most of his time working in a laboratory as a research assistant for the National Rubber Producers' Research Association. There he helped a professor test different kinds of rubber in the quest to find an antioxidant for natural rubber. Cragg describes these bio-chemical experiments as 'quite physical and sculptural'. In retrospect, this all looks like the bedrock on which Cragg's work as a sculptor developed: creating, testing, pushing and pulling materials, seeing what each one did, and trying to figure out why. In order to better understand the experiments, Cragg took to drawing them, until bit by bit the drawings assumed greater significance than the experiments themselves. Excited by the process of drawing, Cragg joined an evening course at a printmaking workshop on the same College campus. Some months later he was offered a job at the workshop, at which point he left the laboratory.

In 1969 Cragg started a Foundation Course at Gloucestershire College of Art in Cheltenham, near to his parents' home in Bristol where his father was working on the Concorde project. He carried out a traditional syllabus of drawing, painting, printmaking, ceramics and sculpture. The following summer he worked nightshifts at the Yates metal stamping foundry, which manufactured components for engines. By chance, he had stumbled upon a physical activity that gave him immense pleasure: working with big, heavy, industrial materials and transforming one form of material into another.

拍摄对象的形式很有限——塑料的鼻子，眼睛，耳朵，嘴巴——艺术家把它们按照某种数列规律添加在马铃薯上，制造成一个个很特别的脑袋。它借用了勒维特（Sol Le Witt）所用的一种观念艺术的方法，有形式主义与极简主义的意味。艺术家把每一个脑袋用黑白摄影拍摄下来，手工给它们上色。顺便说一句，这也是克拉格第一件使用塑料作为材料的作品。1971年春天，学生们到西萨塞克斯郡的柯林平海滩远足，再结合1971年创作的《沙滩发现物品集锦，柯林平海滩》（图2），克拉格萌生出检查、梳理和呈现更进一步的阶段的念头，他要找到、整理这些东西——包括一个薯条包装盒、一些贝壳、一些电线、一把海藻——将它们分类放入用粉笔画的网格里。这是他的第一件户外作品，现在看来，这便是他二十世纪七十年代晚期所作的塑料材质系列作品的鼻祖。

尽管克拉格是在油画系（他曾经试图申请转入雕塑系，但被拒绝了），但他在温布尔登创作的作品都是雕塑作品。他的导师有吉姆·罗格斯（Jim Rogers）和罗格斯·艾克苓（Roger Ackling），后者是不久前刚从圣马丁艺术学院毕业的，仅仅比克拉格本人年长几岁。克拉格1971年七月曾经到艾克苓父母位于怀特岛的邦彻奇（Bonchurch）的酒店工作，在那里，他创作了一大批作品，也都指向了他后来创作的方向。这些作品都是昙花一现，存在时间很短，不过，都用照片的形式记录了下来，里面有他在海滩上捡到的天然或人造物件，艺术家把它们排成行，标记着沙滩。1972年夏天它们回到邦彻奇的时候，艾克苓也拍摄了克拉格做这些海滩“行为艺术”的创作（图3）。

在圣马丁艺术学院的时候，艾克苓与理查德·朗和巴里·弗拉纳根（Barry Flanagan）是同代人，正是通过艾克苓，克拉格在1971年九月见到了朗（Long）。他们成为朋友，一起参与行走艺术。克拉格乐于承认：不论在观念的视角、过程推进的方法还是在用诸如石头一类天然材料表现人类的在场的形式上，朗当时对他的艺术创作都颇有影响。和艾克苓一样，朗对时间性的艺术，诸如行走、寻找、整理以及表现很感兴趣。克拉格采用了一种质疑式的、准科学的方法来整理物件——包括将其归入家族类型——他把对象打包在一起，使用了更为广泛、更不明确的一系列材料，其中包括塑料（图4）。常有人评论说，克拉格这一时期的作品就像是朗的浪漫主义风景作品的城市版本，把石头和小树枝变成了建筑的小碎片。对克拉格来说，从在山水之间进行创作到在一个工作室环境里展示这些物件，之间只是一小步。

这时候，温布尔登艺术学院的外聘教师开始谈论意大利的贫穷艺术，谈论马里奥·梅尔茨（Mario Merz）的作品和朱塞佩·佩娜（Giuseppe Penone）。这种艺术所用的材料是基本的、“贫困的”材料，雕塑家对其改造极少，托尼·克拉格对此产生了浓厚的兴趣。这也是一种专属于欧洲的现象。六十年代末七十年代初，在英国的各大积极进取的艺术院校里发生着积极地转变，尤其是在圣马丁艺术学院，这种转变挑战着美国艺术的霸权地位（贾思博·约翰、罗伯特·劳申伯格、波普艺术），而追随拥戴当时兴起于欧洲的更为观念化的艺术风格。在波普艺术家曾经赞美消费文化的地方，贫穷艺术家则以一种更具有启发性的、更慎重的，也更具有政治批判性的方式来处理材料。由哈拉尔德·塞漫（Harald Szeemann）于1969年初在伯尔尼美术学院做的“当态度成为形式”展览是克拉格所尊崇的艺术的典范，这个展览后来又巡展至伦敦的当代艺术院。约瑟夫·博伊斯（Joseph Beuys）、卡尔·安德烈（Carl Andre）、伊娃·海塞（Eva Hesse）、乔凡尼·安塞尔莫（Giovani Anselmo）、、简尼斯·库耐利思（Jannis Kounellis）和约瑟夫·孔素思（Joseph Kosuth）等艺术家在这次展览中集体亮相。几乎在同一时段，约瑟夫·博伊斯在英国的名声越来越大。1972年，由于建筑工期的延误，泰特美术馆不得不迅速安排一些短期的当代艺术展览，其中之一就是博伊斯个展。克拉格参加了博伊斯1972年3月在怀特查佩尔美术馆做的一次“活动”，这个活动就是泰特美术馆这场个展的一部分。博伊斯成为反体制的英雄并不仅仅是因为他的艺术面貌，或是他对材料的非传统处理方式，还有一个原因是，当他在面对历史、科学、人智学、哲学、历史文化以及最重要的政治之时，

图.3 |《无题（石头的曲线）》，1972
Fig.3 | *Untitled (Stones Curved on My Body)*, 1972

图.4 |《无题》，1970
Fig.4 | *Untitled*, 1970

图 2 《沙滩发现物品集锦，柯林平海滩》, 1971
Fig.2 *Combination of Found Beach Objects, Climping*, 1971

He worked there again the following summer. As with the laboratory work, it can be seen that this experience is echoed in his later sculpture.

In the autumn of 1970 Cragg enrolled at Wimbledon College of Art. Much of the work he did there – little of which survives except in photographic record – is prescient of his later work. *Combinations of Potato Heads*, a photographic piece done in his first months at Wimbledon, late in 1970, was composed from a limited dictionary of forms – plastic nose, ears, eyes, mouth – each added to the potato in sequential permutations to create a different head. It borrows a conceptual approach used by Sol Le Witt for formalist, minimalist means. Each head was photographed in black and white and hand-tinted. This was, incidentally, Cragg's first work to incorporate plastic. In the spring of 1971, the students were taken on a trip to Climping in West Sussex. *In Combination of Found Beach Objects, Climping*, 1971 [fig.2], Cragg took the idea of examining, sorting and presenting a stage further, laying an assortment of found objects - including a crisp packet, some shells, a bit of wire, a handful of seaweed - in a chalked-out grid pattern. This, his first outdoor work, now looks like a direct forebear of the plastic floor pieces of the late 1970s.

Although officially in the painting department (he tried to move across to the sculpture department but was ejected), all Cragg's work at Wimbledon was sculptural. His tutors included Jim Rogers and Roger Ackling, the latter a recent graduate of St Martin's College of Art and only a couple of years older than Cragg himself. Cragg worked at Ackling's parents' hotel at Bonchurch on the Isle of Wight in July 1971, and produced a body of work which again points forward to the later work. These works, all of which were ephemeral but were recorded in photographs, included natural and man-made objects which he picked up on the beach, laid out in lines, marking the sand. Ackling also photographed Cragg doing some of these Land art 'performances' when they returned to Bonchurch in the summer of 1972 [fig.3].

Ackling had been a contemporary of Richard Long and Barry Flanagan at St Martin's, and it was through Ackling that Cragg met Long in September 1971. They became friends, participating on walks together. Cragg readily acknowledges the influence Long had on his work at the time, in terms of a conceptual outlook, a process-driven approach, and the use of natural materials such as stones as markers of human presence. Like Ackling, Long was interested in a time-based art centred on walking, finding, sorting and presenting. Cragg introduced an interrogatory, quasi-scientific approach, sorting objects – including into family types – and bagging them up together and also employing a broader and more ambiguous range of materials, including plastic [fig.4]. As has often been observed, Cragg's work of the period is like an urban equivalent of Long's Romantic, landscape-based work, exchanging stones and twigs for builders' debris. For Cragg, it was a short step from making work in the landscape to presenting objects on the floor in a studio setting.

Around this time, external tutors at Wimbledon College of Art began speaking of the Arte Povera movement in Italy, and the work of Mario Merz, and Giuseppe Penone. This was an art of basic, 'poor' materials that were only lightly reshaped by the sculptor's hand and as such it held great interest for Tony Cragg. It was also a specifically European phenomenon. There was a shift operating within progressive art schools in Britain in the late 1960s and early 1970s – particularly St Martin's – which challenged the hegemony of American art (Jasper Johns, Robert Rauschenberg, Pop art), and embraced the more conceptual type of work then emerging in Europe. Where the Pop artists had glorified consumer culture, the Arte Povera artists treated materials in a more suggestive, circumspect and politically-charged way. The kind of art Cragg admired was exemplified by the groundbreaking exhibition When Attitudes Become Form, organised by Harald Szeemann at the Kunthalle Bern early in 1969, and which travelled to the Institute of Contemporary Art in London. It included work by artists such as Joseph Beuys, Carl Andre, Eva Hesse, Giovani Anselmo, Jannis Kounellis and Joseph Kosuth. Around the same time, Joseph Beuys began to be heard of more and more in

所采取的知识分子立场。

1973年从温布尔登艺术学院毕业之后，克拉格进入皇家艺术学院研修雕塑专业硕士课程。导师中有伯纳德·梅多斯（Bernard Meadows）、肯尼斯·阿米蒂奇（Kenneth Armitage）、卡尔·普莱柯曼（Carl Plackman）、理查德·温特沃斯（Richard Wentworth）和保罗·内亚古（Paul Neagu）等艺术家。在皇家艺术学院，克拉格对极简主义雕塑兴趣更加浓厚，不过，他并不想成为一名极简主义的艺术家。在克拉格全部作品的演进中，我们可以看到在极简主义方法之下他所创作的两类作品占据相当重要的分量：一个是大立方形式的《垛》，始于1975年；还有一系列置于地面的人造物品碎片堆。《垛》是由他在一年多的时间里收集来放在工作室里的人造和自然物品组成的，包括：石头，木料，书籍，盒子，杂志还有各种各样的垃圾。一层层小心地堆积起来，看上去就像地质层，它们将脏乱的城市现实以唐纳德·贾德和卡尔·安德烈式的冷酷而形式化的极简主义融在一起（图5）。从规模，数量和质量上来说，这也是一个新的发展。比如1976年的《四个盘子》这件作品，里面的四个盘子逐渐变得越来越碎，表现出一场部分与整体之间的对话（图6）。原本还有第五个盘子，散布在伦敦周围，不过也是以同样精确地圆形——这也是他对城市窗框的兴趣的一种预示。《四个盘子》与《垛》两件作品都属于家庭类型，这是克拉格几十年来的创作的一个特征；两者也都显示了他对于所找到的大量生产原材料的一种发明与调查的态度；另外，这两件作品都体现出克拉格对贯穿其作品始终的一个问题的发明式的解决方法，这个问题就是对象（例如一个盘子）、图像（一个圆形板）和材料（瓷）之间的关系。克拉格的作品始终如一地探索这三样相关东西之间紧密而又时常暧昧的关系。1975年，克拉格在位于阿克斯布里奇的布鲁内尔大学图书馆一个群展中展出了几件地面作品。1967年在伦敦创立Lisson画廊的尼古拉斯·罗格斯达尔（Nicholas Logsdail）看了这个展览之后联系了克拉格。1977年，克拉格开始在里森画廊做展览，同一年，他卖掉了一件雕塑作品，是四块石头中的一块，收藏者是南安普顿美术馆。

1977年，克拉格与乌特·莱恩结婚（之前的一年里他们一起住在法国的梅斯，他在那里的美术学院教了几个月的书）。由于女方的教学考试要求，莱恩在德国待了一年，借此机会，1977年的八月，她把克拉格带回了家乡伍珀塔尔城，这时，克拉格刚刚从皇家艺术学院毕业不久。克拉格在莱恩叔叔的木工作坊上建立了自己的第一个工作室。这一原本是临时举措的迁移导致了他艺术创作中另一改变的发生。他对于木头、砖、大地和瓷这样一些天然材料的偏好被鲜亮多彩的塑料给取代了——瓶子、球、玩具、盖子、包装袋和容器——他在莱茵河畔找到了这些被河水冲洗地干干净净的东西。更早些时候的作品里，克拉格也曾用过塑料，但一般与其他材料一起使用。不过在伍珀塔尔，这些材料成为他艺术实践的核心。

塑料在我们的文化中既是一种产品，也是一种症状。它曾经并且直到今天都被消极地视为廉价的劣质产品，不受待见，俗气，与艺术大相径庭。然而，尽管塑料制品被大量生产且无处不在，不知为何，却又有些陌生感。雕塑家很少对塑料产生兴趣。诺姆·伽勃（Naum Gabo）是个特例；他最早使用透明的醋酸纤维产品和树脂玻璃进行创作，对它们进行重塑和创造。尽管波普艺术家也曾集中表现日常所用的包装袋，塑料在当时的雕塑中仍然没什么代表性：你能够在阿尔曼、丹尼尔·施珀里、博伊尔家族、尼基·圣菲勒和克拉斯·奥尔登贝格的作品中看到塑料材料的存在，但它从来就不是主角。考古学家们对青铜器时代的盆盆罐罐感到惊叹，用它们虚拟建造出创造和使用这些器物的人的图像；而克拉格以一种平行的方式，用他找到的塑料瓶子和杯子进行建造图像。塑料与历史、与文化立场或者符号的关系甚少，因此，克拉格着手为其创造出一种新的视觉神话。克拉格在伍珀塔尔创作的第一批作品中有一系列光谱雕塑，由一些塑料物件构成，这些塑料制品里有微小的碎片，也有尺寸较大而未破碎的东西，它们被按照光谱里面渐变的颜色归类分开，整整齐齐地在地上摆放成长方形。其中第一个让克拉格想起了伊萨克·牛顿发现的白光

图.5 |《垛》, 1976
Fig.5 | *Stack*, 1976

图.6 |《四个盘子》1976
Fig.6 | *Four Plates*, 1976

Britain. In 1972, delayed building work forced the Tate Gallery to quickly arrange some short contemporary exhibitions, one of which was a Beuys show. Cragg attended an 'action' Beuys gave at the Whitechapel Art Gallery in March 1972, as part of the Tate project. Beuys became an anti-establishment hero not just for the way his art looked, or for his unorthodox approach to materials, but also for the intellectual stance he took on history, science, anthroposophy, philosophy, historical culture and above all politics.

After graduating from Wimbledon College of Art in 1973, Cragg enrolled on the postgraduate MA course in sculpture at the Royal College of Art. Bernard Meadows, Kenneth Armitage, Carl Plackman, Richard Wentworth and Paul Neagu were among the tutors. At the Royal College, Cragg became more interested in Minimalist sculpture, without wanting to become a Minimalist. This approach led to two original types of work which are central to the evolution of Cragg's whole oeuvre: the big cubic *Stacks*, begun in 1975; and a series of floor-based accumulations of fragmentary man-made objects. The *Stacks* were composed of the man-made and natural stuff that had accumulated in his studio over a period of more than a year: stones, wood, books, boxes, magazines and assorted waste. Carefully piled up in layers that looked like geological strata, they melded messy urban reality with cool, formal minimalism of Donald Judd and Carl Andre [fig.5]. This was also a new development in terms of scale, volume and mass. Works such as *Four Plates*, 1976, in which four plates are progressively more and more fragmented, involve a dialogue between the fragment and the whole [fig.6]. There was originally a fifth plate, scattered around London, but still in the same, precise circular pattern – a harbinger of his interest in urban situations. Both works, *Four Plates* and the *Stacks*, belonged to family types – a feature of Cragg's work over the decades; both displayed an inventive, investigative attitude towards found mass-produced raw materials; and both displayed a peculiarly inventive approach to an issue that runs like a thread through Cragg's work: the relationship between the object (such as a piece of a plate), the image (a circular plate) and the material (ceramic). Cragg's work has consistently mined the close but sometimes ambiguous relationship between these three related things. In 1975 Cragg showed several floor-based works in a group show at Brunel University Library in Uxbridge. Nicholas Logsdail, who had established the Lisson Gallery in London in 1967, saw the exhibition and contacted Cragg. In 1977 Cragg began exhibiting at the Lisson Gallery and that same year he sold a sculpture, One Stone in Four, to Southampton Art Gallery.

In 1977 Cragg married Ute Uberste-Lehn (they had lived together the previous year in Metz, in France, where he spent several months teaching at the Ecole des Beaux-Arts). Her teaching exams required her to spend a year in Germany, and this is what took Cragg to her home town of Wuppertal in August 1977, shortly after graduating from the Royal College. Cragg established his first studio above her uncle's carpentry shop. The move, initially conceived as a temporary one, prompted another change in his work. His preference for natural materials, such as wood, bricks, earth and ceramics, gave way to brightly coloured plastic – bottles, balls, toys, lids, packaging and containers – which he found washed up along the banks of the River Rhine. Cragg had used plastic in earlier work, usually alongside other materials, but in Wuppertal it became central to his practice.

Plastic is simultaneously a product and a symptom of our culture. It was and still is viewed negatively, as something cheap (in both senses), unloved, tacky and the opposite of art. Mass produced and ubiquitous, it is, nevertheless, somehow unfamiliar. Sculptors have seldom shown much interest in plastic. Naum Gabo is the exception; he worked primarily in transparent cellulose acetate and Plexiglass which he shaped and reworked. Although Pop artists focussed on everyday packaging, plastic rarely features in the sculpture of the time: you can spot it in works by Arman, Daniel Spoerri, Boyle Family, Niki de Saint Phalle and Claes Oldenberg, but it rarely takes centre stage. Archaeologists marvel at Bronze Age pots, and use them to build an image of the people who

里隐藏的看得见的光谱，所以这件作品被命名为《新石：牛顿色调》(图7)，这是一个双关语，同时还暗示了他已经结束了做大地艺术的时代。克拉格1978年首次在巴黎展出这些光谱作品，次年又在Lisson画廊的个人展览上将其展示了出来。

像科学家一样的好奇心与奇思妙想是克拉格的创作和世界观的中心所在。正如他自己所说，它们是“巨大的储藏室的一部分，开启我们生命存在的过程与原因之门的钥匙就在其中”。他认为自然世界与人造世界之间没有什么区别，一个雕塑家对电（比如说电）的兴趣不应该亚于他对动物和树木的兴趣。他的包罗万象、好奇心十足的创作方法也同样体现在他所用的材料上，对他来说，局限于青铜和石头是没有任何意义的。为什么要控制你的视觉欲望呢？这也部分地揭示了他在材料和技术上非同寻常的处理方式。他不会有意识地去寻找一种新材料来做艺术创作；实际上，他是在不断地调查的过程中，一个又一个雕塑作品就自然地被创造出来，不同材料也不断地加入这一大混合之中，表现了不同的手段、不同的解决方法以及不同的视觉词汇和语言。

克拉格的作品可能看上去有些像卡尔·安德烈或理查德·朗创作的颇具讽刺意味的变体，但对于克拉格来说，讽刺并非他所想要表现的东西。正如安迪·沃霍尔否认自己的作品具有讽刺性的观点，说Brillo箱子与汤罐头构成了他的世界的现实一样，而克拉格的世界的现实，正是他对材料的使用。说到对塑料的兴趣，克拉格说：

“在我眼里，一块材料或者一个物品，都牵扯着相当多的信息。像木头这样的材料本身已经包含着很多信息。而我们工业社会里的东西所包含的信息就很少，因此，即使像塑料这样的可以被用作材料的物品，仍然很缺乏内涵。我们需要做大量工作才能真正为这种材料创造出一个神话来，这个神话必将高于、超越它原本实用的、功利的价值。”

塑料之中所包含的信息有一部分来自它的人造性与实用性，以及因为实用性而拥有的能够体现其使用者特点的特性。普通塑料制品是我们及我们的生活中某一类别的隐喻。克拉格有时非常平实地把这种隐喻表现出来，他让人注意到，许多塑料瓶子，以其颈、肩和身体的造型惊人地拟仿了人类。克拉格的雕塑作品中有许多零件保持了原装，很容易识别——瓶子、把手、纽扣、盖子；这是我们曾经推拉、提起、打开和按下的东西——还有其他的一些零件，则是破裂的碎片，颇有神秘感。克拉格几乎是一团团地将其摆出来，仿佛是要让人检阅这样一种对我们生活和文化的仪式化解说。或者如他自己所述，所有的人造物都是“我们自身的延伸，点点滴滴都围绕自己而建造”。有人说克拉格对消费社会的残羹剩饭感兴趣是出于环保的、“绿色”的缘故，但其实并非如此；作为一个对科学有浓厚兴趣的艺术家，克拉格天生就有一种不受传统制约的好奇心：“我对垃圾从来就不感兴趣；这个字眼过于宽泛，使用它是一种不负责任的行为。如果我们不再使用垃圾这个词儿，我们就能看到它原来包含那么多各种各样的材料，这样，我们才可能将它们区别对待。”

图.7 |《新石：牛顿色调》, 1977
Fig.7 | *New Tones: Newton's Tones*, 1977

一个偶然的机会，克拉格得到杜塞尔多夫艺术学院的一份工作，开车到伍珀塔尔只要三十分钟。他从1979年初开始在这里工作，最初每周只教上几个小时的课。杜塞尔多夫艺术学院的教师阵容和学生们都相当强大，有许多人是誉满天下的名人。约瑟夫·博伊斯被禁止教学，但他仍旧经常出没在学院里；伯纳德·贝克(Bernd Becher)、杰拉德·里希特、白南准和古特·乌克(Günther Uecker)都是这个学院的教师。已经成为父亲的现实和这里的教学岗位让克拉格想要回到英国的愿望再也无法实现了。他1988年成为杜塞尔多夫艺术学院的教授，2009年荣任院长。

1979年在柏林的一次展览中，克拉格用塑料碎片创作了第一件具象的作品。这件题为《红色皮肤》的作品是一个跳舞的印第安红人，是由几百篇红色塑料小心翼翼地摆在地上呈现出来的(图8)。形式上模仿了一个印第安红人的塑料玩具，这个玩具是克拉格找到并保存的大量塑料制品中的一个。如莱恩·库克(Lynne Cooke)所言，这一向着具象化的变化是克拉格作品发展趋势的一部分，也是20世纪七十年代后半期里，与他同时代的诸如伍德罗和迪肯等

made and used them; Cragg works in a parallel way with found plastic bottles and cups. Plastic has little in the way of history, cultural standing or symbolism, so Cragg set about creating a new visual mythology for it. Among the first works Cragg made in Wuppertal were the Spectrum sculptures, in which the pieces of plastic, some of them tiny fragments and some quite big and unbroken, were separated into the graduating colours of the spectrum and laid out in neat rectangles on the ground. The first of them reminded Cragg of Isaac Newton's discovery of the visible spectrum contained within white light, hence the title *New Stones: Newton's Tones* [fig.7], a pun which referred to his move away from Land art. Cragg first exhibited the Spectrum works in Paris in 1978 and the following year at his solo show at the Lisson Gallery.

A scientist's sense of curiosity and wonder lies at the heart of Cragg's work and world view. For him, all mass-produced, functional objects and materials are vital ingredients of the natural world. They are, as he puts it, 'part of the huge storeroom [in which] lie the keys to essential processes and explanations of our existence'. He sees no distinction between the natural world and the man-made world, remarking that a sculptor should be just as interested in electricity (for example), as in animals or trees. The same inclusive, inquisitive approach extends to the material he uses: the idea of restricting himself to bronze and stone makes no sense to him. Why limit your visual diet? This partly explains his extraordinary approach to materials and techniques. He does not consciously look for a new material and make art out of it; rather he is involved in a continual process of investigation in which one sculpture leads to another and different materials get thrown into the mix and suggest different avenues, different solutions, different visual vocabularies and languages.

图 .8 | 《北美印地安人》, 1979
Fig.8 | *Redskin*, 1979

图 .9 | 《五个瓶子》, 1982
Fig.9 | *Five Bottles*, 1982

Cragg's works might appear to be ironic variants of the work of Carl Andre or Richard Long, but irony is the last thing on Cragg's mind. Just as Warhol rejected the idea that his works were ironic and said that Brillo boxes and soup cans constituted the reality of his world, so this is also true of Cragg's use of materials. Speaking of his interest in plastic Cragg observes:

I see a material or an object as having a balloon of information around it. Materials like wood already have a very occupied balloon. The objects of our industrial society as yet have very little information attached to them, so even if something like plastic can be accepted as a valid material for use, it still remains very unoccupied. There is a lot of work to be done to actually make a mythology for this material, over and above its extremely practical and utilitarian value.

The 'balloon' that hovers around plastic partly concerns the fact that it is man-made and functional and that it therefore in some way embodies the user. Ordinary plastic objects are metaphors of a sort for us and our lives. Cragg has sometimes made that embodiment literal, calling attention to the surprisingly anthropomorphic nature of many plastic bottles, with their necks, shoulders and bodies. Many of the component pieces in Cragg's sculptures are readily identifiable and archetypal – bottles, handles, buttons, lids: things we push, lift, open and press - while others are enigmatic, broken fragments. Cragg lays them out in almost regimental form, as if for inspection, as some kind of ritualistic commentary on our lives and culture. Or as he puts it, all artefacts are 'extensions of ourselves, bits and pieces we build on around ourselves'. It is sometimes said that Cragg is interested in the leftovers of consumer society for environmental, 'Green' reasons, but that is not really so; as someone with a keen interest in science, Cragg has a natural curiosity which is not circumscribed by tradition: 'I have never been interested in rubbish; it is a generic term and it is so irresponsible to use it. When we stop using the term we see how many different materials it is made of and then we probably deal with them differently.'

Through a chance acquaintance, Cragg was offered a job at the celebrated Kunstakademie in Düsseldorf, just thirty minutes' drive from Wuppertal. He started early in 1979, initially teaching for just a few hours a week. The Kunstakademie had a legendary teaching staff and student body. Joseph Beuys was banned from teaching, but still appeared there regularly;

人的发展趋势。当时有人觉得，极简主义与形式主义的艺术已经成为唯我论的东西，而一些叙事的或符号的题材与内容，应当代城市生活的需要，可以与一种极简主义的视觉语言共享空间。克拉格的方法依靠隐喻，但他的隐喻是简略而模糊的，在这种隐喻里，塑料物品以一种丰富而引人注目的哲学方式再现了当代生活。克拉格开始制作一系列挂在墙上的作品，这些作品都是极富挑战性的具象主题:《一个牛仔》、《米开朗基罗的大卫》、《自画像》，旁边放一幅英国地图,《从北边看英国》。通过这些作品，他在他所用的物品（瓶子、玩具、勺子与容器的碎片）、材料（塑料）与他以这些东西所创造的画面之间，发起了一场开放性的、甚至可能冲突性的对话。做成瓶子的塑料现在变成了牛仔。

符号学和结构主义的学生或许就此引发关于符号，关于“能指”与“所指”的讨论，或者用索绪尔的“语言”与“言语”去探讨克拉格的作品，但认知语言学并非克拉格的真实深意，他谨慎地将问题与答案折叠在一起，制造出视觉上相当具有挑衅性的东西来。他的工作方式可以追溯到毕加索，毕加索在创作立体主义的拼贴画时，会使用真实的墙纸来表现作品中的墙纸，但他更多时候是以一种反直觉的方式进行创作，例如，他用从报纸上剪切下来的字去表现瓶子或者酒杯。当这些字所谓同义词使用的时候，它更加是一种反义词，因为由此一来，画面语言就被锁定在它与自身所表现的东西之间的斗争中了。若要继续追溯历史上与克拉格的创作平行的艺术，玛格丽特式的荒诞在克拉格的作品中也不少见。他的一些雕塑似乎是要表述时下的表现哲学，例如他那些在墙上摆出的巨大的、象征性的塑料瓶形状的作品——这些作品用一些塑料碎块摆放组成的，其中一些碎块本身就是塑料瓶（图9）。由于所藉视觉语言是从极简主义发展而来，它们看上去既形式化，又充满隐含的内容，意义难以捉摸。一眼望去，首先抓住视线的也许是那个放在洒水壶旁边的塑料枪，尽管他布局和摆放这些碎片多是出于直觉而迅速完成的。在寻找这些物品的时候，他并没有设定任何道德准则之类的东西：其中有一些是从商店购买的。克拉格1980年在布里斯托尔的阿尔诺菲尼画廊和1981年在伦敦的怀特查佩尔画廊的几个早期重要展览中，展出了包括这些在内的一些作品。此时，包括比尔·伍德罗、理查德·迪肯、格姆雷、弗拉纳什、温特沃斯、安尼诗·卡普尔、埃里森·威尔丁以及西拉泽·何塞利等艺术家的作品在内的所谓“新英国雕塑”艺术开始在国际上赢得广泛声誉。所有这些艺术家都曾为行为艺术、装置艺术、大地艺术以及观念艺术所打动，但到了1980年左右，他们都从这些创作方法中跳了出来，迷恋上了用已有的、人造的材料创作自成体系甚至常让人感到不可思议的作品。从其立体性与手工性，以及经常有具象性等特点来讲，这种新的艺术创作定然是“雕塑”无疑。曾有人说，克拉格的创作反映出欧洲的艺术，特别是德国，在这一时期，被彭克(A.R. Penck)、约尔格·伊门多夫（Jörg Immendorff）和鲁培兹（Markus Lüpertz）等艺术家“回归了具象”，但事实上，克拉格的具象——构成其作品的各个部分如此慎重地结构和如此断然地“真实”——更准确地说，是对这种“表现主义”的讽刺甚至是批判。尽管很少被提及，但实际上克拉格的作品中是有一种强大的“反抗”态势的。他对塑料的使用可以说是一种反大地艺术；他的城市垃圾立方堆是一种反极简主义；而他的严谨的看上去如同马赛克图案一样的具象作品，则是反表现主义的。

图.10 | 《Kahzernarbeit》, 1985
Fig.10 | *Kahzernarbeit*, 1985

克拉格的表现对象来自真实世界：一个皇冠、一面英国国旗、还有一个警察，这是1981年，查尔斯王子与戴安娜结婚的这一年，也是布莱克斯顿暴乱的一年。这些作品出自一个身在异国的英国人之手，由无数个塑料碎片构成；它们指涉当代的文化与政治问题，但从创作手法来说，与早期的作品并无太大差异（它是当时的现实：到处都是警察，并且，他的确在人行道上发现了一顶塑料的皇冠）。20世纪八十年代早期，克拉格不仅仅用塑料进行创作，他也使用木材、仿木料以及木板进行创作，有时候部分地施以颜色。这一切表现出1982年左右他在艺术实践上的部分变化，他不再（或说不再仅仅）用找到的东西作为艺术创作的基本材料，而是回到工作室，聘用助手，从头开始制作和构

Bernd Becher, Gerhard Richter, Nam June Paik and Günther Uecker were on the staff. Fatherhood and the teaching position meant that Cragg's expected return to Britain never materialised. He became a professor at the Kunstakademie in 1988 and director in 2009.

In an exhibition in Berlin in 1979, Cragg made his first figurative work out of plastic fragments. A dancing Red Indian entitled *Redskin* (a play on words relating to the subject but also to the visible surface of the sculpture), it was composed of hundreds of pieces of red plastic carefully laid out on the floor [fig.8]. The form copied a plastic toy of a Red Indian that was among the large body of plastic objects Cragg had found and kept. As Lynne Cooke has observed, this move towards figuration was part of a growing tendency in the work of Cragg and his close contemporaries such as Woodrow and Deacon during the second half of the 1970s. There was a feeling that minimalist and formalist art had become solipsistic, and that some kind of narrative or symbolic subject matter and content, geared to contemporary urban life, could share space with a minimalist visual language. Cragg's approach relied on metaphor, but it was an elliptical, ambiguous sort of metaphor in which plastic items re-presented contemporary life in a rich and philosophically arresting way. Cragg embarked upon a series of wall-based works of defiantly figurative subjects: a *Cowboy*; *Michelangelo's David*; self-portraits; a map of Britain on its side, *Britain Seen from the North*. These works play on an open-ended and possibly conflicting dialogue between the objects he was using (fragments of bottles, toys, spoons and containers), the material (plastic), and the images into which he forms them. Plastic becomes a bottle becomes a cowboy.

Students of semiotics and structuralism might here embark upon a discourse about the sign, the signifier and the signified, or discuss Cragg's work in terms of Saussure's *'langue'* and *'parole'*, but cognitive linguistics is not really Cragg's thing and he deliberately folds the questions and answers into each other to produce something that is visually provocative. His way of working can be traced back to Picasso, who in his cubist collages sometimes used real wallpaper to represent wallpaper, but more often worked in a counter-intuitive way, using, for example, cut-out newspaper print to represent bottles or drinking glasses. It is about antonym as much as synonym, in that the pictorial language is locked in combat with the thing it is representing. To continue the parallels with the art of the past, there is more than a hint of Magritte's absurdity in Cragg's work. Some of his sculpture seems to address the philosophy of representation head on, for example, his giant, emblematic plastic bottles composed on the wall from an agglomeration of plastic objects, some of which are bottles themselves [fig.9]. Executed in a visual language that develops from minimalism, they are formal yet full of implicit content, and enigmatic in meaning. Scanning them, the eye might first be caught by a plastic gun placed next to a watering can, although his process of mapping and placing the fragments is largely intuitive and rapid. He has no moral code about finding the objects: some of them are bought from shops. Works such as these were shown at Cragg's first major exhibitions, at the Arnolfini Gallery in Bristol in 1980 and at the Whitechapel Art Gallery in London in 1981. By this date, 'New British Sculpture', as it became known – the work of Bill Woodrow, Richard Deacon, Antony Gormley, Flanagan, Wentworth, Anish Kapoor, Alison Wilding, Shirazeh Houshiary and others – was acquiring an international reputation. All these artists had been touched by Performance art, Installation art, Land art and Conceptual art but they had, by 1980, begun to turn away from these approaches in favour of making self-contained, often hermetic objects out of pre-existing, man-made materials. This new work was self-evidently 'sculpture' in that it was three-dimensional and crafted by hand, and it often had a figurative aspect. It has been said that Cragg's work mirrors the 'return to figuration' in European and particularly German art of the time, by artists such as A.R. Penck, Jörg Immendorff and Markus Lüpertz, but in fact, Cragg's figuration – so deliberately constructed and so emphatically 'real' in terms of its constituent parts – is more a riposte to or even critique of this kind of 'expressionism'. There is indeed a strong 'anti' current in Cragg's work

图.11 | 《臼与槌》, 1986
Fig.11 | *Mortar and Pestle*, 1986

造雕塑，尽管这些雕塑在题材或材料上，或者题材与材料两者上，仍多源自找到的物品的启发。一些在地面上展示的作品中使用了找来的非常大的立体素材，例如轻型建筑用砖、板条箱、椅子和桌子，这些物品按照尺寸和颜色摆放在一起。作品的雕塑性越来越强烈：其中一些显然是用工具制造出来的，而不再是所找到的物品的集结。各种系列作品按照这种从片断的形式到结构体的渐变逐渐进化，例如：以微小的塑料颗粒覆盖的矩阵；以钩子或旋钮覆盖的矩阵；棕色的塑料管道拐角连接在一起构造的作品（图10）。这种向立体的、雕塑化的形式的转变导致了1986年两件巨型雕塑的诞生，既《洗眼器》和《研钵与研杵》（图11），它们都是小的室内物品的放大版本：每一件都有近一米高，是用铁铸造的实心雕塑。这是他最早的铸造雕塑，它们预示了后来《早期形式》系列作品的诞生。克拉格承认，由于亨利·摩尔已经在巨型青铜雕塑方面享有声誉，对他自己而言，转向铸造雕塑作品的创作是一件很困难的事：“我知道，我要用青铜来做这件作品，但我花了将近一年的时间才鼓起勇气这么做；亨利·摩尔的作品像阴影一样压在我们头上，你会觉得‘我不想做那种东西。’”最终决定用铁而不是用青铜铸造这件作品也跟这种想法有一些关系，他宁愿与理查德·塞拉为伍，也不想步摩尔的后尘。

《早期形式》到目前为止是克拉格铸造作品里创作持续时间最长的系列，它演进为一整个系列扭曲和变异为其他形式的容器类系列作品。此系列的大标题指涉的是容器是人造物最早形式之一的这个事实，这种形式充满了人类的基本需求。《早期形式》系列作品中最早的一件是以化学烧瓶为基础制作的，然后，克拉格又开始引入其他类型，他常常故意将古代容器与试管、果酱瓶混为一起，更近一些时期的作品里还与去污剂瓶子等现代容器混在一起。他说：“《早期形式》系列作品总是与容器从一个时空到另一个时空的发展变异有关。容器是自然世界的主体和组织一个强烈的隐喻，而且，从考古学的角度来说，它们是我们衡量自己的文化与别人文化的途径。”1987年创作的《本能反应》现收藏于沃尔夫斯堡美术馆，它是由不锈钢铸造而成的，引入了“变形容器”这个母题——这个作品中使用了弯曲的试管——并且因此被作为《早期形式》系列的开山之作。它成为1987年克拉格在Hayward 画廊的个展中的代表作，同时展出的还有用玻璃、石膏、木头、砖、石头以及钢等材料创作的作品。克拉格是一位对所用材料、技术和方法都丰富地惊人的大师。1988年，他代表英国参加威尼斯双年展，同一年，他赢得了。

克拉格对化学容器的兴趣并不是在简单地提醒他曾经是一名实验室技术员的时光；而是指这样的容器在炼金术事业中的发展：类似于试图将普通金属变成金子以及找到一种包治百病的办法的原始科学。同样，克拉格尝试将塑料和青铜一类的材料转化为隐喻价值丰富的物品。克拉格的一系列蚀刻作品主要表现的是铸造的过程和将金属溶液转变为艺术的过程。炼金术中使用的早期容器的形式常常与自然中一些特别的形式相呼应，因为有一种信念是，一些特定的形式可以产生特别的反应。随着炼金术演化为现代的化学科学，容器也随之变化，变得更为理性，在造型上也更有几何感。克拉格研究了这两种类型，以及可能存在于两者之间的大量潜在类型，以期创造一种新的合成形式。克拉格作品中有很多都处于介乎已知的、已存在的形式“之间”的神秘领域。

泰特美术馆收藏的他1988年的作品《非洲大草原上》（图12），以其鲜明的、歪曲变形的容器形式而成为《早期形式》系列里面最早的成熟作品。正是克拉格想要将这些形从其原有的轴心弯曲和拉伸开来的欲望，使得他选择用青铜来铸造这件作品，因为非常复杂的形式没法用铁或钢来铸造的。青铜的熔点低于其他金属，能够完全成为液态，因此它是克拉格在这件作品里要处理的液态形状最为合适的媒介。这种变化与其说是一种审美上的考虑，不如说是技术要求所致。《非洲大草原上》的混合形制来自真实的容器，但克拉格更感兴趣的是尚未被创造出来的其他形式的无限可能。因此他近期作品多数采取两种或更多种真实的物品，并探索其中可能存在的大量中间形式。同样，《非洲大草原上》这一标题指的是我们所不知道的

图 .12 | 《非洲大草原上》, 1988, 泰特美术馆，伦敦
Fig.12 | *On the Savannah*, 1988, Tate, London

which is rarely noted. His use of plastic could be seen as anti-Land art; his cubes of urban waste as anti-Minimalist; and his precise, mosaic-like figurative work as anti-Expressionist.

Cragg's subjects were anchored in the real world: a Crown, a Union Jack and a Policeman, all date from 1981, the year of the royal wedding between Charles and Diana and the year of the Brixton riots. Made by an Englishman abroad and composed of a myriad of plastic fragments, they referred to contemporary cultural and political issues but in a way that was not so very different from earlier work (it was the reality of the time: policemen were everywhere and he actually found a plastic tiara on the pavement).

In the early 1980s Cragg was working not just in plastic but also in wood, simulated wood and board, sometimes partly painted. These indicated a partial shift in practice around 1982, away from (or rather in addition to) using found objects as the basic material of his work, and going back to the studio, employing an assistant, and making and constructing sculptures from scratch – though the sculptures were generally inspired by found objects in terms of subject or material, or both. Some of the floor-based works incorporated very large, found three-dimensional elements, such as breeze-blocks, crates, chairs and tables, arranged according to size as well as colour. The works became increasingly sculptural: some of them were clearly manufactured using tools instead of being assembled from found objects. Various series evolved out of this gradual shift from fragmented forms to structures, for example: forms covered with tiny plastic granules; forms covered with hooks or knobs; works constructed from the corner sections of brown plastic plumbing fitted together [fig.10]. This move into three-dimensional, sculptural forms led in 1986 to two large sculptures, *Eye Bath* and *Mortar and Pestle* [fig.11], both enlarged versions of small household objects: each stands nearly a metre tall and is cast in solid iron. These were his first cast sculptures and they anticipate the *Early Forms* series. Cragg acknowledged that it was difficult to take the plunge into casting owing to Henry Moore's reputation as the sculptor sine qua non of giant bronzes: 'I knew that I had to make it in bronze but it took almost a year to pluck up the courage; the Henry Moore legacy looms down on us and you think "I don't want to do that."' The decision to cast in iron rather than bronze was partly to do with that, a way of siding with Richard Serra rather than with Moore.

The *Early Forms* are by far Cragg's longest-running series of cast works, evolving into a whole taxonomy of vessel forms which twist and mutate into other forms. The group title refers to the fact that vessels are among the earliest surviving man-made forms, fulfilling basic human needs. The first of the *Early Forms* works are based on chemical flasks, and then Cragg introduced other types, often deliberately mixing ancient flasks with modern vessels such as test-tubes, jam jars or, more recently, detergent bottles. He remarks: 'works in the early forms group are always to do with vessels transforming and mutating into one another in space. Vessels are a strong metaphor for the body and organisms of the natural world and in addition, from the archaeological viewpoint, they are the means by which we gauge our own culture and other cultures.' *Instinctive Reactions*, 1987, now in the Kunstmuseum Wolfsburg, was cast in steel and introduces the motif of the mutating vessel – in this case the bent test-tube – and therefore stands at the start of the *Early Forms* series. It featured in Cragg's solo exhibition at the Hayward Gallery in 1987, alongside work in glass, plaster, wood, brick, stone and steel. Cragg emerged as the master of an astonishing range of different materials, techniques and approaches. In 1988 he represented Britain at the Venice Biennale, and that same year he also won the Turner Prize.

Cragg's interest in chemical vessels does not simply reference his time as a laboratory technician; instead it refers to the development of such vessels in the cause of alchemy – the proto-science which sought to turn base metals into gold and to find a cure for all ills. By the same token, Cragg seeks to transform materials such as plastic and bronze into objects of rich metaphorical value. A series of his etchings focuses on the process of casting, of turning

千万种已经灭绝的动物，以及它们可能在那些幸存至今的动物中间“填补空白”的形式。《早期形式》系列雕塑因此很少是一种形式像跳芭蕾舞一样地变化成另一种形式，而是对一些可能并不存在的新形式的创造。在走向经济化和大生产的路上，工业创造了形式有限的商品，忽视了那些无法满足经济或功能性要求的形式。克拉格要开拓的就是这些格式化的商品之间可能存在的形式的广阔领域。尽管第一眼看上去，克拉格这些年来的作品在风格与方法上都在变化，但实际上，在哲学的出发点上，他的作品都是统一的、有根据的。立体主义雕塑家雷蒙·杜尚－维隆(Raymond Duchamp-Villon)说“艺术的唯一目的既不是描绘也不是模仿，而是从始终存在但并不明显的元素出发，去创造未知之物。”这一观点也许与托尼·克拉格的并不尽然相同。

克拉格作品的特点要素之一是手工性。参观过他的工作室的艺术家朋友们无不惊讶地发现，他的作品仍然在使用石膏这一材料，用手工小心地打磨和抛光，然后经常又以类似罗丹所用过的那种手法相同的方式，切割、重做与重组它们。克拉格有很多助手(当然罗丹也一样有很多助手)，不过他们所执行的克拉格的要求和说明，用绘图传达的时候不会比口头传达的少。每天早上一到工作室的时候，以及这一整天里休息的间隙，克拉格都会去看一圈他们做了些什么，进行检查和修改。如果一件雕塑逐渐成型的时候，看上去不是他要的东西，他就会切割、改变、重新制作或将其废弃。在制造方面，《早期形式》系列作品是以两个或者更多的不同容器横截面的胶合板模板作为开端的；然后在这些东西的基础上用一种纯视觉的方式，用聚苯乙烯、石膏和高分子树脂(一种近似玻璃钢的树脂材料)连接在一起。上世纪八十年代，克拉格设计了一些雕塑作品，在工作室之外进行放大和制作(室外创作是很多当代雕塑的一个共同特点)，但结果他并不满意。他发现手工制作的过程是他所作一切的动力。这不仅是因为从雕塑的观点来说，他发现手工制作过程充满创造性和趣味，同时，在制造一件作品的过程中他能够找到下一个创作的灵感更为重要的原因。正因为如此，他的作品总是成为“族系”中的部分——《早期形式》、《分泌物》、《信封》系列；各种堆积作品，从堆在一起的金属片到不稳定的喷砂玻璃堆；覆盖有石墨商标网的容器形式；瓷；以及许许多多其他的作品皆属于这种族系。谈到他的作品演进的方式的时候，克拉格说：

“久而久之，作品中有了一些需要与其他的‘通道’区别开来的‘通道’。对我来说，保持在思想中区别对待它们是必须的，因此时不时的，无需强求，我的脑海里就会冒出一些标签来，分别表示出哪些是《早期形式》，哪些是《理性生物》。它们成为作品的‘类别’，于是我们由此弄清楚这些雕塑作品属于哪个特定的族系，又有哪些另外的族系，以及这些不同族系之间的关系等问题。并且，我觉得这是很自然的。首先，对我来说这样的分类很方便，其次，这可能就是世界在生物学上进化发展的方式：从简单的细胞，发展成为越来越复杂的、特别化的各种形式。”

《早期形式》系列中较早的作品多数在形制上比较巨大(因此在一个展览中呈现时，会相当夸张)，并且是摆放在地上的。容器形式采取直立状或躺倒在地上。正是在创作《早期形式》系列作品的过程中，“拉伸的孔”这个母题诞生了，描述了一个个容器之间相连的顶部开口，并观察了其中里面的空间。通过一系列的雕塑作品，这个孔变成了一个窄缝，通过这个窄缝，内部空间被瞥见或者暗示。这个窄缝，在狭窄的容器沿或沟槽的强调之下，成为《早期形式》雕塑的一个中心特点。它暗示雕塑本身的某种运动或变形，并且要求观众围着它转动，并体验它，而非仅仅站住不动看着它。此外，这也给了作品一种特定的性别暗示：像阴茎一样的试管形式立在深深地、阴暗的、肌肉发达的孔洞旁边。我们可以看到，由此一来，克拉格在他每一件作品中都设定了大量动态的想法和隐喻，但他又以雕塑的方式严格地控制和利用它们。在此观念之下，视觉语言不断地向前发展。

二十世纪九十年代，这些形式变得更加复杂，窄缝转化为几乎是巴洛克风格的、消极的、蛇一样的形式——青铜与塑料管作品相对应，如1985年的《Kahzernarbeit》(图13)——内

molten metal into art. The forms of early vessels used in alchemy often responded to specific forms in nature in the belief that certain forms might generate particular reactions. As alchemy evolved into modern chemical science, so vessels changed, becoming more rational and geometric in shape. Cragg investigates both types, as well as the myriad of potential types that might exist in between, to create a new synthetic form. Much of Cragg's oeuvre dwells upon this enigmatic area'in between' known, existing forms.

On the Savannah, 1988 [fig.12], in the Tate collection is, with its distinctive, warped, vessel forms, the first of the mature *Early Forms*. It was Cragg's desire to bend and pull the forms out of their axis that led him to cast this work in bronze, simply because very complex forms cannot be cast in iron or steel. Bronze melts at a lower temperature than these other metals, and becomes completely fluid, making it an appropriate medium for the fluid forms Cragg was now dealing with. The move was based on technical rather than aesthetic decisions. The hybrid forms in *On the Savannah* originate in real vessels, but Cragg is more interested in the vast range of forms that have not been created. Much of his recent work thus takes two or more real objects and investigates the vast range of potential forms that lie between them. The title '*On the Savannah*' likewise refers to the thousands of extinct animals that are unknown to us, and how their forms might 'fill the space' between those that have survived. The *Early Forms* sculptures are therefore not so much about one form balletically morphing into another, but about the creation of new forms that would otherwise not exist. In the drive towards economy and mass production, industry has created a limited range of formatted goods, and ignored all those forms which do not serve the purpose of economy or functionality. Cragg addresses the vast terrain of potential forms that lie between these formatted goods. If, at first glance, Cragg's work over the years seems to have shifted in style and approach, it is in fact united and grounded in this philosophical starting point. The cubist sculptor Raymond Duchamp-Villon declared that 'The sole purpose of the arts is neither description nor imitation, but the creation of unknown beings from elements which are always present but not apparent'. This statement might equally have been made by Tony Cragg.

One factor which characterises Cragg's work is that it is handmade. Artist friends who have visited his studio have been astonished to find that the work is still made in plaster, is carefully filed and polished by hand, and is often cut up, reworked and reconfigured in an approach that is basically the same as that used by Auguste Rodin. Cragg has a number of assistants (as of course did Rodin), but they carry out his specific instructions, which are transmitted through drawings as much as through speech. On arriving at the studio every morning, and at intervals throughout the day, Cragg will inspect what is being done, and check and correct. If, as a sculpture grows, it doesn't look right, he will cut, change, remake or scrap. In manufacturing terms, the *Early Forms* works begin as two or more plywood templates of the cross-sections of different vessels; these are then built upon and connected together, in a purely visual way, using polystyrene, plaster and jesmonite (a resin-based material similar to fibreglass). On a couple of occasions in the mid-1980s Cragg designed sculptures and had them enlarged and manufactured outside the studio (a common feature of much contemporary sculpture), but the results were not to his liking. He found that the process of making something by hand was the stimulus to everything he did. Not only did he find the hand-making process creative and most interesting from a sculptural point of view, but it was through making one work that he found inspiration for the next. It is because of this approach that his work has often formed itself into 'family groups' – the *Early Forms*; the *Secretions*; the *Envelope* series ; various types of stacked works, ranging from stacked metal discs to precarious assemblages of sandblasted glass; vessel forms covered in webs of graphite marks; ceramics; and many others. Commenting on the way his work has evolved, Cragg has stated:

Over time, there are passages in the work that need to be distinguished from one another.

外部相互转化，创造出非常自由的体积。这可以在一些作品，例如1997年的《早期形式圣加仑》中看到，这件作品中，扭曲如螺丝一般的形式看上去像在与自己角力，内里的面翻了出来。一种形式置于另一种形式的内部的观念，以及将内与外折叠在一起的观念，在《信封》这个系列的作品中得到了表现。在这些作品中，一个青铜的外壳被刺地满面是孔，使眼睛能够看到这件雕塑的内部结构，并且实际上直接看穿了它。还有另一个系列的作品，题为《有孔体》，它是由被钻了上千个孔的大石膏形体组成的，表现一个被钻孔的表面外壳；还有《分泌物》系列，表面上覆盖着成千上万个骰子；还有其他一些系列的作品，例如表面覆盖以钩子、门把手、颜料、或凸起的数字；或者是用高度抛光的反射着光芒的钢为材料制成的作品。这些都表明克拉格对事物表面以及对揭露其外壳下掩藏之物的迷恋。

克拉格创作于20世纪九十年代晚期的《早期形式》作品在形式上变得更加有机和灵活，到2000年左右发生了完全的改变，此时，他开始创作一组更加几何化的作品，表现出更有力量的内部结构，其中代表作品有《棒》、《康康舞》和《辛巴德》。新世纪最初几年，他的创作中又出现了一个新的维度：色彩。当然克拉格在上世纪70年代晚期和80年代早期的塑料作品中就已经探索过色彩的问题，但要在青铜表面使用传统的黑色、棕色或绿锈颜色之外其他永久性颜色，防止划痕与破碎，是很有难度的。克拉格借用德国汽车工业的新式喷漆技术，创造出他自己令人惊叹的色彩作品来，这些作品至今在伍珀塔尔地区仍然颇有影响力。这些色彩作品中最早的一件是2000年创作的《辛巴德》。在他更晚一些时候的作品里，克拉格还结合了大量普通容器的形式。举个例子来说，其中一件2006年创作的《卸马具》，是用另外两种容器将一个有螺纹的油桶一端变形，做出洗发水瓶子的形状来的一个作品。这件作品的标题或许看上去很是神秘，但它们多来自克拉格的生活。比如漆为蓝色的青铜作品《麦科马克》是根据艺术家的主要助手约翰·麦科马克命名的，而《路加》则来自《旧约全书》，不过实际上这是麦科马克儿子的名字。近年来《早期形式》系列雕塑作品中的另一演变是它们离开地面，走向高处，如《赤纬》这件巨大的，重达两吨半的漆为黄色的青铜雕塑（这一标题来自与太阳相关的一个天文术语），就灵巧地三足站立着。

克拉格始终如一地同时进行几个显然毫不相干的系列作品的创作。在继续《早期形式》系列的创作的同时，他还在推进《理性生物》系列，这也是他在过去的十年多的时间里工作的重要部分，可以追溯到上世纪九十年代的中期。《理性生物》系列作品是以高大的圆筒形作品为典型的，当观众围着它们走动的时候，面部轮廓时而出现，时而消失。这个系列的源头可以追溯到1990年的《大教堂》，这件作品包含四件垂直圆柱状的物品堆，堆积这几个圆柱的物品是一些找来的圆柱状的东西。这件作品有许多变化，但每一件都是物品层层堆积，且完全只依靠地心引力保持它们垂直于地面的状态。物理规律决定了这些作品的外观，它们必须百分之百地保持垂直一线，并且由下往上的尺寸必须依次变小，否则就容易倒塌。为了拓展这一族系的作品，克拉格开始在一个固定的垂直中轴上堆积物，这样一来，自下往上依次增大而非变小的垂直作品也可以被实现。这种尝试的结果是创作除了诸如1988年的《废料》这样的作品：切好定型的圆形玻璃钢部件，一个堆积在另一个上面，制造出新式的、有机的、雕塑化的形式来。玻璃钢的圆圈作为制造过程的一部分，仍然清晰可见，起到结构元素的作用。而克拉格从这一点出发开拓的作品则不再是平面形式的堆积垒砌，而是一些充气的物品，平衡和压缩在一起的样子看上去摇摇欲坠，在整齐的垂直轴心上左右鼓出来：就是题为《脊柱》(Wirbelsäule)（这个作为作品标题的名词在德语里面是"脊椎"的意思，但也暗含"压缩之意"）的这些作品。这些采用椭圆形状而非正圆的作品后来引向了《理性生物》系列作品的诞生，后者有一些堆积垒砌在一起的椭圆形物品构成，但它们有着较为复杂的内部结构。

《理性生物》雕塑群的创作是从一些铅笔草稿开始的。克拉格画了大量的草图，并且通过这个过程，最终画出一幅表现一个立体形状

It becomes necessary for me to keep them apart in my mind, and so every now and again, without forcing it, a mental tag crops up in my mind, as indicated with *Early Forms* and *Rational Beings*. These become 'species' of work and so we get sculptures belonging to a certain family, and then there are other families, and then there are relationships between these families etc., and I think this has happened quite naturally. Firstly, it's convenient for me and, secondly, it's possibly the way the world just developed biologically anyway: from simple cells developing into more complicated, specialised forms.

The earlier works in the *Early Forms* series were generally large in scale (often human in size, and therefore quite theatrical when approached in an exhibition) and placed on the floor. The vessel forms stand upright or lie on the ground. It was through making the *Early Forms* works that the motif of the stretched hole appeared, describing the top of one vessel connecting with another, and giving a view of the internal space that was created in between. Through a sequence of sculptures, this hole became a narrow slit, through which the internal space is glimpsed or implied. This slit, emphasised by a narrow lip or groove, as often found on vessels, became a central feature of the *Early Forms* sculptures. It implies some kind of movement or metamorphosis in the sculpture itself, but also asks the viewer to move around the work and experience it, rather than simply stand still and look at it. Additionally, this has given the work a certain sexual charge, with phallic test-tube forms standing alongside deep, dark, muscular holes. We can see, then, that with each work Cragg sets a range of ideas and metaphors in motion, but controls and harnesses them through strictly sculptural means. The visual language develops in tandem with the idea.

During the 1990s the forms became more complex, with the slits forming almost Baroque, negative, snake-like forms – bronze counterparts to plastic pipe-works such as *Kahzernarbeit* of 1985 [fig.13] – and the insides and outsides turning into each other to create very open volumes. This can be seen, for example, in Early *Forms St Gallen*, 1997, in which the twisting, screw-like form seems to be wrestling with itself and turning inside-out. The idea of one form inside another, and of the folding together of inside and outside, found expression in the *Envelope* series. In these works, a bronze skin is pierced all over with holes, allowing the eye to see the internal structure of the sculpture, and indeed see right through it. There is another series, the *Forminifera* works which comprise big plaster forms drilled with thousands of holes to present a perforated surface skin; there is the *Secretions* series, in which the whole surface is covered with thousands of dice; and there are other series covered with hooks, doorknobs, coloured paint, embossed numbers, or made from highly polished, reflective steel – for example. These all testify to Cragg's fascination with the surface of things, and the role that surface performs in simultaneously revealing and hiding what lies beneath.

Cragg's *Early Forms* works of the late 1990s were increasingly organic and elastic in form, leading to a volte face around 2000, when he made a group of more geometric works, with more structured internal dynamics, such as *Rod*, *Can-Can* and *Sinbad*. In the early 2000s a further dimension was added: colour. Of course Cragg had exploited colour in his plastic works of the late 1970s and early 1980s but bronze presents problems in terms of permanently fixing a colour other than a traditional black, brown or green patina to a metal surface so that it will not scratch or chip. Cragg has produced his astonishing coloured works using new paint technology borrowed from the German car industry, which is still strong in the Wuppertal area. The earliest of these coloured works is *Sinbad*, 2000. In his more recent works, Cragg has also incorporated the forms of a broad range of ordinary vessels. A work such as *Outspan* 2006, for example, is based at one end on a ribbed oil can which transmutes via two other vessel shapes into a shampoo bottle. The titles of the works may appear enigmatic but are often grounded in Cragg's life. The blue-coloured bronze *McCormack* is, for example, titled after the artist's chief assistant, John *McCormack*, while *Luke* is not a reference to the *Old Testament*, but is actually the name

的前面与侧面的样子的图来。其中每一件雕塑都是用许多椭圆形的木头薄片构成，这些木片被切好之后一个个堆砌起来，制造出草图模型的三维版本。2006年，克拉格为都灵的冬季奥运会做了这样一件雕塑，在取得安全证书的过程中，他遇到一位工程师，这位工程师开始引导他使用数码和计算机技术。从那以后，克拉格开始使用电脑来协助自己的创作，尽管一开始他仍然用铅笔在纸上进行构思。他把计算机描述为“就像是在用一种工具，一个顺手的好工具，来完成我想要做的东西”。他先画出一件雕塑作品的轮廓，然后CAD 技术就能够准确计算堆砌所用的椭圆形物件。切割所有的部件仍然是纯手工的，而数字化的式样往往需要返工。克拉格用计算机技术制作的第一件作品是《数码皮肤》，这也是《早期形式》系列作品的其中一部分，不过它的外壳上覆满了凸起的二进制数字1和0（同一时期的素描和水彩画作品表现的也是同样的数字矩）。克拉格把计算机形容成是一个在制作作品方面很有用的工具，但认为它在做决定和确定形式上毫无用处。他仍然喜欢用铅笔画草稿，或者用粘土做泥模，并且他常说，雕塑是关于物的思考。

克拉格自2008年以来着手创作的最新的系列作品是《篱笆》系列。或许篱笆不太像是一个雕塑家的创作对象，但对于克拉格来说，它就是一种暗含力量的外壳，地下藏着某种活的东西——如同一片小小的树叶能够容纳成千上万的昆虫和动物。它既是障碍，也是避难所，它不完全是封闭的面，但要判断它的深度，内容和“生命的迹象”（在此借用他近期一个展览的题目），也并不容易。谈及篱笆的时候，克拉格说到米开朗基罗与罗丹。这或许乍听上去显得有些荒诞，但他的意思是，这两位雕塑家都对表面之下掩藏的生命及雕塑化的方式充满兴趣，罗丹那遍布指力之痕迹和令人印象深刻的表面，以及米开朗基罗肌肉发达的结构和将皮肤交待到令人骄傲的清晰的血管，皆可以表现出来他们对重新创造生命的兴趣。显然乏味而单调的篱笆实际上是一种复杂到让人难以置信的、灵活多变的形式，它有力地脉动着，提供着躲避农夫化学药剂的避难所。它是一种赠与生命的力量，是山水的静脉与动脉。这需要一位像克拉格这样的雕塑家去发现它。

图.13 | 《大教堂》，1990
Fig.13 | *Minster*, 1990

of McCormack's son. Another evolution in the *Early Forms* sculptures in recent years has been their elevation from the ground, as in *Declination*, a big, two-and-a-half ton yellow-painted bronze (the title derives from an astronomical term connected with the sun) which stands nimbly on three points.

Cragg invariably works on several apparently unrelated series at the same time. While the *Early Forms* series was in progress he was also developing the *Rational Beings* series, which has been a major component of his work in the past decade or so, and dates back to the mid-1990s. The *Rational Beings* works are, typically, characterised by tall columnar works in which facial profiles emerge and disappear as one walks around them. The origins of the series can be traced back to *Minster*, 1990, a sculpture of four stacked vertical columns composed of an assortment of found cylindrical objects. [fig.13] There were several variants of this work, but in each, the objects were stacked on top of each other with nothing else keeping them upright other than gravity. The laws of physics determined the appearance of these works, in that they had to be exactly vertical, and they had to feature objects of diminishing size, otherwise they might topple over. In an effort to extend this family type, Cragg began to stack forms on a fixed vertical axis and by doing so was able to produce works which enlarged vertically, rather than diminished. This in turn led to works in which circular fibreglass forms were cut out and fixed, one on top of each other, to produce new, organic, sculptural forms, as in *Flotsam*, 1998. The fibreglass circles which are part of the manufacturing process remain clearly visible and act as structuring elements. From this point, Cragg went on to develop works which were not stacked with even planar forms, but were composed from pneumatic forms which appeared precariously balanced and compressed so that they ballooned out to left and right of the neat vertical axis: the *Wirbelsäule* works (the name comes from the German for 'spine', but also alludes to 'compression'). Made out of elliptical forms rather than circular ones, these led to the *Rational Beings* works, which are composed of elliptical forms stacked on top of each other, but often on a complex internal structure.

The Rational Beings sculptures start out as pencil drawings. Cragg makes vast numbers of drawings and through this process eventually achieves a drawing showing the front and side views of a three-dimensional form. Each sculpture is constructed from dozens of elliptically-shaped pieces of laminated wood, cut and stacked on top of each other to achieve a three-dimensional equivalent of the drawn model. In 2006 Cragg produced such a sculpture for the Winter Olympic Games in Turin, and through the process of gaining a safety certificate met an engineer who introduced him to digital and computer technology. Since then Cragg has used computers to facilitate the manufacture of his works, although the starting point always remains pencil on paper. He describes the computer as 'really just like using a tool, an adequate tool, to make the thing I want to make'. He begins by making drawings of the profiles of a sculpture, which CAD (computer-aided design) technology can then calculate in terms of stacked elliptical forms. All the cutting of the forms remains a manual task, and the digitally-realised patterns are usually reworked. The first work Cragg made using computer technology was *Digital Skin*, which is part of the *Early Forms* series, but is covered with a skin embossed with binary 1 and 0 numbers (drawings and watercolours of the same period are composed of this same matrix, [fig.1]). Cragg describes the computer as a useful tool in terms of making a work, but useless in terms of making decisions or determining a form. He still prefers to draw with pencil or model in clay and he often repeats the idea that sculpture is about thinking with material.

Cragg's most recent series, underway since 2008, is the *Hedge* series. A hedge is perhaps an unlikely subject for a sculptor, but for Cragg it is a supreme example of an outer skin hiding something that is alive with energy underneath – a curtain of little leaves enclosing thousands of insects and animals. It is simultaneously barrier and haven, not exactly a closed surface, but difficult to judge in terms of depth, content and 'signs of life' (to borrow the title of one of his recent exhibitions). When he talks about hedges, Cragg speaks of Michelangelo and Rodin. The references might appear absurd at first, but his point is that both sculptors were interested in the life that lies beneath a surface and in using sculptural means – Rodin's fingered, impressionistic surface, Michelangelo's taught muscular structure and proud veins which articulate the skin – to recreate that life. The apparently dull, unglamorous hedge is in fact a fabulously complicated, flexible form that pulses with energy and provides a haven from the farmer's chemicals. It is a life-giving force, the veins and the arteries of the landscape. It takes a sculptor such as Cragg to see that.

条款和条件：托尼·克拉格访谈

乔恩·伍德

引言

“雕塑的未来才刚刚开始，其潜力之大前所未有，未来一切皆有可能。雕塑语言和形式才刚刚开始演变……”

你可能会听到艺术家TC·克拉格这样的叙述，无论是在演播室，还是在访谈中，抑或在讲座时、会议上、教室里，或者工作之余的小酌中。克拉格对雕塑一贯的尊奉和对当前雕塑地位及功能的复杂性的执着探索已经带给他在当代艺术圈子里耐人寻味而又不同寻常的地位。克拉格是一名仍旧制作独立雕塑的雕塑家，拒绝接受现成品及装置的主导统领。克拉格对材料和意义的结合，以及形式的内容抱有兴趣，他的观点是唯物主义的。同时他还是一位将全部想象都放在雕塑本体动态上的雕塑家，专注于表达本体动态的语言，以及着眼于今天如何讨论这个问题和明天如何设想它。他依然宣扬“雕塑”，在这样一个焦灼于媒介为基础的各种定义的时代。

那么今天作为一名“雕塑家”的真正意义何在？特别是在我们对雕塑的概念已经通过观众参与和互动模式，大胆地拓展到表演、摄影、电影和数字媒介的时候。今天，应该怎样去畅想和表达媒介的前景？甚至是材料的前景？在现代科技面前，雕塑家该怎样发扬雕塑在呈现并塑造科学理念方面的重要作用，而又让一切听起来不像是捍卫日益衰亡的传统？那些著文描述过雕塑的雕塑家经常会觉得面对现代化和科技日新月异的世界时，特别是现代化产品如此经常地直接对雕塑构成挑战时，应该说出他们的感觉，那就是雕塑与这一切都有关联。过去是一个雕塑主导的时代，但未来却不一定如此，雕塑家们认为有必要阐释：雕塑不仅仅和现代世界有关联，而且是与现代世界紧密契合的。当你聆听克拉格关于雕塑的访谈时，你会被他言语中不时流露的未来主义所震撼。同样值得注意的是，你还会从早先雕塑家的口中，不时听到和他相同的观点。

下面的文字可以用5个关键词来概括，揭示了克拉格对于当今雕塑的看法，这5个关键词贯穿于雕塑语言中，开启并探究雕塑语言的特殊之处：

* 材料
* 体量
* 表现
* 重量
* 繁殖

这些词不仅仅能引发关于雕塑表面基础要素的讨论和质疑，还会促进关于雕塑和超过雕塑本身的谈话，因为这些词汇应用范围和关联的内容很多。有些时候它们在社会、政治和伦理方面衍生出的思考，与它们在形式和美学方面产生的讨论一样多。很多时候这样的探讨出现，实在不足为怪。雕塑，对于克拉格来说，代表一种考问世界的积极方法，也是增强我们敏感性的催化剂。对他而言，必要的不仅是想象、塑造和展示复杂的想法，还有探索物质世界、揭示材料的各种可能性。因此，生物、化学和物理引导他去思考雕塑，反思雕塑在今天的作用，猜想它的潜力。正如这篇访谈所阐明的，这种潜力超越雕塑家在工作室中的实验，进入我们所有人的生活和想象。

材料

乔恩·伍德（以下简称JW）：材料从来都不只是“东西”，是不是？

托尼·克拉格（以下简称TC）：完全不是。我知道对于雕塑家来说有一个习惯，那就是称雕塑材料为“东西”，我觉得怪怪的，并且也无益于对于材料的真正思考。

JW：因为这个称呼会让材料听起来没有生命力？

TC：是的，因为这样听起来没有生命力，这个称谓听起来就像是仅能填充空间的东西。我更愿意把材料当成与自身密切相关的东西——我周围的一切都是材料。每看到任何材料，我都会将其与自己的思想结合起来，这样我就会被周围的事物所影响而发生改变。其实对于每个人来说都是这样，尽管我们不大可能意识到身边每件东西都是怎样影响到自己的。无论是空气的温度，空气的运动，空气中的光线，空气的颜色，还是我们坐着的椅子……我们身边的一切都会带来无数的影响，影响着我们的健康、我们的感觉和我们的思想。

JW：想到这些，再考虑到众所周知的你对罗丹作品的欣赏，可能我们应该以他对材料的评价和他著名的等式开始我们的访谈：“泥土等于生命，石膏等于死亡，青铜等于复活。”这种非常古老的说法赋予材料以隐喻，在这种情况中是赋予宗教或精神的意义，我想知道今天你对此怎么看？

TC：嗯……首先，罗丹作为一名雕塑家并不具备对所有材料的认识。雕塑对他来说仅是模仿而已。雕塑作为发现真实材料世界的一个学科在他生活的年代尚未开始，因此他赋予了雕塑语言一些隐喻。其实是我们今天仍旧在做的事情。我的意思是：在我们的文化中，我们认为黑色压抑、与死亡相关，而白色就意味着生、希望、启迪或愉悦，等等。

Terms and Conditions: An Interview with Tony Cragg

Jon Wood

Introduction

'The future of sculpture has only just begun. Its potential is greater now than ever before and its possibilities are just starting. Its language and its forms are just beginning to evolve...'

These are the kind of statements that you are likely to hear from the artist Tony Cragg - whether in the studio, during interviews, in lectures, at conferences, in the classroom, or over a drink after work. Cragg's constant espousal of sculpture and his dedication to the complexities of sculpture's status and function today have given him an intriguing and somewhat unusual place within contemporary art. Cragg is a sculptor who still makes freestanding sculpture and who refuses to accept the dominance of the ready-made and installation projects. Interested in coalitions of material and meaning and in the content of form, Cragg's outlook is a materialist one. He is also a sculptor imaginatively preoccupied with the textual dynamics of sculpture - with the language used to talk about it and with looking at how it might be discussed today and envisioned tomorrow - promoting 'sculpture' in an age of anxiety about such medium-based definitions and about such a term in particular.

So what exactly does it mean to be a 'sculptor' today, especially when our ideas of what sculpture can be have been expanded so radically into performance, photography, film and digital media, and through other modes of viewer and visitor involvement and interaction? How can a medium specific - or even a material specific - outlook be imagined and articulated nowadays? And how can a sculptor promote an important role for sculpture visualising and giving shape to scientific ideas without sounding like a guardian of a dying tradition in the face of modern science and technology? Sculptors who have written about sculpture have often felt the need to articulate their sense of sculpture's relevance in the face of modernity and in a technologically changing world - especially when the products of modernity, as has so frequently been the case, offered direct challenges to sculpture. Whilst the past has often been on sculpture's side, the future hasn't, and sculptors have often felt the need to explain how their sculpture is not only in touch with the modern world, but also in direct sympathy with it. When you listen to Cragg talk about sculpture, it is striking how futuristic his words sometimes sound. By the same token, it is also noteworthy that, from time to time, you will hear the voices of other earlier sculptors echoing in what he has to say.

The group of texts that follows reveals Cragg's thoughts on sculpture today by taking five terms that have common currency within the language used for sculpture and opening them up, exploring their particularities, through interview discussion. These terms are:

* Material
* Scale
* Demonstration
* Weight
* Generation

The idea is that these terms and conditions will not only allow discussion and interrogation of the ostensible basics of sculpture, but will also enable the conversation to extend elsewhere, within and beyond sculpture, because of their more general application and relevance. Sometimes it is their social, political and ethical ramifications that emerge as much as their formal and aesthetic aspects. In many ways it is not surprising that the discussion takes this turn. Sculpture, for Cragg, represents an active way of interrogating the world and a catalyst for heightening our sensitivity to it. It is needed, for him, not only to visualise, shape and demonstrate complicated ideas, but also to explore the material world and uncover its possibilities. Thus biology, as much as chemistry and physics, guides his critical thinking about sculpture and enables him to rethink its role and imagine its potential today. A potential that, as this interview reveals, extends well beyond the laboratory of sculptor's studio and into the lives and imaginations of us all.

Material

Jon Wood: Material is never just 'stuff', or is it?

Tony Cragg: Not at all. I know there's a tradition for sculptors to call the material of sculpture 'stuff', which I think is a very odd and very unhelpful way of actually thinking about material.

JW: Because it makes it sound dumb?

TC: Yes, because it makes it sound dumb, and because it also makes it sound like something that merely fills the space. I would like to think of material as something that is closely related to myself - because I'm material and the 'stuff' next to me that I'm supported by is material, and everything around me is material. As soon as I look at any material, I combine my thoughts with that material, and so I'm changed because I become influenced by everything that's around me. This is actually so for every human being, even though we cannot possibly be aware of how influenced we are by every single piece of material that's around us. Whether it's the temperature of the air, the movement of the air, the light in the air, the colour of the air, the chair you're sitting on etc...everything surrounding us is a myriad of effects and affecting our well being, our senses and our thoughts.

JW: Thinking of this and given your relatively well-known admiration for Rodin's work, perhaps we can start with his evaluation of materials and with his famous equation: 'Clay is life, plaster is death and bronze is resurrection'. I want to know what you think today of these extraordinary older claims for materials and this investing of materials with metaphorical meaning, in this particular case a religious or spiritual meaning.

TC: Well, first of all Rodin as a sculptor didn't have the horizon of all the materials we have. The practice of making sculpture then for him was basically modelling. Sculpture as a discipline for discovering the physical material world hadn't started in his life. So he gave the language

JW: 你是否也赋予了材料类似的喻意呢？例如，泥土对于你来说，是否由于它通常的原初功能，而就与生长或发源有所关联呢？那么，今天我们回头来看，纤维板、中密度纤维等材料又具备怎样的意义呢？

TC: 这是两码事，因为如果你取20种材料，赋予这些材料20个称谓，那么你就有了20个名词，但还可以赋予它们更多称谓，我们甚至能命名出来2万种称谓。但这样就成了一场名词之争，一场从语言角度来判断哪个更为重要的战争。我们无时无刻不在接受他人对于这个世界的评判，但做雕塑却是自己返回并开始评价的一种方法，因为你真正经历过、体验过。所以我不知道是否有2万种名称，可能只有2千种，但现在的确有很多名词。在任何情况下，我们都无法掌握事物有多复杂，我们的语言已然成为一个体系，一个去除并最终开始减少各种可能性的体系。最简洁的商业用语就是最简洁的语言，但接下来就会有越来越复杂的词语，然后你就会面对词语的边缘，随后就是词典的边缘，最后就必须要开始发明新的词语。

JW: 但不管现在材料和名词的范围是否已经界定，你都要利用泥土、石膏和青铜进行创作。这些传统的雕塑材料是否仍旧与你的雕塑创作和构思紧密相关呢？

TC: 绝对相关。我认为泥土是打发时间的好材料。不对，应该说是值得构思的好材料，因为它让人思考。所以我可以将泥土作为一种材料来讨论，我觉得它也是影响世界发生变化的工具，和征服世界的方法。雕塑只是征服广阔世界的一种方法，一种寻求新的形式、考问我们生活的世界和现实的方法。

JW: 你是否认为有些材料会比其他材料更适合表达某种意义和信息？你有时暗示提出一种“材料实质”的更新版本，以此作为描述材料对你的影响和你对材料的影响之间关联的方法，暗示主体与客体之间一种“乒乓球”似的关系。

TC: 我觉得在某种程度上说是有一种“乒乓”效应，但如果你明白我的意思就会知道，对于我来说“材料实质”就是“为什么米老鼠是用火柴棍做的原因”。我想我的意思就是“更适合”。“适合性”把我们放在一个流动的平面上。材料世界貌似复杂，因为材料有各种各样不同的外观。而外观总在变化，因此，在材料的某一给定形式的有形凝固与一切都尽在变化这一事实之间就存在一种冲突。此外，我们与材料之间的关系也在改变，从而在材料世界中就存在着大量的变化。所有这些都会在思索和赋予材料标签的时候发挥作用。

JW: 那么如果说我们生活在一个所谓“后媒介”的时代，也就是生活在一个材料更具相关性、意义性和有效性的时代了？

TC: 媒介只是一种材料现象，不管你说的是摄影、电脑还是CD……材料并不一定过分简单——把玩一块泥只是初级阶段，这就是我们如何开始的方法。同样这也不意味着现在探讨“媒介”就是要利用最为复杂的科技产品。在面对材料的时候，有方方面面异常复杂的问题需要考虑，而我们在面对这些问题时仅仅才做出最基本的努力。我们对于材料的许多特质，都无从知道如何利用，以及如何以其表达自己。如果材料具有某种潜力，那么我们要做的就是熟知更多的材料语言，以及让这些材料能够表达自身的方法。

JW: “材料的潜力”对于你来说关系重大，是你的论题，这也是你在柏林艺术学院举办的展览采用的主题。

TC: 是的。这些问题对于我来说非常重要，因为我的一些作品中使用了新材料。这些材料带来一种新的视觉体验、一种新的思想体验。还有其他一些作品，材料或多或少地已经消失，以致在整座雕塑中你不会在意材料是什么。在较早的雕塑作品中经常会看到这种情况。例如，你不会注意到罗丹的作品是用青铜雕塑而成的，也不会留意材料的“青铜属性”，而是会关心其它方面。我们甚至可以讨论亨利·摩尔的某些铜塑作品，你不会注意它们的材料，只会注意作品的轮廓，看到作品的表面，还有各种量的接合。

JW: 如果有那种雕塑，它的材料“消失”了，我们可能更多去关注轮廓、形体和神态。但就你的作品来说，材料就是关键，是应该悉数显现的东西。对你而言，没有材料就不会有雕塑吗？

TC: 我觉得在很多作品中，材料占有相当重要的地位，因为材料是载体，但材料到底承载了什么呢？这就又回到了这个问题上：“制作雕塑做什么？”、“有什么好处？”。有人诚实坦言雕塑家需要材料，没有材料就没有雕塑家。但首要问题是材料究竟是什么？一个人用材料究竟能成就什么？我个人认为：材料就是一切。我们由材料构成，我们所在的空间也是由材料构成，那么我想不出有任何现实是与材料无关的，包括作为材料现象的光和电，包括同样是材料产物的智力的思索过程，包括在非常复杂和高度进化的材料过程中产生的情感。这并不是说没有神秘的东西存在，因为这些都是人类的终极的大问题。我们目前能够切实把握的，就是有充分的证据证明，我们处在一个异乎想象的、复杂的材料世界，并且（据我们所能认识到的）很多东西完全不为我们所知。即使今天，宇宙论和神经学仍只触碰到材料的各种可能性的表面。因此，我对于材料，尚且抱有极大的期待，其潜力仍旧很大。

JW: 你是否认为通过与材料发生密切关系，雕塑就能成为处理和解决这些“终极的大问题”的有效方法？

TC: 依我看来，科学研究并不是我们了解物质世界的唯一方法。尽管知识获取和改变的速度有快有慢，但我认为艺术（尤其是发展较快的雕塑艺术）也是探索研究物质世界的有效方法。

JW: 怎样才能做到用艺术探索物质世界呢？

TC：嗯，不仅仅是因为艺术的物质特性、它的

about sculpture some metaphoric meaning. This is something that we still do anyway. I mean we decide in our culture that black is depressive and to do with death, and white is to do with birth, hope, revelation or joy or something.

JW: Do you find yourself ascribing quasi-metaphorical meaning to materials? Does clay, for example, have germinative or originary associations for you, because of its usual preliminary function? And perhaps looking back today what meaning do plastic, fibreboard, MDF etc. have?

TC: It's a different thing, because if you just take twenty materials and give them twenty terms, then you have a language of twenty terms and you can still do a lot. My understanding is that there are twenty thousand or so materials. So then it becomes a battle of terms, a battle of what's important with language. All the time we are obliged to accept other peoples' evaluations of the world, but making sculpture is a way of actually going back and starting the evaluation oneself because you actually experience it. So I don't know if there are twenty thousand - maybe there are just two thousand - but there are a lot of terms now. In any case, we can't grasp how complicated things are, and our language is already a system that cuts out and eventually starts to reduce possibilities. The simplest commercial language is also the simplest language, and after that there are more and more complicated words. Then you are faced with the edge of the words and, after that, the edge of the dictionary, and then you have to start inventing some new words.

JW: But despite this range of materials and terms available now, you work in clay, plaster and bronze. Are these traditional sculptural materials still deeply relevant to your practice and your envisioning of sculpture?

TC: Absolutely. I think clay is a good material for just fooling around. No, it's a good material to kick around, because it lets itself be kicked around. So I can talk about clay as a material that I feel lends itself to effecting change in the world as a tool too, as a method of dealing with the world. Sculpture is only a method of dealing with the big world - it's only a method of looking for new forms and of formulating questions about the world we live in, about reality.

JW: Do you think that some materials are more appropriate for certain meanings and messages than others? You have sometimes implied an updated version of 'truth to materials' as a way of describing a connection between the effect the material has on you and the way that you have an effect on the material, hinting at a kind of ping-pong between subject and object.

TC: I think there is a ping-pong effect on some level, but for me 'truth to materials' means 'why make a Mickey Mouse out of matchsticks', if you know what I mean. I guess I just mean more 'appropriate'. And 'appropriateness' already puts us on a very fluid plane. The material world looks complicated because there are lots of different appearances for materials. Also these appearances change all the time so that there is a conflict between the tangible frozenness of material on a given form of the material and the fact that the whole thing is in flux, incredibly in flux. In addition, we are changing our position relative to them as well, so there's an enormous amount of flux going on in the material world. All of this plays a role in thinking about materials and about giving them labels as well.

JW: So if we are living in a so-called 'post-medium' age, we're also living in an age in which materials become even more relevant, meaningful and effective.

TC: The medium is only a phenomenon of material, whether you are talking about photography, computers, CDs etc...Material doesn't have to be simplistic - playing around with a piece of clay is only the beginning of things, that's how we start. It also doesn't mean that to talk about 'media' now means just dealing with the most complicated technological things. There are just unfathomably complicated facets to be considered when dealing with material, and we really only make rudimentary efforts in tracking those down. There are many, many aspects of the material we just don't know how to use, and how to express ourselves with. And if there is a potential of things, it is somehow in understanding more about the vocabulary of material and the ways in which it can express itself.

JW: The 'potential of things' being a highly relevant and topical phrase for you, as it was the working title for your exhibition at the Akademie der Künste in Berlin.

TC: Yes, these issues are important to me now because there are some sculptures of mine that introduce new materials. They offer a new seeing experience, a new thinking experience. Then there are other sculptures where the material more or less falls away, so that whatever's coming through the sculpture, you're actually not really concerned with what the material is. That often happens if it's an older sculpture. For example, you don't really look at the bronze of the Rodin, you're not concerned with the 'bronzeness' of the material, rather you're concerned with other things. And maybe we can even argue that in some cases with Henry Moore's bronze sculpture, you don't look at the material, you look at the silhouette, you look at the surface and you look at the articulation of the volumes.

JW: But if there are sculptures where the material 'disappears' and we attend perhaps more to outline, image and patina, for you and your work material is key and all-appearing. Without material there is no sculpture, as far as you are concerned?

TC: I think there are a lot of works where the material is of course important because that's the carrier for them, but then what the hell's it carrying? So that leads back to the question, 'what is making sculpture about?' 'What's it good for?' One can say with honesty that a sculptor needs material, and you would hardly be a sculptor without the material. But the first question is then, what does the material mean, what does one achieve by using the material.

构成和历史，当然这些因素构成人类与这些知识、现象和物质世界关系的基础，但是还是因为这些因素和社会的关联。当人们看到雕塑时，通常会想：“噢，这是形式，那内容在哪里呢？有没有什么政治或社会意义？”。但对于我来说，雕塑或绘画已经是非常激进的政治声明了。超越功利主义，以一种非常特殊的方式，用材料传达某种意思和某种生活，或人类强加给材料的意义，这本身就是一种非常罕见、与众不同，或者说非常神秘的过程。

这种过程本身也具有很大的社会和政治价值，因为它使用材料来创作雕塑的这种责任感。这是一个宣言：人类需要热爱并尊重物质，需要和物质材料建立更为复杂的关系。乐观一些说，人类对材料世界的实践将至少延续几个万年，而我们和物质材料的关系也将更加复杂。不仅仅我们对材料的理解要改变，还得不断调整我们对这个世界的心理预期。我们要习惯于生活在那种由分子构成、不断有放射性物质穿过的房间里。我们掌握的所有知识——伽马射线、X光、可见光子、相对论，以及所有一切，都可能只是冰山一角。仍有很多很多知识等着我们去了解。在我看来这种用艺术探索物质世界的意义仅在于：我，作为一个忠实信仰物质材料的雕塑家，可以说我能够从物质材料的角度，了解这个世界和人类生活。我的意思是，当你真的认识了物质材料、真正关注物质材料，并且真正信仰物质材料的时候，你才能解决物质材料的问题。因此，我觉得雕塑家对手中微不足道的那点材料肩负着巨大的责任。这样才是以一种特殊的方式，真正凝聚围绕着材料的智力和物理能量。

JW：是否可以说，你所关心的一个问题是，作为一名雕塑家，要从各个方面，强调或者说提醒人们“无形”世界和有形世界的物质特性，并对它承担责任？

TC：是的，在人类感知范围以外，有很多其他事物存在，就像100年以前我们的曾祖对我们现在不证自明的事物毫无概念一样。但这不仅仅是物质的差异，某种程度上还是精神的差别。这就是说：“看，物质是惊人地具有启发性，你知道的。”唯物主义可以被看作是一种初级的、不那么高明的哲学，但如果你接受了全部的唯物主义知识，你会发现它依然极具启发性，也意味着你会对物质承担责任，并在一个完全不同的高度来与它相处。作为人类，我们可能只是一个短暂的存在，在某个时候就会消失（尽管我们没有放弃希望，要去逃脱那种在消失后产生的无边黑暗阴冷）。所以，在短暂的生命中，我们承担着道义与伦理上的职责和义务去塑造、去描绘，只有这样，任何复杂的生物才能得以承受最小的伤痛，甚至我们还可以把这种关爱和责任延伸到周围其他没有生命的事物。我认为雕塑是一种感知活动，有催化更多敏感思维的作用。这是唯物主义者的工具，我希望它能让我们身边这个世界的思想更为开明。

体量

JW：你经常会举出关于体量的例子，如海滩上的鹅卵石、手中的沙粒或种子、风景中的人体等。你所有的雕塑都是按照与人体的体量关系创作的吗？

TC：作为人类，我只有这种自己身体角度的体量概念。我没长到2米，但一个2米高的人肯定会有不同的理解。他可能会觉得这间屋子很小，也肯定会认为那扇门很小。同样，一个孩子会觉得“在那儿的那个柜子真大，太大了。”所以，在人类中已经存在着多种的体量范围和体量的不同。这也和相对于人类最初认知的其他经验的积累有关。但对于那些真正的大体量的事物来说，又会怎样呢？例如，有人告诉你人类大脑中有2万亿个神经细胞时，你会觉得这可真是个很大的规模，不是吗？但另一方面，我们同时面对着一个无穷无尽的宇宙。因此，就体量而言，只有在对我们产生直接影响时，才能有直接的意义。

JW：在直接“有效”于文化领域方面，体量又是怎样的呢？

TC：在文化领域中，体量关系到事物的大小及这种大小所产生的影响。拿教堂的尖顶来说吧，大多数教堂在修建时都是很大的，尖顶高高耸立是为了（在没有收音机、电视机和其他手段时）便于与距离这一精神生活中心较远的地方进行沟通交流。那时，钟也造得特别大，这也是为了钟声能够覆盖到很大面积。在一定时间段内，教堂是人类修建的最大建筑，这也是很多类似的纪念性建筑的特点。再比如金字塔，也是人类修建过的最大建筑，其影响也因其体量而生。

JW：那我们来讨论一下体量的伦理，或者说体量所承载的责任。作为一名雕塑家，你是否觉得自己有义务去把东西制作得很小或者很大，或者要制作那种尺寸和人体紧密相关的东西？

TC：不管怎样，我都觉得我们应该创作在尺寸上和人体有关联的作品，作品的尺寸在某种意义上和你想要表达的内容，以及你想通过作品传达的信息有关。如果你想表达支配的欲望，或者想夸大其词，那么就应该制作体量很大的雕塑。我认为，我们在当下目睹了太多的“图样”和“图样装置”，它们到处都是，并且有众多建筑师和艺术家参与其中。我发现这样的作品不断涌现，规模很大，它们在概念和形体上都非常的法西斯主义。这些作品毫无必要地充满了整个空间，从而吸引了太多的注意力在作品表达的意义上。这是一种空间策略，一种空间占领。最近还出现了一系列文化产品，它们试图在知性和感性上征服你。

JW：我们来考虑一下体量和那些巨大的当代展览空间吧……当面对那样巨大的空间时，你是否会特别想要制作相对来说体量很小的雕塑？

TC：我不觉得相对于那样巨大的当代展示空间来说，我的作品会显得很小。但我会尝试从外部解决问题。我没准备“因地制宜”地创作或者特别为一个场地去度身创作。我只对自己在作品中表达的关注抱有兴趣，对作品展出的视觉效果并不在意。我宁可把作品放在一个我觉得不太合适的地方展出，也不愿为了在展览空

And from my point of view, I believe that material is everything. We consist of material and the room we are both in consists of material, and so I can't think of any reality that isn't material. That includes light and electricity as phenomena of the material, that includes the thought processes of our intellects which are also properties of material, that includes our emotions, which are also caused by very, very complicated and highly evolved material processes. This is not to say that there's not something very mysterious about all that, because these are the ultimate big questions. What we really do have in front of us is enough evidence of an incredibly complicated material world, which is (as much as we know something about it), for the vast proportion still totally unknown. Even now, cosmology and neurology are still just scraping the surface of the possibilities of material. So for me there is great expectation and an enormous potential in material.

JW: And do you think that sculpture, through this close relationship with material, offers a good means of approaching and dealing with these 'big questions'?

TC: Scientific investigation, from my point of view, can't possibly be the only method of informing ourselves about the material world. And although there are different speeds of knowledge gain and knowledge change, I think that art (and especially the relatively fast developing art of sculpture) is also a very good method of investigating material.

JW: How?

TC: Well, not just because of its physical properties, its constitution and its history, although these factors definitely provide a basis for the human relationship to this knowledge, to these phenomena and to the material world, but also because it has social connection. When people look at sculpture, they tend to think, 'Oh, it's formal, where's the content? Does it have a political or a social meaning?' But for me, to make a sculpture or make a painting is a radical political statement already. To work outside of the utilitarian system, to take some material and to transfer in a very special way some meaning and some life, some human significance onto the material, is quite a rare, very special and, in some ways also, very mysterious process.

This activity also has a great social and political value to it because of the responsibility of working with material, of making sculpture. It's a declaration of the need to love and respect material, and the need to get into a more complicated relationship with material. If we're being optimistic, the human race may have a few more hundred thousand years practice with the material, if not longer, and our relationship to it will have to become much more complicated and sophisticated. And it's not just our understanding of it that will change, but we will also have to continually readjust the psychological parameters of our world. We will have to get used to the idea of sitting in this room made of molecules with radioactivity rushing through it. All the things we know about - gamma rays, X-rays, light photons, relativity and all that sort of knowledge - is really probably only the tip of the iceberg. There's still much, much more to come of this knowledge. And from my point of view, one simple significance of this is that I, as a sculptor who obviously invests a great deal of faith in material, can say that I understand the world and human life in terms of material. The point being that, when you actually turn and focus on our awareness of material, our faith in the material, then one starts to solve problems in material terms. And so I think that sculptors bear an enormous responsibility for the bit of material they get in their hands. Through this there is a real concentration of intellectual and physical energy around the material that they're dealing with in a very special way.

JW: Is one of your main concerns as a sculptor also to try to emphasise or remind people of, and take responsibility for, the materiality of the, to all intents and purposes, 'invisible' world, as well as the visible world?

TC: Yes. Beyond the scale of human perception, there are a lot of other things, just as our great-grandparents a hundred years ago had no awareness of any of the things that for us are self-evident. But it's not just a physical difference, it's also a spiritual shift in a sense. It's to say, 'Look, the material is awe inspiring, you know.' Materialism can be taken as a somewhat shoddy and inferior philosophy, but if you accept the full compilation that it offers, it's always awe inspiring and also means that one takes responsibility for the material and deals with it on a completely different level. We as human beings are possibly here for only a temporary period of time and we'll just disappear at some point (even though we haven't given up the hope of avoiding the ultimate cold darkness of non-existence). So in our short life span we have a moral responsibility and an ethical obligation, I think, to structure things and to make things so that there's the very least amount of pain inflicted on any complicated creation and even extend our care and responsibility to the non-living constituents of the world around us as well. I think that sculpture is a kind of sensitising activity and that it has a role in being a catalyst that may lead to more sensitive thinking. It's a materialist's tool, which I would hope would also lead to a more open-minded approach to the world around us.

Scale

Jon Wood: You have often made references to the highly scale-orientated examples of the pebble on the beach, the grain of sand or seed in the hand, the body in landscape etc. Is all your sculpture on a scale with the human body?

Tony Cragg: As a human being, I only have this bodily concept of scale. I'm not two metres high, but maybe a two-metre high person has a different understanding. He might think this is a small room, and he would definitely think that was a small door. Similarly a child would think 'that's a great, big, enormous cupboard over there'. So there are already some ranges and changes of scale in human beings. It is also

间中看起来更协调而改变作品。

JW: 那么你怎样解决基座问题呢?

TC: 当然，体量和基座问题总是多少会纠缠在一起。通常我会说，我不是跪在地上去塑造或者雕刻，这样就把问题解决了。如果作品是在桌子上创作的，那么使其形象化的力量，也就是我创作和欣赏作品的方式，就会与之相符，作品可能也只适合在桌子高度的平面上欣赏。如果作品体积足够大，能够立在我旁边，和我的身高相仿，也就是和一个人的体量相仿，那么我就会感觉应该把它放在地上。说了这些以后，可能你不太想让雕塑和自己是1:1的比例，或许以我们平时看身边他人的那种角度来欣赏雕塑的这种方法过于熟稔。所以你更愿意加一个基座或者平台，把雕塑和你身边的世俗平庸世界分割开来，赋予它一种特殊的地位或者别的什么东西。

JW: 同样，从室内到室外，从美术馆到雕塑公园，仍旧需要处理体量的问题，以及体量比例关系的变化。

TC: 是的，是存在体量变化的问题，但迄今为止我在室外展出过的很多雕塑都能够妥当地安置在室内。当然，也有一些例外的情况。但我认为问题的关键和挑战是在于你想在哪里创作，想做成怎样的体量，并且是在你对将要放置作品的空间完全未知的情况下。对自己的作品将会放置的那个空间十分熟知并不是什么优势。

JW: 真的吗?

TC: 嗯，我觉得这根本不是什么优势。如果我知道作品最终会放在哪里，那么我就会更多地考虑那个地方的语境，我对此可毫无兴趣。我并不是说对别的艺术家来说也是这样，这只是我不想解决的问题。创作下一个作品时，我会带着一个问题，不断考虑如何解决它，并在制作过程中不断改变它，直到得到让我惊喜的东西，我非常高兴这样。这就像那个的说法(其实我并不同意这种说法)，“艺术就是你做不出来或者不知道如何去做的东西，或者说艺术是你没能力表现的东西。”

JW: 我还想到体量和艺术市场的关系，通常较小体量的作品才较易被收藏和购买。我记得你说过，有时会有参观者到你的工作室四处搜罗能塞在胳膊底下带回家的小雕塑。这样的小型雕塑会不会在某种程度上引起你的兴趣呢?

TC: 我认为对于人们来说，有一个可携带的体量。在我的作品当中，我觉得“可携带”的小型作品非常之少。我制作1米以下高度的小型作品，通常是为了专门研究这种形态，或者专门寻找一种形态。我觉得那些仍未完成的小型作品是因为在它们身上找不到我想要的形态。有时我也能创作出我觉得很成功的小型雕塑，但数量很少。对此我真的不想过多妥协，我觉得我的工作不是去促进雕塑的收藏。我的工作是挑战周围世界中雕塑对象的极限。对我来说，这样才更有意思。制作那些容易收藏的东西对我来说不如去做那些我认为重要的东西。但可笑的是，雕塑于我重要(听起来可能有点自恋)，却也需要别人的呵护，所以我对这些作品得以被人收藏颇以为意。

JW: 我想了解激发雕塑家制作大型作品的动力是什么。同样，制作小型作品的动力又是什么。把巨型作品和孩子般大小的微型雕塑(有模特和设计草图)结合起来很有意思，在两者之间盘旋似乎是很多雕塑作品的特点，或许你的作品也包括在内?

TC: 可能是吧。首先，体量和内容之间有一种说不清楚的关系，因为在这种关系中内容立即成为一个对其它方面产生影响的问题。如果创作的是一件非常巨大的雕塑，你就不可能假装这是为你自己一个人做的。从设计草图开始，有一条很长的路要走，不是吗? 所以艺术家自顾自地在工作室里创作作品的那种私密性就当然要打个折扣，并且很自然地就会让步为一种影响他人的需要。人们可以在罗素和罗丹雕塑体量的不同中看到这种情况：一位是社会主义的人道主义艺术家，明显是非常谨慎适中地表达对于人类的关怀；而另一位加大了作品的体量，从而给世间留下了更为深刻的印象。当然，最终这就成了谁给你留下的印象更深刻的问题，因为最后还是由观众选择自己更感兴趣的雕塑体量。通常，观众的兴趣不在更大的体量上。例如莫斯科红场或者天安门广场，规模巨大，但收效甚微。这比“更大就是更强”要复杂得多，因为在这里更大可能也就更无力：它承载着更大的感染力，同时也就更没有意义。

JW: 你说体量免不了要和内容相关，似乎体量也免不了地要和职业发展相关。所以随着艺术家越来越成功，越大型的作品就会产生出来。我在尝试能够想起哪怕一位雕塑家，他/她在经济上逐渐稳定之后，制作的作品却越来越小。

TC: 我认为大多数雕塑家都不可避免地想创作更大的作品。如果是你在雕琢一种材料，仅是对使用这种材料的好奇就会促使你去想要尝试能不能用它做出更大的雕塑? 或者你的雕塑以及你对这种材料的设想在遇到更大的体量时会如何应对。但如果你认为这是推动整件作品创作的原因——即体量变成作品创作的动力，那就是完全不同的另一回事了。

JW: 是否工作室这一大多数雕塑最初产生时的框架，也成为雕塑作品要去突破的东西?

TC: 是的，你自己独立工作时你能使用怎样的工具传达什么东西，而当你有更多人在身边协助时情况又是怎样，从这个角度上讲，我对你这个问题的回答是肯定的。体量和尺寸大小并不是同一件事。一个人拥有更多力量、更多工具、更多帮助、更多关注，体量就会发生变化；我认为有这样的一种倾向。我知道我可以做许多更大的作品，但是我有抵触，不想将它们做得更大。我很少创作像在都灵的作品那么大的雕塑，我觉得在我这里来说，那件作品可能已是极限了。

to do with the accumulation of other kinds of experiences that relativise that initial perception. But what about all those really large scales? For example, as soon as someone tells you there are two trillion neurons in the human brain, that's an enormous scale, isn't it? And on the other side of things, we are faced with a universe that is infinite. So in terms of scale, it can only directly have meaning when it has a direct effect on us.

JW: What about scale in directly 'effective' cultural terms?

TC: Scale in terms of culture has to do with the relationship between the size that something has and the effect it has. So take a church spire: at the time most churches were built they were quite big. The spire went up high because (in the absence of radio, television and any other such means) it was a way of communicating from a relatively large distance where the centre of spiritual life was. And then the bells were very big because their noises also had to cover a lot of terrain. At a certain time churches were the biggest things that humans were making, and this has also been the case for a lot of such monumental things. The pyramids, for example, were the biggest things human beings ever made - their effect was issuing from their scale.

JW: So let's talk about what we might call the ethics of scale, or the artistic responsibility that scale carries with it. As a sculptor, do you feel you have something of an obligation then to make very small things or very big things, or things that have a close relational dimension with the human body?

TC: I think we will make things that have a dimensional relationship to the human body anyway, and the size of the things has to do partly with the expression you want the things to have, in a sense; the message you want these things to send. If you want to dominate or to be bombastic, then you'll make very big things. We can also, I think, witness this strategy today with 'patterns' and 'pattern installations', which are everywhere, with lots of architects and artists involved in them. I find these endless structures, which can be very large, both conceptually and physically, incredibly fascistic. They unnecessarily fill up the space and take too much attention for what they offer in return. It's a territorial strategy, a kind of territorial gain. But they are recent examples in a long line of cultural products that are meant intellectually or emotionally to subjugate you.

JW: Thinking about scale and about the sometimes huge contemporary exhibition spaces...when you're faced with such spaces is there a temptation to make very small-scale sculpture in relation to them?

TC: I don't think my work would be small in relation to many such contemporary spaces. But I'm past the point with my work where I would be attempting to solve the problem from outside. I'm just not prepared to make sculpture in order for it to become 'situational' or tied specifically to a site. I'm interested in the concerns that I develop in the work, and I'm not really interested in the effect it's going to have on the stage. I would rather put a work I'm convinced about within an unfortunate physical framework, than have to change the work so that it somehow looks better in that framework.

JW: How do you deal with the plinth problem now then?

TC: Of course, scale is also slightly mixed up with the question of the plinth. I generally resolved the plinth problem by saying that I don't kneel on the floor to model something or carve something. If it's made on a table, then the visualising energy - the way I've made it and seen it - should then be adhered to and the work maybe should be seen on a table height surface. If the thing is big enough to stand next to me and rival my own physicality, some measure of a person or whatever, then there is a sense that it should stand on the floor. Having said that, maybe you don't always want to give an object a one-to-one parity with yourself - maybe it's too familiar to have a sculpture judged like the bodies of other personalities around us. So maybe you want to give him a base or a platform to stand on that separates him from the mundane and banal world around you, so it gives him a special status or something.

JW: And moving from indoors to outdoors, from galleries to sculpture parks for example, one is still surely dealing with the question of scale and important changes in scale relationships.

TC: Yes, there is a change of scale, but a lot of the sculptures that I've shown outside so far have managed to go well inside as well. Though there are of course some exceptions. But I do think the test of the matter and the challenge is to make the work you want to make, where you want to make it and the size you want to make it, and in an unknown space. It's not an advantage to know the space you think the work's going to end up in.

JW: Really?

TC: Well, I think it's no advantage at all. If I know where it's going to end up it, then I start to think more about the context, and that is just not what I'm interested in. I'm not saying it's not an interesting thing for other artists to do, it's just not the problem I want to solve. I have a problem as it is making the next work, working out how I'm going to physically get around things, and while I'm making it, to keep changing it so that I arrive at something that surprises me, and that I am happy with. It's like that stupid saying - that I simply do not agree with - that 'art is what you can't make or don't know how to make, or that art is the thing that you can't do'.

JW: Thinking of the relationship between scale and another framework, namely the art market, the smaller scale is often a highly collectable, consumable scale. I remember you saying once that you sometimes get visitors to your studio looking around for little sculptures to tuck under their arm and take home with them. Does this small-scale intrigue you in any way?

TC: I think there is a carrier scale for people. In my own work, I think there are perhaps very few small-scale 'carry-able' works. The times that I've

JW: 有些作品体量大了是不行的。

TC: 是的，说的很对。形态的转译当中存在重要而微妙的差异。在克拉斯·奥尔登堡的作品和托马斯·舒特的泥塑中就能看到这些差异。奥尔登堡的作品中结合了一种抽象的体量变化和不太刻意的设计结构，体现出一种病态和他性。如果他像我们今天一样找一个物体，将其放大到1:100的比例，物体之间的巨大张力看起来绝对会非常惊人，但他没有。在上述两个案例中，较小的体量会更有效。这个问题不好解决，因为你用的工具是手指，你没办法把作品做得更小，除非你有非常精细的工具或者别的什么东西。但只要你用手指来创作，或者用手塑造作品的形态，你就会无意识中或者非目的性地到达一个点，在这一点上，关于作品的视觉效果，相比你能自己操纵决定来说，材料更有发言权。让材料自己说话有时很有意思；雕塑家在某种程度上，总是会给材料一个平台，让它自己来表情达意。所以，当你的作品制作由于你的手指笨拙而被迫停顿，当你的手工制作变得无能为力时，一旦作品被弄大，作品的体量就变得很有意思。它会具有一种自然流露的表达效果和难以预见的品质，因为它不是我们通常习惯看到的东西。

大胆改变作品体量，突破工作室空间限制，这也很有意思。对我来说，史密森的《螺旋形防波堤》就是很好的例子。这件作品猛地提出了一个不寻常的想法，要做一件从天上也能看到的作品，这是巨大的体量变化。 通过创作这样一件从天上能够看到的作品，艺术家想到了飞机、太空旅行、外星人等等……这是通过客体本身而表现出的巨大体量变化。我也认为马塔·克拉克的作品以一种不可思议的方式改变了体量，因为他突然就脱离了空间，留下你去看空间里剩下了什么。所以，这是通过延伸更大空间中的活动而改变体量的范例。但这些作品以这样的体量，不免流于形体巨大，细节简化、甚至缺失。例如，塞拉会做特别大型的雕塑，但表面总是粗糙，这是工业制作的结果。我觉得，对于作品投入的努力与专注和实际使用到作品中的材料总量应该是对等的。

表现

乔恩·伍德：我想用“表现”这个词来探讨你雕塑中的“运动”问题，展开关于你的雕塑是怎样让运动凸显，以及你的雕塑如何像是被电荷、气流赋予能量并受到驱动。绘画可能是进入这个话题最简便的方式。无论是在纸面上，还是在雕塑上，绘画似乎能促使你说明或展示你的雕塑形态的生命力，表述它们的物质和感情定位。或许我们可以从你近期的绘画开始谈起。

托尼·克拉格：是的，我有一些绘画或多或少是为了它本身而创作的，而不是作为雕塑作品的草图。它们是我为绘画而画的，这种情况通常是我想在绘画中表达些什么，不是单纯的技术问题或直接的雕塑问题。它们甚至会是我在雕塑中不能解决的问题。

JW: 是那些只能存在于纸上的不可能完成的雕塑吗?

TC: 是的，存在于纸上的雕塑。有很多雕塑永远都不会做成，因为需要耗费的时间太长，但却是我觉得值得去在纸上记录或完成的。但即使是草图通常也是在某些方面建立在过去的雕塑制作中所经历的东西上。这种情况也发生在雕塑身上。《理性生物》这件作品属于也源于作品《大教堂》，只是因为它是关于收集的，它在毫无意识的情况下与物质活动相关，它是一次材料探险。我所知道的就是我想要很多环形物体，并且把它们码放起来估计也不是难事，因为以前我就这样做过，我要继续使用之前的方法和成果来进行堆积码放材料的过程。我甚至还有过螺旋形状的画。我最近找到了一些《大教堂》的草图，不知道为什么我把“大教堂”画出来，因为我知道在画之前我已经将它做成雕塑了。但当这些图画组合起来以后，就有了雕塑不可能实现的几百万种可能。

JW: 这些后期绘画(与准备性的前期绘画相对)记录了你在作品完成后又是如何解读作品的，它们是否重新想象了作品经历的过程，并重新为这个过程注入活力?

TC: 没错。经常有人问我，“你的作品是从哪里来的?”，我希望我能说“是神的启示!”。但大多数作品其实来自于过去的经历。这适用于作品的方方面面，感情、理念、形式和制作过程。有些经历在当时看起来不重要，但后来和别的不相关的经历结合起来变得重要了。我会保留一些材料，甚至是“不成功的”作品，重新审视完成的作品并进行绘画。这些都是我回忆作品，甚至重新燃起对作品的兴趣或关注的方法。

JW: 你的作品中，形状和形式都不那么常见，视觉上也不容易预测，观众不容易找到坐标。而通常工业制成的部件——工字梁、金属管等——都有自己的“说明”，看的人更容易理解。你是否使用绘画作为引路的方式，来引导观众、向他们展示雕塑内部、外部和周围的能量? 这些画中的线条是否最终为作品的意义给予评注与提示?

TC: 在某种程度上，工业制造的环境和艺术品都是雕塑家的敌人。它们为我们提供了最有效的生存架构，并且我们对其依赖很深。显然，我们需要能够按照我们的目的来构建有用的环境。在我们周围的真实物质世界、以及我们伴随物质世界的感觉和思维中，实用主义和工业体系占主导地位。有时甚至很难找到任何可以替代的其他真实存在。我们已经远离了源于自然世界的丰富形式语言。折中的自然和工业的物种已充斥于我们的现实。任何不遵循工业生产系统基本原理的绘画或材料使用都能带给我们创造新形式和新梦想的希望。另一方面，我有时也很难把握是选择二维的还是三维的方法，更别提将这方法自如地展示给别人了。

JW: 可能我脑海中印象最深的图像是Coracle 出版社发表的你的作品，其中有些是你在大幅的雕塑照片上画的漩涡和螺旋，它们都静止地摆在你的工作室里。你能告诉我们你在这些组合起来的形象中要表达什么吗?

TC: “静止”是一个很有意思的词，因为这个词显然是指不动的物体。但同时，这个词也让

made smaller works, less than a metre tall, have usually resulted from a specific investigation of the form or a specific search for a form. I think that most of the smaller attempts that still hang around have been failures to find the form I've been looking for. The ones that I felt were successful in some cases exist as smaller sculptures, but there are very few. I don't want to compromise that much really. I don't think that it is my job to facilitate the collecting of sculpture. My job is to push the envelope of sculptural objects in the world around me. That's much more interesting for me. Making things highly available is less interesting for me than making things that I think are important. But, funnily enough, their importance to me (it might sound pretentious) also demands that somebody looks after them, so I'm obviously very interested in them being collected.

JW: I want to know more about what motivates sculptors to make large works and, by the same token, what's motivating the making of very small things. That combination of gigantism and then almost childlike miniaturisation (with models and maquettes) is very intriguing. The sculptural spin between those two seems characteristic of many bodies of work, perhaps your own included?

TC: Possibly, yes. Well, first of all there is an inexplicable relationship between scale and content, because immediately the content becomes a question of an effect on others. You can no longer pretend, if you make a very big sculpture, that you're only doing it for yourself. It's a very long way from a sketch, isn't it? So the privacy of creation and of creating things that artists have in their studio when they're on their own certainly is compromised - and willingly compromised by a need to effect others. One sees it in the difference of scale between Rosso and Rodin: one is a socialist humanitarian kind of artist, apparently modestly concerned for human beings, and the other ups the scale of the works to make a greater impression in the world. In the end, of course, it's a question of which made a greater impression on you, because in the end the viewer comes to the scale of sculpture with their own set of interests. Often the interests of the viewer can be very dismissive of a larger scale. Red Square in Moscow or Tiananmen Square for example, are enormous but the effect is very strange. It is much more complicated than 'bigger is more powerful' because bigger here is maybe also more pathetic - it can carry more pathos, more meaninglessness with it.

JW: You said that scale is inextricably related to content, and it also seems that scale is also inextricably connected to career development. So as an artist gets more successful then the bigger the work becomes. I'm trying to think of a sculptor who, as he or she becomes more financially secure, makes smaller work.

TC: I think that most sculptors will inevitably want to make larger work. If you're dealing with material, just a curiosity of working with the material will drive you to want to know if you can actually make a larger work or to see how your sculpture and how your vision of the material will work in a larger size. But then it's very different if you feel that this is the motor driving the oeuvre - if the size then becomes a motor for the work.

JW: And does the studio, the primary frame or container for much sculpture, become the frame to break out of as much as work within?

TC: Yes, in terms of what you can carry when you're on your own or do with whatever tools you can deal with on your own or if you had more people around you. Scale and size are not the same thing though. Scale does change the more power one has, the more equipment one has, the more help one has, the more attention one has; I think that there's a tendency to do that. I could make many bigger works, I know that, but I have a resistance to make them much bigger. The few times I've made a really big work like the work in Turin, I felt that that was in my terms perhaps a limit.

JW: And some works don't work quite on the larger scale.

TC: Yes that's right, there are important and subtle differences in the translation of form. You can see that in the work of Claes Oldenburg and in the plasticine works of Thomas Schütte. There is morbidity and an otherness in Oldenburg's works that comes through a combination of a sort of abstract scale change and a less conscious design structure. If he'd taken an object, as you could today, and blown it up on a one to a hundred scale, it could really have looked absolutely amazing to see the enormous tension between those objects. But he didn't. In both cases the small scale is more effective. It can't be resolved because the tool you're using is your fingers - you can't make it any smaller, unless you've got a very fine tool or something. But as long as you're just modelling it with your fingers, or just manually twisting the form around, you get to a sort of unconscious or intentionless point where the material has a bigger say in what it looks like than you can determine with your manipulations. Letting the material have its say is sometimes very interesting; the sculptor is always, to some extent, giving the material a platform to let it express something of itself. And so the scale at which your manipulation breaks down because your fingers are too clumsy to do it - your manual ineptness - becomes very interesting when the work then gets blown up. It has an unconscious expressive quality and an unseen quality, since it's not something we're used to seeing.

What's also interesting is when there are radical changes of scale brought about through breaking out of the studio. A good example here for me would be Smithson's 'Spiral Jetty'. Suddenly there's an extraordinary mentality here in making something that should be seen from the heavens, and that's a big change of scale. By making something for somebody who can see it from the heavens, he speculated on air flight, space voyage, aliens etc... That's a dramatic change of scale through the object itself. I also think that Matta-Clark's work is a fantastic way of changing scale because he suddenly just leaves the room, leaving you to see what was left of the room. So that's an example of changed scale by extending the activity over a bigger space. But those works tend to become

你知道并没有这样的东西。它暗示着某种电荷或其他潜力，比如说静电。潜在能量受到抑制，但仍旧不断散发涌动。化学能量在我们认知水平以下沸腾，核能以违反定义的形式和状态存在。我们这个狂野宇宙的物质部分的每一粒微尘，任何艺术作品的各种可能性，我们自身存在的潜能，所有一切都如此宏大和不凡，以至于不能成为简单绘画的主题，但恰恰这些才是每件艺术作品的核心。光是坐在装满静止材料的工作室中——也就是你提到的那些作品的主题，就是一种镇静的方式，如果你不设法克服这种平庸的状态并不让材料把你带上征程的话。

JW：那么我们离开平面上的画，来看看雕塑上的绘画。我们发现你的作品，从《战车》（1983）和《山之性》（1984），到容器《信风》（1995）和《诗行》（1997），再到用骰子做的《分泌物》（2001）都有一个特点。为什么你总是特别关注雕塑的皮肤和表面呢？

TC：以前我画自己作品有几个原因。大多是因为对于作品来说有这个必要。我第一次画物体是在20世纪70年代初，当时是我想标记那些找到的物件和使用的材料，用来区别于其他材料。这也成了把材料放在一起的方法。这些绘画就是草草而就的示意图。后来我意识到，画图能帮我在轮廓、延展、甚至颜色等方面界定作品的表面。20世纪80年代初，我创作《晚祷》和《回声》时再次使用了这种绘图技术。胶木表面上的黑白蜡画绘出了其它方式无法表现的棕色和灰色，有时这种方式还能确定作品形式的走向。从那里，就很容易使用以前我在关于作品表面的画作中画箭头的方法（我在创作《信风》时就用了这种做法）。这样就能赋予形式一种气氛，或者一种预示内部动力的表面动态。我觉得很兴奋，因为制作雕塑的前景很有意思，在这种前景中，形式成为内在原因的结果，无论是真实存在还是凭借推断的。其他作品如骰子制成的《分泌物》，甚至是表面浮雕在铸造前凿成阴型的作品《构想》都是处理这个问题的方法。

JW：当想到“内部动力”，我通常会联想到你的雕塑，用语言学词汇表达就是名词和形容词的交叉。既静止、具体，同时又活跃、具有描述性，既是一件物体又是一个过程，实际上就像“雕塑”这个词在今天英语词汇中的状况。引用一个拉丁词汇，我觉得这种雕塑就像一个动名词，在意义上十分活跃，好比是“Ars scribendi”（写作过程的艺术）或“ars sculpendi”（雕塑过程的艺术）。

TC：这个解释方法不错。我相信用绘画和符号激活形态表面的潜力巨大。我的意思是，如果仅作为欣赏一种材料美学品质的平台，无论是大理石的，还是塑料的，这对于雕塑来说都不是真正重要的功能。而仅仅光是在雕塑上进行绘画，对于画家们来说，也并不会比在画布上绘画产生更好的表面效果。画家们并不关心颜料下面蕴藏着什么，而雕塑家却在意。

JW：绘画是否一直存在于雕塑的结构当中？并且既在雕塑内里进行“呈现”，又脱离雕塑进行“呈现”？

TC：是的，从表现角度而言，雕塑的形式有一种语法或者说句法结构。在不锈钢柱子中，就像作品《狂热者》，通过2条轴线和4处视点，各种东西缓慢累积。这个围绕这件作品的结构并不立即显现出来。各种东西凸显出来，又遁形而去，从雕塑中心处来，达到雕塑表面，随即淡出视线。相对于你的位置，会有一种定位的感觉。观看雕塑几分钟之后，你就会清楚地看到那些轴线，因为轴线上清晰可见的轮廓明明灭灭，已经给你一些导引。我并不是说这种做法合乎逻辑，而我仅仅在最开始时即兴地使用绘画，而一旦进入制作阶段，就会改变雕塑的形态。所以会有纵向线条，有频率地出现，卷曲着，部分暗示着我们已经知道的事物，比如脸颊。作品的另一部分反映不为我们所知的事物。同时还有作品的反射，它闯入雕塑以外、观众身后的空间，也使得观众的形象出现在作品上。

JW：说到经历和意识的提升，你谈到了周围事物的辐射，那些我们可能无意识中注意到的东西。我想知道“辐射”是不是“气场”的另外一种说法，也是回避那些有关艺术作品气场潜力的各种焦虑的一种方式。“辐射”，甚至“共鸣”，这些词都回避了形而上或者说意识形态的关联。

TC：我这里基本上是指物体和物质材料的效果。但因为这种形而上的关联和物质的关联已经被占用，我所感兴趣的是建立我周遭的事物与物质材料的关系，同时并不使用我们对于一门已被占用的语言所惯有的预想。这有点像弃用一个基督教名，使事物失去个性。我的意思是，这是从我的角度所做的一种尝试，重新建立与材料的关系，我觉得雕塑家必须要这样做。

JW：现在人们越来越意识到，你作品的这一方面在试图抓住和控制观者。你能讲讲自己期望提高哪种敏感性吗？你认为自己的作品表现的什么，为什么而表现？你的雕塑会引发什么样的思考？

TC：嗯，有这样一种态度，在看待事物、看待物体和材料的时候，要基于一种沉思和冥想：即“一沙一世界”的观点，或者甚至是某些宗教观点，通过这样，你能够真正在另一个高度与物质世界沟通，比你在平日能够显然达到的任何层面都要深刻，是一种存在于你的普通经历之外的不同寻常的层面。

我并不是说这种态度没意思或者不重要。但我认为这种态度为日常生活留下了一片战场，由那些非沉思的和非冥想的思想来占领。这听起来可能像是术语的混合，但我认为，即使在那种每天的、“每分每秒”的生活层面上，即生活的体验层面上，也有一项工作要做。我觉得这项工作就是提高对于物质世界的认识，提高思考这种认识的能力，要把把物质世界看作自身的延伸，如果不是自己，那也就是社会行为的延伸，你置身其中的文化行为的延伸。

JW：如何从个人思考体验发展成具有群体性质的思考呢？

materially huge and it's inevitably quite likely that the detail is going to suffer or not even be in existence on this scale. Serra, for example, makes very large-scale works, but their surfaces are un-worked, as a result of their industrial making. For me, there is an equation between the effort and concentration and the amount of material that you can actually bring to it.

Demonstration

Jon Wood: I would like to approach the question of 'movement' in your sculpture through the term 'demonstration' and open up a discussion about how your sculptures make movement manifest and how they seem animated or energised by charges, directions and currents. Drawing is perhaps the easiest way into this issue. Drawing, whether on the page or actually on the sculpture, seems to allow you to indicate or demonstrate the life of your sculptural forms and articulate their physical and emotional orientation. Perhaps let's start with your recent drawings.

Tony Cragg: Yes, these are drawings that are made more or less for their own sake, rather than working sketches. They are the drawings that I do as drawings, if I want to express something in drawing which is not just a technical problem or a directly sculptural problem. It may even be the things I can't solve in sculptures.

JW: So impossible sculptures that can only exist on the page?

TC: Yes, sculpture on the page. There is a lot of sculpture that's never going to be made, because it would just take too long, but that I feel is somehow worth doing or recording as a sketch. But even the sketches generally have a basis somewhere in something that's been experienced in making. It occurs in the sculpture too. '*Rational Beings*' really belong to and begin with '*Minster*', simply because it was about collecting, and to do with a physical activity without even really knowing it, an adventure with the material. I just knew I wanted loads of circular objects, and then stacking them up is probably not that complicated because I'd done that in the past, as well as taking the formula and getting consequences out of it for the stacking process. There were even drawings of the spires. I've recently found some sketches of '*Minsters*'; I don't know why I'd draw a 'Minster' because I know I made the 'Minsters' before I drew them. But after they were fixed, there are already a few million possibilities that can't all be worked out through sculpture.

JW: So were these post-work (as opposed to preparatory) drawings - records of how you subsequently interpreted the work, reactivating it and re-imagining how it could be experienced?

TC: Exactly that. I am often asked, 'Where does the work come from?' And I would love to be able to say 'Divine inspiration!' However, most of the work results out of what has gone on before. This applies to all facets of the work, in terms of emotions, ideas, forms and making processes. Sometimes it is the things that did not seem important at the time which later, possibly in combination with other unrelated experiences, become important in a different way. Keeping some of the material, even 'failed' works, looking again at the work I have made and making drawings are amongst the ways in which I can recall and even restart an interest or, concern in the work.

JW: Within your work, shapes and forms are less familiar, less visually predictable and it is less immediately possible for viewers to get their co-ordinates. Whereas industrially formatted units - I beams, metal piping and tubing etc - come with their own 'instructions' which viewers can more easily follow. Do you use drawing as a way of leading the way, guiding viewers and showing them the energies in, over and around a sculpture's surface? Are these lines ultimately providing commentaries and indications of meaning?

TC: In some sense the industrially produced environment and its artefacts are the sculptor's enemy. They offer us the most efficient existential framework and we rely on them greatly. Obviously, we need a useful world that we can form to our purposes. Utilitarianism and industrial systems dominate the real material around us and with that our senses and our thoughts. It even becomes difficult at times to see any alternative reality. We have moved along way away from the rich vocabulary of form resulting out of the natural world. Mediated nature and industrial species populate our reality. Any drawing or, any use of material that does not obey the rationale of industrial production systems offers the hope of providing us with new forms and new imaginations. On the other hand, at times I barely have a grip my own two and three dimensional alternative routes, let alone having a hand free in order to show others the way.

JW: Perhaps the images that come to mind most strongly for me are the prints you did with Coracle Press, some of which contained swirling, spirals drawings you had drawn over large photographs of your sculpture, which stood static in the studio. Can you say what you were trying to articulate in these combinatory images?

TC: 'Static' is an interesting word because it obviously refers to an object at rest. At the same time, however, it lets you know that there is no such thing. It infers some kind of charge or other potential, for example static electricity. Potential energy held in check, but still pushing. Chemical energy seething under the level of our perceptions. Nuclear energy in forms and states that defy definition. Every grain of material part of a violent cosmos, the possibilities of any art work, the potential of our own existences. All much too grand and pretentious to be the subject of some simple drawings, but it is exactly concerns like this that are at the heart of every artwork. Just sitting in a studio full of inert material, which is the subject of those prints, is a downer if you don't manage to get over the banality of the situation and let the material take you on a trip.

JW: Moving from drawing on page, to drawing on the sculpture itself. We find this across your

TC：从主要来看，只有群体性。你能为自己做的事情，就是说自己的话、做合自己胃口的饭、穿适合自己的衣服，其它你必须接受的每一件事都是由他人为你而做的。显然，这些事情即使没有得到你的允许，也都存在着，并且各方都接受这样，不是吗？尽管你不喜欢，好像你也没试图改变。而且或许这里还有一些积极的东西存在着。我的观点是：即使我不喜欢，也无法改变许多，但我还是要在我认为重要的大方向上播下改变的种子。这是对一个人承担多少改变责任的衡量。在周围的视觉世界里寻找更多，寻找更多语言，在某种程度上来看，这是强化敏感性、扩充词汇的一种方式，而延伸对于词汇的反应也是强化敏感性的方式。我不是政客，但我觉得我仍旧生活在一个催眠和神秘偶像大行其道的世界，这些东西非常分散我们的注意力，因为它们妨碍我们真正尝试去面对现实。

重量

乔恩·伍德：重量是雕塑的一个重要条件，但我总是感到惊讶，为什么重量很少与材料名称、尺寸、日期和来源等一起被标注在作品标签上。

托尼·克拉格：在最近的一本古德伍德的画册上，作品标签上就标注了重量。

JW：好吧，可能这只是这一规则的一个例外而已。

TC：是的，可能是唯一的一次例外吧。我知道这有点莫名其妙！

JW：古德伍德展在重量问题上很有意思，因为你展示的多是大型户外"重量级"雕塑，如果可以这样说，每件作品都在探索"重量"的问题。有一些看起来真的不会屈服于爱情或者钱财的层叠状石头雕塑；明黄的金属塑像在绿草茵茵的地上卷曲着，像希腊的科林斯王一般；有的作品外框钻洞，轻一些，但仍然矗立着并且结构上完整无缺。或许从其他角度来说，作品被打磨的多么有光泽是用来使雕塑的曲面更加难以捉摸复的一种方式，使重量便变得更加模糊不清，难以判断。不过，你仍旧是"重量级"雕塑的制作者。

TC：是的，所有的事都是相关的。不谈密度就没法讨论重量，因为密度、重量和体积都相互关联。例如，你能制作体积较小的作品，气球或除聚苯乙烯以外的东西（木头密度也不大），但随后就会进入现实的重量问题。举例来说，如果你有一立方米的木头，尽管体积不大，但重量大约900kg；但如果你有一立方米钢，重量就能达到大约6吨……因此，重量就是作品的一部分意义。中空的作品则必须考虑真空的问题。

JW：你说过，最初开始制作铜雕塑时，对铜制作品里中空的问题有点焦虑，这些作品中间"仅仅"就是空气。

TC：我想是这样的。我觉得我的多数铜制作品都以某种方式表现它们自己，揭示它们重量和体积的关系。在一些作品中表现得非常明显，如《信封》，因为你能看到体积里面，并且非常清楚地意识到"皮肤"。《早期形式》也展示了这种一对一的关系，因为作品有外表面和内表面，还有引导从一个表面到另一个表面的洞（入口或出口）。作品《理性生物》有些细微的差异，因为我用正外部的横截面处理了它。

JW：你之前也说过，有的雕塑（你提到亨利·摩尔用重量级材料制作的作品，如铜）轮廓超越了雕塑本身。透过它们，你是否在某些时刻感到材料和重量瞬间消失？你还可以用抛光的方法达到目的，光泽让雕像消失。你能谈谈这些吗？例如，像《狂热者》那样高度抛光的表面？

TC：是的，我正试图克服这些零散的部件，不管是我的、你的，还是一块石头、桌子上的一个瓶子。我知道这就像一个物体周围有一个坚硬的轮廓，但这比我们想象的周围其他的事物更为完整。例如海滩上的石子，自古以来这就是海滩的一部分，它们并非无关紧要，相反却和周围事物有着相同的温度。石子也反射光线。即使仅是一块石头，也会和空气发生化学反应；蒸发、辐射、吸收辐射。你不能把石头从原来的地方拿走，而不再放上去任何东西——这里不能留白。它们起着支持的作用，扮演着辅助性的角色。

所以，如果你觉得这就是一块石头而已，那么你再考虑一下我们的身体，我们的共鸣、本质、发出的气味或温度、头发生长、微笑、语言、思想、行为、和物质世界的相互作用。我们存在于社会的大语境之中。

我知道，我们必须保持头脑清晰，因此把事物划分为分散的物体，但在另一个层面上，事物却又完全混合在一起。材料是一种开放自我并能带给你深邃观点的东西，因此使用材料和这种认知有关。你知道，物体进入空间，像我们进入空间一样，同时物体也会把空间推出去。作品的具有反射性的表面也是同理，你不可能脱离作品所处的空间来看作品，作品进入空间同时也被空间推回。看作品表面时，你看到了什么？你被推回到正在观察的房间和你的脸。这就是物体和空间之间相互关系的方面。

JW：你之前还说过，体量和内容相互关联，但重量和内容呢？

TC：如果你对材料有一定的敏感性，在某种程度上，比例就是重量。例如，塞拉的小型立方体作品，甚至是乌利希·路克里姆的雕塑，都充分体现了这一点。这些都不是很大的雕塑，但事实上，一块立方米的石头重两吨已经说明一种体量上的尺度。可能材料的金钱价值也是一个规模问题，所以一立方米黄金的体量应该非常之大，而一立方米水就没那么大了。这和价值有关，但价值和材料的稀缺性有关，因此材料可用性有明显的结构参数。

JW：从雕塑的可运输性而言，如何理解重量？艺术、道德标准和经济学之间有一种很有趣的关系，特别是近年来，随着大批年轻雕塑家制作能够轻松周游世界的轻型作品以来，两吨的

work: from works like '*Chariot*' (1983) and '*Mountain-Nature*' (1984), to the vessels of 'Trade Winds' (1995) and '*Verses*' (1997) and then to the dice works like '*Secretions*' (2001). Why are you consistently drawing attention to the skins and surfaces of sculpture?

TC: There are several reasons why I have drawn on my work in the past. Most of them have resulted as a necessity arising out of the work. The first time I drew on objects, and this was in the early 1970's, it was intended to mark the found objects and materials I was using to give them a distinction apart from other materials. It was also as a way of fixing them together. The drawings were rough gestural meshes. Later I realised that the drawing helped define the surface in terms of its contours, its extension and even its colour. I reused this kind of drawing technique in the early 1980's again, for works like '*Evensong*' and '*Echo*'. The black and sometimes white wax drawing on the formica surfaces brought out the pigmented colours of the otherwise non-descript browns and greys, and at times gave the forms some kind of a direction. From there it was an easy step to drawing the arrows that I had used in earlier drawings on paper on the surface of the work as I did with '*Trade Winds*'. This gave the forms a climate or, a surface movement which inferred an internal dynamic. I found that exciting because the prospect of making sculptures where the form is the result of an internal cause, whether real or inferred, interesting. Other works such as the '*Secretions*' made of dice, and even '*Formulations*' where the surface relief is gouged into the negative form before casting, are also ways of dealing with this concern.

JW: Thinking of this 'internal dynamic', I have often thought of these kinds of sculptures of yours, in linguistic terms as being a cross between nouns and adjectives. At once static and specific, but also active and descriptive - so both a thing and a process – actually very like the word 'sculpture' is today in English. And using a term from Latin, I think this kind of sculpture as being like a gerund, a verbal noun which is active in meaning. Like 'Ars scribendi' (the art of writing) or 'ars sculpendi' (the art of sculpting).

TC: That is a good way of putting it. I believe that there is an enormous potential for activating the surface of forms with drawings and notation. I mean, it is not really a very important function for sculpture if it is only a platform to admire the asthetic qualities of a material, whether it is marble or, plastic. And, simply painting on the sculpture rarely provides a better surface for painters for their images than the canvas does. They don't care what is underneath the paint anyway but, a sculptor does.

JW: Does drawing continue inside the structures of your sculptures and 'demonstrate' from within as much as from without?

TC: Yes, in terms of demonstration, there is a kind of grammar or sentence structure to the form of the sculpture. In a stainless steel column like '*The Fanatics*' there are all sorts of things that are slowing accumulating, through the fact that it's got two axes and four points of view. It is the structure around the thing that is not immediately apparent. They go out, they cut in, and they come from the centre of the sculpture onto the surface and then out and beyond. There's a kind of orientation relative to your position. Once you've looked at the sculpture for a few minutes you become very aware of those axes, because on those axes the recognisable silhouettes blink at you. So there's already some navigation going on there. I'm not saying it's logical, it's just simply me playing and improvising with the drawing initially, and then once you get into the making stage, modifying the sculptural form. So there are vertical lines that definitely take up a frequency, which take up curves, which partly hint at things we already know about, like faces. And then part of the work is reflecting on things we don't know about. There's the reflection, which is breaking into the space beyond the sculpture and behind the viewer and also allowing the viewer to be seen in the work.

JW: Thinking about this heightening of experience and awareness, you have talked about the radiation of the things around you, the things we're maybe not consciously picking up on. I was wondering if 'radiation' is just another way of saying 'aura', and also a way of sidestepping the anxieties around discussion of the auratic potential of a work of art. Aren't terms like 'radiation', and 'resonance' even, terms that also avoid any metaphysical or ideological associations.

TC: I basically mean the effectiveness of the object, of the material. But because the metaphysical and the physical association are already occupied, I'm interested in somehow establishing some relationship with the materials and the things around me without using the preconceived notions of an already occupied language. It is a bit like taking away a Christian name and depersonalising something. What I mean is that it's an attempt on my side to restart the relationship with the material, which I think sculptors have to do anyway.

JW: Thinking of the increased awareness that this side of your work tries to capture and harness in the viewer, can you say a bit about the kind of sensitivities that you would like to see heightened? What do you see your work as demonstrations of and for? Your sculptures are triggers for what kind of thinking?

TC: Well there is an attitude to looking at things and to looking at objects and materials which is based on a meditative tradition of contemplation: the universe in a grain of sand idea, or maybe even religious ideas where you actually get in contact on some level with the material world, on a deeper level than the one that you obviously are capable of reaching in an everyday situation, so on an extraordinary level, outside of your ordinary experiences.

I am not saying that that's not interesting or important. But I also think that this leaves the battleground for the everyday life to be governed by non-contemplative thought and non-meditative thought. And this may sound like a mixing of terms, but I think that there is a job to be done even on an everyday, 'second-for-

雕塑可能成本巨大，或者根本就不能长途旅行。

TC：用电子邮件发送？

JW：绝对是这样。我的意思是思考关于重量的可能的道德标准，重量是不是一种条件，让艺术家能更清楚地意识到艺术责任？

TC：我认为重量是资源，同时也需要资源，但雕塑只是整个制造界中渺小的、微不足道的一个成分，从更大的视角来看，实在无足轻重。相比雕塑，当今的纸杯数量更大，实际上成吨的是纸杯。有很多东西是用成吨的迷你雕塑做成的。作为将生产剩余和经济逻辑关联的必要手段，这非常重要。第二，有的东西，我们认为很轻，但它的制作需要巨大的能量，比如制造DVD或影像光盘，需要计算机以及大量其他相关物件。生产DVD机就需要巨大的工业体系。

繁殖

乔恩·伍德：我想提出关于再生产、复制、铸造等问题……这是一整个体系，通过“繁殖”这个词，制造出随后的作品。看来你似乎很关注这个名词（和它的生物学隐喻），你是一个不断创作出被称为“可繁殖”的作品的雕塑家，这些作品具有自我繁殖结构或者格式，能够促进后来的作品生成。

托尼·克拉格：是的，绝对是，我认为大块的物体和能量需要被繁殖，任何有效的改变都应该被繁殖。在我的作品中，“繁殖”于我而言就是在特定时期自己繁殖的作品，具有自生成特点。现在我正在做的作品具有可行性是因为三四个月前的作品，而三四个月前的作品可行是因为九个或十二个月之前的作品……即使不是线性发展，一切也在繁殖。我认为材料天生拥有自我传播、自我繁殖的能量。甚至“繁殖”这个词，从“种类”来说，不管是创造一个相互关联的群体或是创造人口、物种，它就是创造物体族群的概念。

JW：我们来看一下在你的雕塑中，这个生物模型是怎样组织并面对一件真正表达自我的作品的。

TC：是的，我必须承认，尽管似乎我用了很多年来认可或接受这种工作方法。实际上，没有其他清晰、系统的工作程序时，我被迫进入这种工作方法。我已经创作作品十多年了，经历了跳跃、中断、平行发展，作品千差万别。但作品的主题没有改变，在某种程度上我对作品的期望也没有改变。每一件新作品带来的新信息总是让我惊讶。对我来说，真正有价值的是不知道作品完成时会是什么样子。这意味着我并不能准确地知道作品的样子，不知道它对这个世界会有什么影响，感觉如何，能够传达什么思想。这就是为什么我从来都不做表达已存在事物的作品，这也是我极少以表现前置信息为目的来着手创作的原因。比起回头溯源，我更愿意向前探索新体验和新知识。向前看的倾向对我来说具有繁殖的性质。这就是为什么我们要繁衍后代为，是为了将自己的一部分融入未来。我们会一度忙于塑造和教导后代，而某一天他们会开始引导我们和他人。我们把他们归入家庭、类别和物种。

工业理性倾向于，通过最低标准的决策、规定材料和使用低廉的可持续的几何形式来决定造型的可能性。制作雕像的其他方法看起来相对有机。我在学生时代迷恋极简派艺术之后，我曾有意识地不去制作构造型铁盒和仿制工业品。有时巨大的商业生产系统似乎延续着达尔文式的方式，适者生存的法则保证了系统的动力，至少是有机动力。但不幸的是，这样的方式却忽略了一个事实：达尔文的进化论假设了大量生物环境，大量物种在生物生境中生息繁衍。这绝对不是“世界是我的牡蛎”的新概念。市场营销通过打压一切不相关的敏感性和文化环境来做好准备，然后在所有的地方倾入ipod和宝马。相比物种繁多的植物群系帮我们创造新语言、新思想和新观点，文化更像一个过于密集的鳄鱼池。制作雕塑是填满“形式水池”的好办法，即使你从来不觉得这是符合逻辑的、合理的，甚至本质上正确的。

JW：在填充“形式水池”方面，你是否不仅把大型展览或回顾展视为展示雕塑“繁殖”的机会，同时也为了描绘不同材料、不同阶段、不同尺寸的作品之间及其内部的“基因”联系吗？

TC：我喜欢在大型展览中展示作品，而不是作为单个艺术品。我希望带来一种进行雕塑创作二十年的感觉，也希望展览有一种更为与世隔绝的特质，以一种不太一样的方式来欣赏作品；可能还要有历史深度，并且为展示形式的演化和形式的意义提供一个机会，至少有一组作品是这样的。在某种意义上，也会有一种错误的处理：把雕塑排成一排，一个挨一个，将其作为整个长故事的某个独立单元来对待，这样会不可避免地影响它们各自的状况。

JW：有没有一个雕塑家作品中天马行空的多样性让你担忧或者焦虑？

TC：完全没有。相反，我的想法或许比较冷血，如果一件作品没有某种程度的复杂性，甚至有点无法控制，可能他们应该去当设计师！

JW：“繁殖”和“萌芽”等等的生物概念，像是自然的进化和生长，取代了实验、错误和未能发展或繁殖出后续作品的“不育”作品，“死胡同雕塑”在任何地方都无法占据主导。在你对事物的计划中，这些雕塑发生了什么？

TC：我们讨论后代时，我们能够想象的万物相生观念就像一丛灌木或一棵树。这样的形式是为了扩大生长和保持持续分化的潜力。任何对生长发展不起作用的东西都会衰退，成为废物。有一点是可以肯定的：没有什么是浪费的。

JW：探讨这种有机变化作用于雕塑，以及与整个雕塑史的关系时，我想问：
为什么你认为雕塑家常常会自觉地关注漫长的雕塑史和雕塑表面上的起源？你提到金字塔，很有意思。如果你采访画家，他们不大可能提到洞穴壁画或者类似的例子，而雕塑家却会提到金字塔。埃及雕塑——金字塔和斯芬克斯等

second' level of life - on the experiential level of life. I think there is a job to be done here in improving the quality of contemplation about an awareness of the material world - the material world seen as an immediate extension of oneself, and if not oneself, then an immediate extension of the communal social effort, the cultural effort that you are part of.

JW: How does it move from being an individual contemplative experience to being one that has a communal relevance?

TC: In the main part it only has communal relevance. All you can do for yourself is formulate your sentences, cook yourself a meal that suits you, get dressed in the fashion that suits you, and everything else you have to put up with as having been made by other people for you. But obviously, even if they didn't ask your permission, there's something consensual about that, isn't there? Even though you don't like it, it doesn't look like you're making an effort to change it. And maybe there's some active thing there. My idea is that even if I don't like it, I wouldn't be able to change a great deal of it, but I could sow the seed for some change in the direction that I would feel would be important. It's a measure of how much responsibility one takes for the change. Looking for more in the visual world around me and looking for more language, in a sense, is one way of heightening sensibilities and expanding a vocabulary and then expanding the responses to a vocabulary is a way of heightening sensibilities. I'm not a politician, but I think we still live in a world that is greatly dominated by mesmerism and mystical models, which are very distracting because they actually stop us from really trying to face reality.

Weight

Jon Wood: Weight is such an important condition of sculpture and it always surprises me that it so rarely gets listed in catalogues alongside the usual inventory of material, dimensions, date, provenance etc..

Tony Cragg: It is in the recent Goodwood catalogue.

JW: Well maybe that's one of the exceptions to the rule.

TC: Yes, perhaps the only exception. I knew it was relevant somehow!

JW: The Goodwood exhibition is very interesting, however, in relation to the question of weight, because you showed a lot of large, outdoor, 'heavy' sculptures there - but sculptures that each explored 'weight', if I can put it that way. There were layered stone works that looked like they really wouldn't budge for love nor money, bright yellow metal sculptures that had been rolled almost Sisyphus-like onto the top of grassy mounds and works whose frames were punctured with holes, lighter but still standing and structurally intact. Or elsewhere it was a question of how shine and polish were employed as ways of trying to complicate a sculpture's surfaces so that weight becomes more ambiguous and difficult to judge. Nevertheless, you are still a maker of 'weighty' sculpture.

TC: Yes, all things relative. You can't talk about weight without talking about density, because density, weight and volume are interestingly linked. So, for example, you can make volume-less things, like an air balloon or things out of polystyrene (and wood is also not so dense). But then you get to the practical reality of the weight question. For example, if you've got a cubic metre of wood, then even though it is not a very big volume, it weighs about 900kg, and if you have a cubic metre of steel, it weighs about six tonnes…and so immediately the weight is a part of the meaning of the work. As is hollowness, when you have to start considering vacuums.

JW: You said at one point that when you first started making bronze sculptures you were slightly anxious about the fact that they were hollow, and that there was 'just' air inside them.

TC: I think I was. I think that with most of my bronze sculptures I've tried in some way to get the sculptures to reveal themselves, to reveal the relationship between their weight and their volume. It's obvious in works like '*Envelope*' because you can see inside the volume and become very aware of the skin. The '*Early Forms*' also have a one-to-one relationship because there is an outside surface and an inside surface, and a hole (an entry or an exit) which leads from one to the other. It's slightly different in the case of the '*Rational Beings*' body of works, because I'm dealing with a peripheral cross section.

JW: You also said earlier on was that there are sculptures (and you mentioned Henry Moore's work and sculptures made out of a weighty material like bronze) where you look at the silhouette, beyond the sculpture. Do you also end up looking through it so that in a way the material and the weight disappears at those moments? You also get this with polish, a kind of evaporation of the sculpture through shine. Can you talk about this, for example, in relation to the highly polished surface on a work like '*The Fanatics*'?

TC: Yes, I'm still trying to get over this description of a discrete body, whether it's mine, yours or a stone, or a bottle on the table. I know it seems to have, to our perception, quite a hard contour around it, but it's much more integral to everything else around it than we imagine. Take the example of a stone on the beach. First of all it's integral historically to the beach and it also has the same temperature as the things around it, which is not insignificant. It's also letting light be reflected off it. It's also, even if it's only a stone, chemically reacting with the air around it; it's evaporating, it's radiating and it's absorbing the radiation. You can't just take where that stone is and put nothing there - there cannot be a blank there in its place. It's a supportive component, it plays a supportive role.

So if you think that's just a stone, well think then about our bodies, with our vibrations and

都会带来一种“雕塑史很漫长”的感觉。这是否也是雕塑家对“繁殖”的一部分想象?

TC：如果在你面前有一首曲子，那么节奏、和声、音高和作曲的标准创造了旋律。雕塑的标准和概念也类似。长寿是材料的一种特性，某种程度上也是跨越时空的坚固桥梁。这是及时留下一条相对持久的信息的方法。看到雕塑成为不同时空之间的桥梁是一件很有意思的事情。雕塑在延长时间的同事也收缩了时间。你可以走进一个房子，里面的东西可能有三千年、三百年或三十年历史，有些东西可能上周才做好。不知何故，在时间的碎屑里留下的东西让我们反思人类的特征，读出我们熟悉事物的变化：人类的关注（有的善于表达，有的幽默，有的高贵，传递美的观念，真理、伦理和道德问题等）在一种材料和一个具体形式中汇聚起来。因此，对我来说，最终认定我想要做雕塑是符合逻辑的，因为雕塑必须要因为材料而被关注，材料将带来更为深远长期的意义。回首过去是另一方面，某种程度上，过去给我们提供了人类关注和价值的实证材料。

JW：“回收”这个词有用吗？你的作品采用了回收策略吗?

TC：我不由自主地说“是的”。不过，因为自身的特殊经历，我觉得你能用这个词解释生态时尚，但我总是有意避免这些词汇，因为如果你避免不了，就真的可会做出来一些丧失真实价值的东西。当被冠以一些简单的争议或社会内容时，真实价值就已经丢掉了。这是最近的趋势，艺术家塑造了某个形象或对象，赋予其预先描述的政治或社会意义，这是很普遍的。但对此我没有兴趣，我愿意发现新的意义，而不是让雕塑仅仅成为暗喻。

JW：“被冠以”这个词让我想到自己应该在哪里停手或者中断创作。就好像人口增长，在什么地方画出停止创作的时间线？或者一直做下去？雕塑像兔子一样繁殖，像野火一样蔓延，去向哪里?

TC：嗯，当你沿着街道行走，却没走出多远，因为你遇到了雕塑，那么你这个问题就出来了。我想，除非你的起居室、厨房和卧室堆满了雕塑，如果不是这样，那么我们距离被“雕塑”这个物种灭绝就还有很长一段距离。

我认为雕塑是难以置信的稀有的人类产品，事实如此。我觉得这个世界的未来需要雕塑来决定很多事物的形式和结构：我们会需要雕塑和雕塑型思想。我想把雕塑思想应用于生物机械、政府机构、社会结构等。我并不是说决定什么结构，但却是为了采用形式分析，甚至将其与理想、甚至道义责任关联。我能够想象艺术家的工作变成其他形式，比如政治机构、教育实践、农业、林业、生态、营养、人类关系、公平和解决争端。这听起来可能有些遥远，但因为我在材料中找到了解决所有这些问题的方法，雕塑是解决这些问题的有效准则。雕塑的未来将更加完备，能够解决复杂的实质性问题。我相信，比起其他艺术或文化活动，雕塑有时可能是更好的建设世界的工具。

[注]：“条款和条件：托尼·克拉格访谈”（“材料”、“体量”、“表现”、“重量”、“繁殖”），发表于《托尼·克拉格：游走于材料内外》，2006，艺术学院，柏林；科隆：Walther König，第13-125页。

our essences, our smells or the temperature we let off, our hair growth, our smile, our words, our thoughts, our deeds, our interactions with the material. We are existing in a big social context.

I know we have to keep our sanity and therefore separate things into discrete objects, but on another level there is an enormous integral mix of things. So using material that is opening itself up and letting you have in-depth visions relates to this awareness. Objects suck in the room, you know, as we suck in the room, and they push out the room at the same time. That works in the same way with the reflective surface, which you can't look at without the image of the room being sucked into the object and at the same time pushed back. And what do you see when you look at the surface? You get pushed back into the room you're looking at and your own face. So they are facets of an interaction between the object and the space.

JW: You said earlier that scale and content were interconnected, but what about weight and content?

TC: Scale is weight to some extent, if you have some degree of sensibility for what materials are. That's definitely exploited in the small cubic works of Serra, for example, and even maybe with Ulrich Rückriem's sculptures. They're not exceptionally big sculptures, but the fact that one cubic metre of stone weighs two tonnes is already a measure of scale. Maybe the financial value of the material can also be a matter of scale - so a cubic metre of gold would be a very big scale and a cubic metre of water is perhaps not a very big scale. It's to do with value and the value has to do with the rarity and scarcity of the material and so there are clear structural parameters to the material availability.

JW: What about the ethics of weight in terms of sculpture's transportability? There is an interesting relationship between art, ethics and economics here, especially in recent years with a lot of younger sculptors making very light work which can travel around the world very easily, whereas a two tonne sculpture either might cost a lot or might not travel at all.

TC: Or be sent as an email?

JW: Absolutely. I mean just to speculate on a possible ethics of weight here - is weight a condition that entails a much greater awareness of artistic responsibility?

TC: I think that weight is resource and one which in turn demands resources, but sculpture is such a small and insignificant amount of the material of the total manufacturing world that I think it pales into insignificance when seen within the bigger picture. There are more paper cups - tonnes of paper cups actually - being made today compared to any sculpture. There are so many things being made that the tonnage of sculpture is miniscule. This is important as a necessary means of relativising the rest of the production and the economic logic. Secondly, some things which are deemed to be very light, like videos or DVDs, require enormous power to produce the computer parts and everything else that is needed to make them. There is an enormous industrial system necessary to produce a DVD player, for example.

Generation

Jon Wood: I would like to raise the question of reproduction, replication, multiplication, casting etc...that whole terrain of the making of subsequent work, through the term 'generation'. You seemed to be deeply concerned with this term (and its attendant biological metaphors) and a sculptor who is constantly looking to make what one might call 'generative' sculpture, works that have a self-generating structure or format and that can facilitate the creation of further works.

Tony Cragg: Yes, absolutely, and I think mass and energy need to be generated - any effective change has to be generated. It's to do with a positive directed initiative to change things. 'Generative' for me, in terms of my work, is the fact that within my own work within any given period the works generates itself and there is a self-generating characteristic. The work I'm making today is only possible because of the previous work of three or four months ago and that was only possible because of the work of nine or twelve months ago...Even if it's not a linear thing, things are generating. There is a sort of self-propagating, self-generative energy that is inherent in the material, I think. And even in the term 'generative', from 'genus', is the idea of making a family group of things, whether making an associative group of things or creating a population, a species of things which 'relativise' generation.

JW: Let's look at how this biological model for organising and envisaging an oeuvre actually works and plays itself out within your sculptures.

TC: Well, I must admit that although this seems to be something approaching a working method it took many years for me to recognise or, accept it as such. In fact I was forced into seeing it in this way in the absence of any other clear systematic working process. I had already made works for over ten years with jumps, breaks, parallel developments and made a lot of quite different looking work. However, the themes in the work and to some extent my expectations in the work had remained constant. What always amazed me was how much new information I took away with me after every new work. For me it is only really worth while making a new sculpture when I don't know what it will be when it is finished. That means that I do not know precisely what it will look like, how it will react in the world, how it will feel, and what ideas it will convey. This is why I have never found it interesting to make sculptures that represent existing objects and I rarely set out with the intention of presenting a pre-described message. I prefer looking forward to a new experience and a new acquaintance than to looking back at a source. This tendency to look forward has for me a generative quality. That is why we have offspring, in order to project part of ourselves into the future. For a period we are preoccuppied with forming and informing them and at some point they start to inform us and others. We relate to them in catagories of family, genre and species.

Industrial rationalism tends to censor the possibilities of form by lowest common denominator decision making, formatting materials and using cheaply producible geometries. Any other way of making things looks relatively organic. After my initial infatuation with minimalism as a student, I made a conscious effort to stay away from constructive tin box making and industrial parodies. Sometimes it seems that big commercial production systems act in an almost Darwinian manner where the survival of the fittest ensures the dynamic of the system, at least somewhat organic. Unfortunately this ignores the fact that Darwinian evolution assumes a multiplicity of biological niches in which a multiplicity of species can develop. This is absolutely not the case in the new 'the world is my oyster' concept. The marketing media prepare the ground by crushing any disparate sensibility or, cultural niche and then they off-load their i-pods and BMWs everywhere. The culture is more like an overpopulated pool of crocodiles, than a rich flora of many species which could then help us to create new language, new thoughts and new perspectives. Sculpture making is a good way of replenishing the form pool, even though, you shouldn't imagine for one moment that it is logical, rational or, even intrinsically right.

JW: And in terms of replenishing this 'form pool', do you see the large exhibition or retrospective as a chance to show not only 'generations' of sculptures, but also bodies of work in different materials and at different stages and sizes, in order to map out the 'genetic' connections within and between the works?

TC: I like to show sculptures in large exhibitions not as individual artworks. I want there to be a sense of almost twenty years of sculpture making. I also want the display to have a more insular quality to it and give the opportunity to see the work in a slightly different way; perhaps also to have a historical depth and maybe offer a chance to show an evolution of form and an evolution of the meaning of the form as well, within at least one group of works. In a sense, there will also be a kind of mistreatment as well - just bunching the sculptures up next to each other and treating them as individual unit parts of a bigger story will inevitably impinge on their individual statuses.

JW: Does a more anarchic diversity in a sculptor's oeuvre worry you or make you anxious?

TC: Not at all. On the contrary. If an oeuvre does not have a certain degree of complexity or, is even slightly out of control, I suspect some kind of cold-hearted strategy, perhaps they should become a designer instead!

JW: The biological ideas of generation and germination etc... seem to foreground natural evolution and growth etc. and displace the role of experimentation, of mistakes and of 'infertile' works that don't develop or generate further work - 'cul de sac or dead end street sculptures' that don't lead anywhere. What happens to these sculptures in your scheme of things?

TC: When we talk about offspring or, the idea of one thing stemming from another we can imagine forms like a bush or, a tree. In order for forms like this to extend to their full potential they grow and divide continually. Anything that does not manage to contribute to the general growth falls off and becomes compost. One thing is for sure: nothing is wasted.

JW: In terms of this organic metaphor's application to sculpture, and in relation to the larger history of sculpture, I want to ask you why you think it is that sculptors often have such self-conscious preoccupation with sculpture's long history and about the idea of sculpture's ostensible origins. You've already mentioned the pyramids, which is really interesting. If you interview a painter, they're not likely to mention cave paintings or some such example, whereas sculptors seem strangely likely to mention pyramids. Egyptian sculpture, the pyramids and the sphinx etc... immediately present a very long sense of sculpture's history. Might that also be part of a sculptor's imagining of 'generation'?

TC: If you've got a piece of music in front of you, you have rhythm, harmony, pitch and certain criteria that make a melody. There are similar criteria and concepts around sculpture. Longevity is a quality of material and so in a sense material is a good bridge through time. It is a way of leaving a relatively lasting and durable message in time. It's also interesting to observe that it's a bridge over different times. On the one hand it expands time, but it also contracts it. You can walk into a room where there's something which is 3,000 years old, 300 years old, 30 years old and something that was made just last week. Somehow, what's left in that residue of time makes one reflect on human characteristics and read variations of things that are familiar to us: human concerns (some expressive, some maybe humorous, some with dignity, some ideas of transported beauty, questions of truth, of ethics, of morals etc..) grouping up together in a material, concrete form. And once again, ultimately, it is logical as a result of this for me to say that I want to make sculpture - because sculpture has to be concerned with the material and material will carry a deeper, long-term meaning into the future. Looking back into the past is the other side of the coin - it's proof in a sense that the past provides us with material witnesses of human concerns and values.

JW: Is recycling a useful term? Is there a recycling policy operating within your work?

TC: Spontaneously I'd like to say 'yes', but because of my own particular history I feel that you can play into the hands of ecological fashion with such a term. I'm always concerned to avoid those terms, because if you don't you can actually make something where the real value of it gets lost, when it is capped with some simple political or social content. It's a sign of the times if you like, and it's very prevalent that an artist gets some image or object and transcribes onto it a pre-described political or social meaning.

That's not what I'm interested in doing. I'd like to discover new meanings rather than just let things be metaphorical.

JW: That term 'capping' makes me think of where you might stop or discontinue a body of work. Using the analogy of population growth, where do you draw the line with stopping making sculpture. Or does it just carry on? Sculpture breeding like rabbits, spreading like wildfire…where will it all go?

TC: Well, that question becomes relevant when you're walking down the street and you don't make much progress because you're bumping into sculpture! Or your living room, your kitchen and your bedroom are cluttered up with sculpture! If that's not the case then we're a long way from being endangered by sculpture, by the species of sculpture.

I think that sculpture is an incredibly rare human product, it really is. And I think the world will need sculpture in the future, in order to decide about the form and structure of many things - we will need sculpture and sculptural thinking. I would like to apply sculptural thinking to biomechanics, to government institutions, to social structures etc. I don't mean in terms of dictating what the structures would be, but in order to use the analysis of form and relate that to ideals and to moral imperatives even. I think that I could imagine the work of artists becoming much more integral to the form of social political institutions, of educational practices, to agriculture, to forestry, to ecology generally, to nutrition, to human relationships, to justice, to the resolution of conflicts. It may sound far-fetched, but because I find the solution to all of these problems lies in the material, sculpture is a good discipline for approaching these problems. And in the future sculpture will become even more equipped to deal with complicated material problems. I do believe that sculpture, perhaps sometimes more than any other artistic or cultural activity, is a tool for building a better world.

[Note]: 'Terms and Conditions: Interview with Tony Cragg' ('Material', 'Scale', 'Demonstration', 'Weight' and 'Generation'), in *Tony Cragg: In and Out of Material*, 2006, Akademie der Kunst, Berlin; Köln: Walther König, pp. 13-125

艺术家生平及部分展览
ARTIST'S BIOGRAPHY & SELECTED EXHIBITIONS

托尼·克拉格
生平及部分展览

生平类条目以粗体标示
有重要出版物的展览都以星号* 标示
出版物的标题以*斜体*标示

1949年
4月9日出生于利物浦

1966年8月
实验室助理，全国橡胶生产者研究协会，韦林花园城，英国

1969年至70年
基础课程，格洛斯特郡艺术学院，切尔滕纳姆，英国

1970年至73年
文学学士，温布尔登艺术学院，英国

1973年77年
文学硕士，硕士研究生雕塑课程，伦敦皇家艺术学院，英国

1975年
群展，布鲁内尔大学，阿克斯布里奇，英国

1976年
任教于梅斯美术学院，法国

1977年
Lisson 画廊，伦敦，英国
从皇家艺术学院毕业并前往伍珀塔尔，德国

1978年
JA-NA-PA III，巴黎
任杜塞尔多夫艺术学院教员，德国

1979年
Lisson 画廊，伦敦，英国

1980年
阿尔诺菲尼画廊，布里斯托，英国
康拉德·菲舍尔画廊，杜塞尔多夫，德国
Lisson 画廊，伦敦，英国

1981年
艺术和工业博物馆，圣埃蒂安，法国
新博物馆，里昂，法国
*托尼·克拉格**，Von der Heydt 博物馆，伍珀塔尔，德国
白教堂美术馆，伦敦 ，英国

1982年
Badischer Kunsverein，卡尔斯鲁厄，德国
Kroller-Muller 国家博物馆，奥特罗，荷兰

1983年
伯尔尼美术馆，瑞士

1984年
路易斯安那州现代美术馆，弗雷登斯堡，英国
图斯罗索画廊，都灵，意大利

1985年
现代美术馆，慕尼黑，德国
*托尼·克拉格**，美术宫，布鲁塞尔，比利时
ARC，巴黎现代美术馆，法国
克斯特纳协会，汉诺威，德国

1986年
布鲁克林博物馆，纽约，美国
美国加州大学美术馆，加利福尼亚，美国

1987年
*托尼·克拉格**，海沃德画廊，伦敦，英国
一场静悄悄的革命：1965年以来的英国雕塑，芝加哥当代美术馆，美国

1988年
*托尼·克拉格：英国馆**，第四十二届威尼斯双年展
获特纳奖，英国
任杜塞尔多夫艺术学院教授，德国

1989年
*托尼·克拉格**，北莱茵 - 威斯特法伦州艺术收藏，杜塞尔多夫，德国
*托尼·克拉格：1988年特纳奖得主**，泰特美术馆，伦敦，英国

TONY CRAGG
BIOGRAPHY AND SELECTED EXHIBITIONS

biographical entries are shown in **bold**
exhibitions accompanied by a major publication are marked with an asterisk *
the titles of publications are shown in *italic*

1949
9 April, Born in Liverpool, UK

1966-8
Laboratory Assistant at the National Rubber Producers' Research Association, Welwyn Garden City, UK

1969-70
Foundation Course, Gloucestershire College of Art, Cheltenham, UK

1970-73
BA, Wimbledon College of Art, UK

1973-77
MA, Postgraduate Sculpture Course, Royal College of Art, London, UK

1975
Brunel University, Uxbridge, mixed exhibition, UK

1976
Taught at L'école des Beaux-Arts, Metz, France

1977
Lisson Gallery, London, UK
Moves to Wuppertal, Germany

1978
JA-NA-PA III, Paris, France
Appointed to teaching staff of Kunstakademie Düsseldorf, Germany

1979
Lisson Gallery, London, UK

1980
Arnolfini Gallery, Bristol, UK
Konrad Fischer Galerie, Düsseldorf, Germany
Lisson Gallery, London, UK

1981
Musée d'art et d'industrie, St Etienne, France
Le Nouveau musée, Lyon, France
Von der Heydt-Museum, Wuppertal, Germany, *Tony Cragg* *
Whitechapel Art Gallery, London, UK

1982
Badischer Kunsverein, Karlsruhe, Germany
Rijksmuseum Kro.ller-Müller, Otterlo, The Netherlands

1983
Kunsthalle Bern, Switzerland

1984
Louisiana Museum of Modern Art, Humlebaek, UK
Galleria Tucci Rosso, Turin, Italy

1985
Staatsgalerie Moderner Kunst, Munich, Germany
Palais des Beaux-Arts, Brussels, Belgium, *Tony Cragg* *
ARC, Musée d'art moderne de la ville de Paris, France
Kestner-Gesellschaft, Hanover, Germany

1986
The Brooklyn Museum, New York, US
University Art Museum, University of California, US

1987
Hayward Gallery, London, UK, *Tony Cragg* *
Museum of Contemporary Art, Chicago, US, *A Quiet Revolution: British Sculpture Since 1965*, mixed exhibition *

市立范阿贝博物馆，埃因霍温，荷兰

1990年
*托尼·克拉格：1975年至1990年雕塑**，港美术馆，新港，美国

1991 年
维也纳分离派会馆，维也纳，奥地利
The Power Plant，多伦多，加拿大
凡纳贝美术馆，埃因霍温，荷兰
休斯敦当代美术馆，美国
Concoran 艺术画廊，华盛顿特区，美国
卡内基美术馆，匹兹堡，美国

1992年
IVAM 胡里奥·冈萨雷斯中心，瓦伦西亚，西班牙
电车和当代艺术中心，格拉斯哥，英国

1993年
Het kruithuiss 博物馆，'s-Hertogenbosch，荷兰

1994年
南特美术馆，法国
*托尼·克拉格**，Civica 当代美术馆，特伦托，意大利
艺术协会，圣加仑，瑞士
被委任为皇家院士，英国

1995年
布拉格国家美术馆，(前) 捷克斯洛伐克
索菲亚皇后美术馆，马德里，西班牙

1996年
亨利·摩尔基金会，哈利法克斯，英国
Mucsarnok 美术馆，布达佩斯，匈牙利
Middelheim 雕塑公园，安特卫普，比利时
Lehmbruck 博物馆，杜伊斯堡，德国
*托尼·克拉格**，当代艺术博物馆，蓬皮杜艺术中心，巴黎，法国

1997年
国立美术馆，斯科普里，马其顿
国立美术馆，索非亚，保加利亚
丰田市立美术馆，日本
国立美术馆，布拉迪斯拉发，斯洛伐克
新南威尔士美术馆，悉尼，澳大利亚
国立当代美术馆，首尔，韩国
国立美术馆，华沙，波兰

1998年
维尔纽斯当代艺术中心，立陶宛
*安东尼·克拉格：材料 - 对象 – 形式**，
St.dtische Galerie im Lenbachhaus，慕尼黑，德国

1999年
Sara Hildénin taidemuseo，坦佩雷，芬兰
大会堂艺术画廊，斯图加特，德国
皇家艺术学院，伦敦，英国

2000 年
*一个呼吸的新事物：托尼·克拉格最新作品**，
利物浦泰特，英国
巴特勒画廊，基尔肯尼，爱尔兰
MuKHA, 安特卫普美术馆*，比利时

2001年
马尔默美术馆，瑞典
Kunstsammlungen Chemnitz，德国
任柏林艺术大学教授直至 2006年，德国

2002年
Dunkers Kulturhus，赫尔辛堡，瑞典
被授予大英帝国CBE 勋章，英国

2003年
CAC，马拉加，西班牙
MACRO，罗马当代美术馆，意大利
*托尼·克拉格：生命的迹象**，波恩，德国

2004年
当代美术馆，波尔图，葡萄牙

1988

British Pavilion, XLII Venice Biennale, *Tony Cragg: British Pavilion* *

Awarded the Turner Prize, UK

Appointed Professor at the Kunstakademie Düsseldorf, Germany

1989

Kunstsammlung Nordrhein-Westfalen, Düsseldorf, Germany, *Tony Cragg* *

Tate Gallery, London, UK, *Tony Cragg: Winner of the 1988 Turner Prize* *

Stedelijk Van Abbemuseum, Eindhoven, The Netherlands

1990

Harbor Art Museum, Newport, US, *Tony Cragg: Sculpture 1975-1990* *

1991

Wiener Secession, Vienna, Austria

The Power Plant, Toronto, Canada

Van Abbemuseum, Eindhoven, The Netherlands

Houston Contemporary Art Museum, US

Concoran Gallery of Art, Washington DC, US

Carnegie Museum of Art, Pittsburgh, US

1992

IVAM Centre Julio González, Valencia, Spain

Tramway and Centre for Contemporary Art, Glasgow, UK

1993

Museum Het kruithuis, 's-Hertogenbosch, The Netherlands

1994

Musée des Beaux-Arts, Nantes, France

Galleria Civica di Arte Contemporanea, Trento, Italy, *Tony Cragg* *

Kunstverein, St Gallen, Switzerland

Appointed Royal Academician, UK

1995

National Gallery, Prague, Czechoslovakia

Museo Nacional Centro de Arte Reina Sofia, Madrid, Spain

1996

Henry Moore Foundation, Halifax, UK

Mücsarnok Kunsthalle, Budapest, Hungary

Middelheim Sculpture Park, Antwerp, Belgium

Lehmbruck Museum, Duisburg, Germany

Musée national d'art moderne, Centre Georges Pompidou, Paris, France, *Tony Cragg* *

1997

National Gallery, Skopje, Macedonia

National Gallery, Sofia, Bulgaria

Toyota Municipal Museum of Art, Toyota, Japan

National Gallery, Bratislava, Slovakia

Art Gallery of New South Wales, Sydney, Australia

National Museum of Contemporary Art, Korea, Seoul, South Korea

National Gallery, Warsaw, Poland

1998

Contemporary Art Centre of Vilnius, Lithuania

St.dtische Galerie im Lenbachhaus, Munich, Germany, *Anthony Cragg: Material – Object – Form* *

1999

Sara Hildénin taidemuseo, Tampere, Finland

Kunsthalle Galerie der Stadt, Stuttgart, Germany

Royal Academy of Arts, London, forecourt, UK

2000

Tate Liverpool, UK, *A New Thing Breathing: Recent Work by Tony Cragg* *

Butler Gallery, Kilkenny, Ireland

MuKHA, Museum van Hedendaagse Kunst Antwerp, Belgium *

2005年
卡斯雕塑基金会，古德伍德，西萨塞克斯，英国
中央艺术家之家，莫斯科，俄罗斯
新美术馆，纽伦堡，德国

2006年
Visive Pescheria 艺术中心，佩萨罗，意大利
*托尼·克拉格：潜在的物质**，艺术学院，柏林，德国
Recoleta 中心，布宜诺斯艾利斯，阿根廷
任杜塞尔多夫艺术学院教授，阿根廷

2007年
吉尔·德卡斯特罗文化基金会，MAVI，圣地亚哥，智利
*托尼·克拉格-潜在的物质，雕塑、素描和版画**，Stiftung Wilhelm Lehumbruck 博物馆，杜伊斯堡，德国
利马美术馆，秘鲁
雕塑家画廊，赫尔辛基，芬兰
Stelline 基金会，米兰，意大利
Nordiska Akvarellmuseet, Skarhamn，瑞典
被授予日本艺术协会雕塑大奖，日本

2008年
*托尼·克拉格与F.X. 梅塞施密特**，丽城，维也纳

2009年
Beelden aan Zee，席凡宁根，荷兰
*托尼·克拉格：第二性质**，卡尔斯鲁厄美术馆，德国
任杜塞尔多夫艺术学院院长，德国
雕塑公园开幕，克拉格基金会，伍珀塔尔，德国

2010年
Lisson 画廊，伦敦，英国
布罗斯美术馆，瑞典
*4D 托尼·克拉格**，Ca'Pesaro，威尼斯当代美术馆，意大利

2011年
*托尼·克拉格：Figure Out, Figure In**，卢浮宫，巴黎，法国
*安东尼·克拉格：思想上的事物 **，梅启明现代美术馆，杜伊斯堡，德国
托尼·克拉格：雕塑与绘画，苏格兰国家现代美术馆，爱丁堡，英国
Nasher 雕塑中心，达拉斯，美国
超有机：首届CAFAM 泛主题展，中央美术学院美术馆，北京，中国

2001
Malmö Konsthall, Sweden
Kunstsammlungen Chemnitz, Germany
Appointed Professor at the Universitat der Kunst, UdK, Berlin, Germany, to 2006

2002
Dunkers Kulturhus, Helsingborg, Sweden
Appointed CBE, UK

2003
CAC, Málaga, Spain
MACRO, Museo d'Arte Contemporanea, Rome, Italy
Kunst- und Ausstellungshalle der Bundesrepublik, Germany
Deutschland, Bonn, Germany, *Tony Cragg: Signs of Life* *

2004
Museu de Arte Contemporanea, Fundação Serralves, Porto, Portugal

2005
Cass Sculpture Foundation, Goodwood, West Sussex, UK
The Central House of Artists, Moscow, Russia
Neues Museum, Nuremberg, Germany

2006
Centro Arti Visive Pescheria, Pesaro, Italy
Akademie der Künste, Berlin, Germany, *Tony Cragg: Das Potential der Dinge* *
Centro Recoleta, Buenos Aires, Argentina
Appointed Professor at the Kunstakademie Düsseldorf, Germany

2007
Fundación Cultural Plazaq Mulato Gil de Castro, MAVI, Santiago, Chile
Stiftung Wilhelm Lehumbruck Museum, *Duisburg, Germany, Tony Cragg – Das Potential der Dinge. Skulpturen, Zeichnungen und Druckgrafiken* *
Museo de Arte de Lima, Peru
Galleria Sculptor, Helsinki, Finland
Fondazione Stelline, Milan, Italy
Nordiska Akvarellmuseet, Skarhamn, Sweden
Awarded Praemium Imperiale for Sculpture, Japan

2008
Belvedere, Vienna, Austria, *Tony Cragg versus F.X. Messerschmidt* *

2009
Beelden aan Zee, Scheveningen, The Netherlands
Staatliche Kunsthalle Karlsruhe, Germany, *Tony Cragg: Second Nature* *
Appointed Director of Kunstakademie Düsseldorf, Germany
Opening of Skulpturenpark Waldfrieden, Cragg Foundation, Wuppertal, Germany

2010
Lisson Gallery, London, UK
Konstmuseum Boras, Sweden
Ca'Pesaro, Galleria Internazionale d'Arte Moderna, Venice, Italy, *Tony Cragg IN 4D* *

2011
Musée du Louvre, Paris, France, *Tony Cragg: Figure Out, Figure In* *
MKM Museum Küppersmühle für Moderne Kunst, Duisburg, Germany, *Anthony Cragg: Dinge im Kopf / Things on the Mind* *
Scottish National Gallery of Modern Art, Edinburgh, UK, Tony Cragg: Sculptures and Drawings
Nasher Sculpture Centre, Dallas, US
The 1st CAFAM Biennale, CAFA Art Museum, Beijing, China

托尼·克拉格：雕塑与绘画展

主　办：中央美术学院美术馆　成都当代美术馆
　　　　上海喜玛拉雅美术馆　英国大使馆文化教育处
协　办：苏格兰国立现代美术馆　伦敦霍特曼艺术公司

中央美术学院美术馆
展览时间：2012/3/2-2012/4/15
学术顾问：潘公凯　托尼·克拉格
学术主持：徐冰
展览总召集：王璜生
展览协调：唐斌　王春辰　岳君瑶
展览视觉设计：纪玉洁
展览执行：朱永康　吴鹏　宿世存　马亮 /John McCormack, Michael Lamitch, Dariusz Piatek, Zbitniew Gula（托尼·克拉格工作室）
媒体联络：杜隐珠
展览推广：李纲　薛江
公共教育：任蕊
出版支持：中央编译出版社

成都当代美术馆
馆　长：吕澎
副馆长：何蕾　蓝庆伟
公共教育与媒体推广专员：钟红豆

上海喜玛拉雅美术馆
艺术总监：王纯杰　魏星
项目总监：黄玥霖
项目协调：张爱东
媒体推广：顾耀峰　黄汉娟
教育推广：刘麟　吴芳
视觉设计：黄盛开
项目工程：成宏　张民

TONY CRAGG: SCULPTURES AND DRAWINGS

Organizers: CAFA Art Museum, Museum of Contemporary Art Chengdu, Himalayas Art Museum, Cultral and Education Section of the British Embassy
Exhibition organized in collaborated with the Scottish National Gallery of Modern Art, Edinburgh and the Holtermann Fine Art, London

CAFA Art Museum
Date: 2012/3/2-2012/4/15
Art Adviser: Pan Gongkai, Tony Cragg
Art Director: Xu Bing
Exhibition Organizer: Wang Huangsheng
Exhibition Coordinator: Tang Bin, Wang Chunchen, Yue Junyao
Exhibition Visual Desgin: Ji Yujie
Installation Team: Zhu Yongkang, Wu Peng, Xu Shicun, Ma Liang / John McCormack, Michael Lamitch, Dariusz Piatek, Zbitniew Gula (Tony Cragg Studio)
Media Contact: Du Yinzhu
Marketing & Development: Li Gang, Xue Jiang
Public Education: Ren Rui
Publishing Support: Central Compilation & Translation Press

Museum of Contemporary Art Chengdu
Curator: Lu Peng
Deputy Curator: He Lei, Lan Qingwei
Public Education and Media Promotion Specialist: Zhong Hongdou

Himalayas Art Museum
Artistic Director: Wong Shun-kit, Wei Xing
Project Director: Yoyo Huang
Project Coordinator: Zhang Aidong
Media Promotion: Gu Yaofeng, Huang Hanjuan
Education: Liu Lin, Wu Fang
Designers:Huang Shengkai,
Installation Team: Cheng Hong, Zhang Ming

活动主办方
ORGANISED BY

CULTURAL AND
EDUCATION SECTION
BRITISH EMBASSY
英国大使馆文化教育处

“艺述英国”是迄今为止在中国举办的规模最大的英国艺术节。为了庆祝伦敦奥运会和纪念中英建交40周年，“艺述英国”旨在把中英两国的艺术机构、艺术家和艺术爱好者们更紧密地联系在一起。

2012年4月至11月，“艺述英国”将在中国的17座城市举办数百场活动，以展览、音乐会、演出和合作性教育培训计划来呈现英国最高水准的艺术和创意。

“艺述英国”由英国大使馆文化教育处主办，并由来自中国和英国的合作伙伴们共同呈现。该艺术节已经得到以下创始赞助商们的大力支持：博然思维、博柏利、帝亚吉欧、汇丰控股有限公司、洲际酒店集团、捷豹路虎、诺顿罗氏国际律师事务所、英国保诚集团、渣打银行、太古。

UK Now is the largest ever festival of British arts and creative industries to take place in China. Coinciding with the London Olympics and the 40th anniversary of the resumption of ambassadorial relations between our two countries, the Festival aims to bring British and Chinese arts institutions, artists and art lovers closer together.

With hundreds of events in 17 cities from April to November 2012, UK Now will highlight the best of UK arts and creative industries with exhibitions, concerts and performances as well as collaborative education and training programmes.

UK Now is organised by the Cultural and Education Section of the British Embassy in China in collaboration with Chinese and British partners. The Festival is receiving generous support from its founding sponsors: Brunswick, Burberry, Diageo, HSBC, IHG, Jaguar Land Rover, Norton Rose, Prudential, Standard Chartered and Swire.

www.uknow.org.cn

创始赞助商
FOUNDER SPONSOR

BURBERRY

NORTON ROSE

图书在版编目（CIP）数据

托尼·克拉格：雕塑与绘画 / 王璜生著．--
北京：中央编译出版社，2012.2
ISBN 978-7-5117-1352-0

Ⅰ．①托… Ⅱ．①王… Ⅲ．①雕塑－作品集－英国－
现代②绘画－作品集－英国－现代③艺术－文集 Ⅳ．
①J331②J231③J-53

中国版本图书馆 CIP 数据核字 (2012) 第 026718 号

《托尼·克拉格：雕塑与绘画》

出 版 人：和　龑
出版策划：薛　江
责任编辑：何嗣虎　曹爱云

编　　著：中央美术学院美术馆
学术顾问：潘公凯　托尼·克拉格
学术主持：徐　冰
主　　编：王璜生
副 主 编：吕　澎　王纯杰
编　　辑：王春辰　岳君瑶　高　高
Lisa Zhang（英国大使馆文化和教育处） David Kaluza（托尼·克拉格工作室）
设　　计：纪玉洁
设计协助：张蓝天　朱明月
翻　　译：孙　越　刘炳艳　黄进之
文字校对：高　高　黄进之　刘希言
图片提供：托尼·克拉格工作室

出版发行：中央编译出版社
地　　址：北京西城区车公庄大街乙 5 号鸿儒大厦 B 座
电　　话：010-52612345 / 总编室　010-52612365 / 编辑室
010-66161011 / 团购部　010-52612332 / 网络销售
010-66130345 / 发行部　010-66509618 / 读者服务部
网　　址：www.cctpbook.com
经　　销：全国新华书店
印　　制：北京雅昌彩色印刷有限公司
开　　本：635 毫米 ×965 毫米　1/16
字　　数：240 千字
印　　张：16.25
版　　次：2012 年 2 月第 1 版第 1 次
定　　价：268 元

开放时间：周二至周日（每周一休馆）9:30 至 17:30（17:00 后停止售票）
电话（服务台）：86-10-64771575
传真：86-10-64771699
地址：北京市朝阳区花家地南街 8 号 中央美术学院美术馆 100102
Hours: Tuesday - Sunday: 9:30 am-5:30 pm* Monday: Closed* Last admission at 5:00 pm
Information: 86-10-64771575
Fax: 86-10-64771699
CAFA Art Museum, China Central Academy of Fine Arts
No.8, Huajiadi Nan Jie, Chaoyang District 100102 Beijing, P.R. China

http://www.cafamuseum.org